More praise for
## CHANGING LIVES

"No musical story of our time has proven as captivating and inspiring as that of El Sistema. Tricia Tunstall has illuminated the moving story of its creation. . . . We are fortunate to have the story of El Sistema, with its world of limitless possibility, related so eloquently." —Deborah Borda, president and CEO, Los Angeles Philharmonic

"The key message of this important book is that playing an instrument can indelibly change the trajectory of a child's life, instilling confidence, personal growth, and joy. Tunstall's compelling stories and reflections show that the long-term benefits to society, in the U.S. as in Venezuela, can be incalculable." —Marin Alsop, music director, Baltimore Symphony Orchestra

"This incredibly well-written book reminds us of how arts education can change lives. The book asks much of each of us, but the rewards are extraordinary. . . . Readers will be empowered to dream bigger, act bolder and eschew the incrementalism plaguing public education policy. The lessons for educators, politicians and parents are innumerable." —Gary Stager, *Huffington Post*, one of three Best Education Books of 2011

"Music education is undergoing a major revolution—perhaps its most important in generations, as chronicled in the new book *Changing Lives*." —Jason Issokson, *LA Weekly*

"This passionate and inspiring story should be read by all those interested in music education, community building, and advocacy for the disadvantaged. An essential purchase." —*Library Journal*, starred review

"It's hard not to get caught up in Tunstall's enthusiasm and believe that, as crazy as it sounds, classical music just might save the world."
—John Lewis, *Baltimore* magazine

"An impassioned case for music as a means of effecting social change."
—Nick Shave, *BBC Music Magazine*

"What makes *Changing Lives* . . . work extremely well is a combination of plentiful engaging interview material and an evocative sense of place/event as Tunstall travels from scenes of deprivation in Venezuela to gleaming international concert halls to schools in the USA now lapping up El Sistema. Tunstall has a keen eye for descriptive detail."
—*Classical Music*

"I hope Tricia's well-written and deeply informative book will encourage thousands more musicians, teachers, funders, and fans the world over to embrace El Sistema, a program that transforms children and their communities by using the symphony orchestra as a template for a society based on rigor, compassion, and joy."
—Jamie Bernstein

"Vivid, informative, and exhilarating—this book captures the power and purpose of the El Sistema movement and the towering figures old and young who are transforming lives through music."
—Jude Kelly, artistic director, Southbank Centre, London

"*Changing Lives* is the first work to pull the entire tale together in one volume."
—Reed Johnson, *Los Angeles Times*

"Tunstall soundly probes how it is that classical music has played such a powerful role in the protection, education and elevation of so many children born into poverty. The author does a noble job tracing the history of El Sistema, while managing to keep the narrative as much in the immediate present as possible."
—*Kirkus Reviews*

# CHANGING LIVES

# CHANGING LIVES

*Gustavo Dudamel, El Sistema, and the*
*Transformative Power of Music*

## Tricia Tunstall

W. W. Norton & Company   NEW YORK   LONDON

For information about permission to reproduce selections from this book,
write to Permissions, W. W. Norton & Company, Inc.,
500 Fifth Avenue, New York, NY 10110

For information about special discounts for bulk purchases, please contact
W. W. Norton Special Sales at specialsales@wwnorton.com or 800-233-4830

Manufacturing by Courier Westford
Book design by Brooke Koven
Production manager: Devon Zahn


Library of Congress Cataloging-in-Publication Data

Tunstall, Tricia.
Changing lives : Gustavo Dudamel, El Sistema, and the transformative power
of music / Tricia Tunstall.
p. cm.
Includes index.
ISBN 978-0-393-07896-1 (hardcover)
1. Music—Instruction and study—Venezuela. 2. Music—Instruction and
study—United States. 3. Fundacion del Estado para el Sistema Nacional de
las Orquestas Juveniles e Infantiles de Venezuela—History. 4. Dudamel,
Gustavo—Anecdotes. I. Title.
MT3.V4T86 2012
780.71′087—dc23

2011026504


ISBN 978-0-393-34426-4 pbk.


W. W. Norton & Company, Inc.
500 Fifth Avenue, New York, N.Y. 10110
www.wwnorton.com

W. W. Norton & Company Ltd.
Castle House, 75/76 Wells Street, London W1T 3QT


1 2 3 4 5 6 7 8 9 0

*To the children of El Sistema, past, present, and future—*
*our best teachers and guides to the truth that music can change lives*

# Contents

# Gustavo and Me

MORE THAN FORTY YEARS AGO, A WAVE OF POPULAR fascination with a musical group distinguished by youth, charm, great talent, and exceptional hair was dubbed a form of "mania" by the press. We have not seen such a case of mania again ... until recently, with the emergence of "Dudamania," which concerns another musical phenomenon with ferocious talent, abundant charm, and—yes, exceptional hair.

This time, however, at the center of the excitement is not a rock band but a classical musician, and he wields a baton instead of a guitar. The pull of Dudamania is felt by almost everyone who has experienced the conductor Gustavo Dudamel. It's close to impossible to watch this young man communicate so passionately through music without feeling captivated and moved.

The musicians who work with Dudamel clearly feel the same way. Whether he is leading the Simón Bolívar Youth Orchestra of his native Venezuela or the Los Angeles Philharmonic, where he is music director, orchestra members play for him with all their hearts.

My own case of Dudamania goes beyond the personal and musical charisma of the man. As a lifelong music educator and a writer, I'm keenly aware that he also embodies a compelling idea: that music education can be a means to both individual empowerment and social transformation. Dudamel is not only a brilliant conductor and a youthful celebrity on the world's musical stage; he is also the most famous product of El Sistema, an extraordinary program for children and youth in Venezuela, where music education and social reform have been fused on a national scale with astonishing results. Through the Sistema, a nationwide program supported and financed primarily by the government, nearly 400,000 children spend hours every day intensely engaged in learning music and playing in the country's hundreds of youth orchestras. The great majority of these children are from poor families.

El Sistema's overarching goal is "to rescue the children" from the multiple dangers of poverty, and most importantly from the sense of hopelessness and low self-esteem that can lead to gang membership, drugs, and violence. Dudamel entered the Sistema as a young child, and he has never left. Even as he pursues a high-profile international conducting career, he continues to conduct the Simón Bolívar Youth Orchestra of Venezuela on a regular basis, and he is a tireless ambassador for the Sistema's vision of improving the lives of children and young people by providing them with musical training and orchestral community. "Music saved my life," Dudamel has said. "It has saved thousands of lives in my country. I'm sure of this."

El Sistema was founded in 1975 by the visionary Venezuelan musician and economist José Antonio Abreu. From the very beginning, the Sistema has been dedicated to realizing the simple but radical idea of its founder—that music can save lives, can rescue children, and can in fact be a potent vehicle for social reform and the fight against the perils of childhood poverty.

"When arts education takes the place in our society that it

deserves," José Antonio Abreu has said, "we will have much less delinquency and violence, and much more motivation towards noble achievement. My struggle is for a society in which art is not just an aesthetic dimension of life. It is a primary instrument for the development of individuals and societies."

The growth of the Sistema has taken place steadily for many years, under the international radar. In the past decade, however, attention has begun to be paid—most famously by conductors such as Simon Rattle, Daniel Barenboim, and Claudio Abbado, and classical superstars like Plácido Domingo, Itzhak Perlman, John Williams, and Yo-Yo Ma. These world-renowned musicians have become ardent advocates and champions of El Sistema, visiting Venezuela frequently and conducting or performing with the Simón Bolívar and other youth orchestras. Simon Rattle, conductor of the Berlin Philharmonic, has said: "If anyone asked me where there is something really important going on now for the future of classical music, I would simply have to say—in Venezuela. It is an emotional force of such power that it may take some time to assimilate what we're seeing and hearing." Claudio Abbado, founder and conductor of the Lucerne Festival Orchestra, has declared, "To me, it is the example that every country should follow." And *Star Wars* composer John Williams, on a visit to Venezuela in 2007, said, "This is something unique that has to be seen by the whole world . . . and that we urgently need here in the United States."

The news about El Sistema has spread in the last few years beyond musical celebrities, attracting the attention of musicians, teachers, and advocates for social reform across the world. I have been a music educator for many years and in a variety of capacities—a public school general music teacher, an adjunct professor of music history and appreciation in colleges, a piano teacher in my private studio. And like music teachers everywhere, I have been touched and inspired by the words of Gustavo Dudamel and José Antonio Abreu and by the example of El Sistema.

I know—we know—that music can change lives. We have seen

firsthand its capacity to enliven a shy child and calm an anxious one, to bring coherence and meaning to the often mysterious chaos of feeling. We have seen music lift people out of depression and even despair, and give new spirit and purpose to young lives. Again and again, we have seen students discover in themselves new dimensions of creativity and vitality through playing and loving music.

But the Sistema's vision goes even further than personal transformation to include a clear, unequivocal, and primary social dimension. The fundamental mission of El Sistema is not only to help children but often, literally, to rescue them—and in the process, to effect real and lasting changes in the lives of their families and communities. "The orchestra and choir are much more than artistic studies," Abreu says. "They are examples and schools of social life. From the minute a child is taught how to play an instrument, he is no longer poor. He becomes a child in progress, who will become a citizen."

Abreu's consistent emphasis is the ability of music to heal the emotional and spiritual depredations of poverty. "Poverty is not just the lack of a roof or bread," he has said. "It is also a spiritual lack—a loneliness and lack of recognition. The vicious cycle of poverty can be broken when a child poor in material possessions acquires spiritual wealth through music."

Within the context of the United States, such an ambitious and far-reaching vision is difficult to conceive of, and liable to be met with skepticism—even by musicians and music educators. All music teachers are convinced that music education can have a potent impact on individual lives. Many allow themselves, as I do, to imagine that high-quality, in-depth music education for all children could turn our culture toward a more abundant and communal creativity. But few dare to dream of re-creating social life and challenging poverty through music.

It is especially difficult to imagine such a possibility, I think, given the current state of musical culture in contemporary U.S. society. While music has in some senses become more ubiquitous than ever before, it has been increasingly appropriated by the engines of marketing and mass entertainment, and has been substantially degraded in the process. For many, music has become a kind of universal ambient noise, a half-attended-to soundtrack for modern life.

Classical music, in particular, is so culturally marginalized as to be barely present, even as ambience, in most people's lives. Among my beginning piano students, it is rare to encounter a child whose experience extends beyond the tune of the "Ode to Joy" and the first few notes of *Für Elise*. For music teachers who value the incomparably rich artistic and expressive power of classical music, challenging this massive cultural amnesia can feel like an uphill battle.

The battle can feel particularly arduous in the context of the bleak picture that constitutes music education, and arts education in general, in the United States. In her 2006 book *The Wow Factor*, Anne Bamford reported that elementary school children in the United States spend an average of 46 hours a year in arts education classes—by far the lowest number of any developed country, and a dramatic contrast with countries like Japan and Finland, where the average is 300 hours a year or more. And race- and class-based inequity with regard to access to music education seems ever more stubbornly entrenched. If indeed music can change and save lives, the very children who need it the most are tragically underserved.

These trends have come to seem inescapable and unchangeable facts of life. And so for me, as for music educators throughout the United States, the story of Gustavo Dudamel and the system that produced him comes as something of a revelation. In the context of an international pop culture that has relegated the traditions of the symphony orchestra to near-obsolescence, here is an initiative that has suddenly infused classical music with new energy and relevance. And in the context of many failed attempts at education reform for inner-city and at-risk children and youth in the United States, here is a reimagining of music education as social reform on a scale without precedent anywhere. Can we allow ourselves to yield our well-earned skepticism and to be astonished, inspired, and galvanized?

The door to the world of El Sistema was first opened for me by Jamie Bernstein, whose father, Leonard Bernstein, was a lifelong advocate for music education as well as one of the twentieth century's most beloved conductors and composers; his series of nationally televised "Young People's Concerts" with the New York Philharmonic arguably kindled an entire generation's interest in and love for classical music. In the winter of 2008, I went with Jamie to hear Dudamel conduct the Israel Philharmonic at Carnegie Hall in a concert that included Bernstein's Concerto for Orchestra (*Jubilee Games*), originally written for this orchestra, as well as Tchaikovsky's Fourth Symphony. Jamie is an accomplished musician and performer in her own right, but that night she was an intoxicated Dudamel fan along with the rest of the audience. It was Jamie and our mutual friend Margaret Mercer, who as program director of the radio station WQXR spent many years quietly and expertly helping to keep classical music alive in New York City, who first told me about the Sistema, which they had recently witnessed on a trip to Venezuela. You have to go, they said. You have to see for yourself.

It was an irresistible idea. I was ready for new ideas; the issues confronting music education in the United States had begun to feel increasingly real and concrete in my own private piano practice. The issue of inequitable access to music education, for example, turns up daily in my piano studio. Although I live in a vibrantly heterogeneous town, a suburb of New York City that is a true melting pot of races and ethnicities, most of my students are white or Asian and middle-class. Minority and low-income students often lack both the financial resources to pay for private lessons and a means of transportation to get to them. The question persists: how can I reach, and teach, children from all sectors of my community, not just the most privileged?

With the children who do find their way to my piano bench, the issue of music as a vital and autonomous art form is also very real. For many of these children, music barely exists as something to be encountered and appreciated on its own terms; it is a groove or "beat" half-heard while watching a movie or television show, while shopping, while socializing. It seems to me that the advent of the iPod and the mp3 file, rather than reversing this development, has accelerated it; now that one can carry one's private musical cache everywhere and listen to it anytime, music can be a casual accompaniment to almost any activity—exercising or doing homework or chatting online. How can a piano teacher, or a music teacher of any kind, lead young people toward the possibility of putting their multi-tasking on pause, and simply, deeply, paying attention to music?

Finally, I have found myself more and more aware of my students' lack of experience with music as a communal endeavor. This is, of course, an inherent limitation of the private lesson format, where teaching and learning happens one-on-one and focuses on individual progress rather than group endeavor. And there is a unique and rewarding intensity in the relationship between teacher and student in the context of the private lesson.

Unlike violin students or flute students, however, my students are not likely to find many opportunities to play with others. The satisfactions of the piano as a solo instrument are among its great virtues. But the drawback of its soloistic character is that for most pianists, the experience of making music is, by and large, the experience of making music alone. This drawback comes into often painful focus at the recital I hold each year in June, when my students march one by one to the piano to perform their pieces, gripped by degrees of stage fright that range from mild anxiety to near-hysteria. How much easier it would be for them, I always think—not to mention how much more fun, and maybe even more musically satisfying—if somehow they could all play together.

These questions about the enterprise of teaching music were evolving in me with increasing clarity and urgency when I first went to see Gustavo Dudamel conduct at Carnegie Hall, and first heard about El Sistema. I realized that each of my questions could be illuminated by an exploration of the program that was so dramatically changing children's lives in Venezuela. The primary importance of

wide and equitable access to music education; the need to revitalize
the art of music in the lives of children and the culture; the value
of making music in community instead of in isolation—clearly, El
Sistema had much to teach in all of these areas.

At the heart of the inquiry was the pioneering assumption that
grounds the Sistema—the assumption that music can be a means
for social transformation. The stories I heard about the Sistema
seemed almost too remarkable to be true: the movement of thousands of children from impoverishment to symphonic mastery, the
youth orchestras who play like professionals, the transformation
of a trombone player's son from central Venezuela into an international conducting star. Even after years of teaching music in many
circumstances, I found that these images challenged my long-held
preconceptions about what music education is, and what it might
be. I knew I needed to find out more.

In the years since, I have traveled several times to Venezuela
and to Los Angeles, where "Gustavo" is simultaneously winning
the musical heart of the city and leading a Los Angeles Philharmonic initiative to create an El Sistema–like program for underserved children. I have visited a number of other U.S. cities where
El Sistema–inspired programs are taking root and flourishing. And
I have talked to many people involved in the evolution of the Sistema
in Venezuela and the spread of its goals and principles to this country and elsewhere.

This book chronicles my explorations, and attempts to illuminate
the Sistema's almost magical capacity to inspire artists, educators,
and social activists everywhere. It traces my gradual realization that
within El Sistema, the guiding ideal of the orchestra as a school for
civic community is so strong as to effectively transcend the distinction between musical education and social transformation. And it
describes my growing certainty that we in the United States, and
elsewhere in the world, have much to learn from the Venezuelan
model—and that the fast-growing international movement to

replicate this model is one of the most significant social and artistic developments of the twenty-first century.

A far-flung network of youth orchestras for at-risk children: it is an unprecedented and unorthodox idea. But given the pressing need for new and innovative approaches to social and educational reform, the time may be right for such a leap of imagination. I am convinced that the children of the United States and elsewhere, no less than the children of Venezuela, can benefit greatly from an educational vision that brings them not only skills and training but also community, artistry, discipline, and hope.

# CHANGING LIVES

# CHAPTER I

# *Bienvenido Gustavo!*: Hollywood's Unlikely New Star

I T'S OCTOBER 3, 2009, A BRILLIANT AUTUMN DAY IN LOS Angeles. As the sun hovers low in the late afternoon sky, thousands of people are streaming up Highland Avenue to a concert at the Hollywood Bowl. It is a time-honored civic ritual; crowds have flocked on picture-perfect days to concerts at the spectacular natural amphitheater since it opened in 1922. Most of the legendary musicians of the past century, from Bernstein and Pavarotti to Sinatra and the Beatles, have performed at the Bowl; Baryshnikov danced here, Judy Garland crooned, Jolson sang on bended knee. The Los Angeles Philharmonic makes its summer home under the vast white arch nestled into the Hollywood Hills.

Even against the backdrop of such history, something unusual is happening at the Bowl on this October day. The Los Angeles Philharmonic is appearing in its opening concert with a new conductor, playing Beethoven's Ninth Symphony—the kind of event usually attended by throngs of well-heeled Los Angeles socialites and middle-aged classical music lovers, with a sprinkling of celebrities and paparazzi. But today, among the thousands of people congregating to hear a symphony orchestra play a classical masterwork, many—perhaps even most—are people whose first language is Spanish. Many, perhaps even most, have never been to the Hollywood Bowl before, or to a classical concert of any kind. They have come at the express wish of the new conductor, a twenty-eight-year-old Venezuelan with emotive hair and an impressive career trajectory who has insisted that his opening concert be free of charge and that at least half of the audience be Latino.

They have come to hear and see and celebrate the arrival in Los Angeles of Gustavo Dudamel.

Dudamel is that rare phenomenon, a classical musician who is an international celebrity far beyond the world of classical music. The story of his rapid rise from humble beginnings in Venezuela to a central position on the world's musical stage has an almost fairy-tale dimension: at the age of eighteen he was leading Venezuela's celebrated youth orchestra on international tours, and in his early twenties he began appearing as guest conductor with preeminent orchestras across the world. Dudamel's formidable musical intelligence and expressive power have won him growing acclaim among musicians and music aficionados; his boyish good looks, extravagant mane of curly hair and exuberant stage presence have enchanted audiences on a far wider scale. By the time the Los Angeles Philharmonic announced his appointment, in 2007, Dudamel was being hailed by some in the United States and Europe as the next Leonard Bernstein.

Even in this celebrity-crazed city, the arrival of Dudamel has been a public sensation, and for months Los Angeles has been in the grip of Dudamania. Images of the young maestro in action adorn billboards, banners, and the sides of buses across the city, each with a giant adjective in Spanish: RADIANTE GUSTAVO! ELECTRICO GUSTAVO! PASIÓN GUSTAVO! The local news media are full of stories about the new conductor. On a brand-new "Gustavo Dudamel microsite" launched by the Los Angeles Philharmonic, a three-minute video shows Angelenos of all varieties, from Santa Monica surfers and tutu-clad ballet dancers to Plácido Domingo and an Elvis impersonator, waving at the camera and caroling "Welcome to Los Angeles, Gustavo!" The roadside stand Pink's, a local legend, does a brisk business in the "Dude Dog," a hot dog topped with guacamole, cheese, jalapeños, fajitas mix, and tortilla chips.

The fanfare attending Dudamel's arrival in Los Angeles has been such that when free tickets to the Hollywood Bowl concert were made available to the public two months ago, at noon on August 1, they were gone in less than ninety minutes—the fastest "sellout" in the history of the 18,000-seat Bowl. Most of the people who had arrived at the box office as early as 5 A.M. to stand in line for hours in the summer heat had walked away without tickets. In the days that followed, disgruntled bloggers and newspaper letter-writers accused the L.A. Phil of handling the ticket distribution unfairly, with a high dudgeon more often associated with sports events or political rallies than with Beethoven symphonies. "We are outraged!" they wrote. "Where did all the tickets go?"

On this October afternoon it is obvious where the tickets went. The Spanish-speaking community of Los Angeles is almost half the city's population, but often—particularly at major cultural events—a relatively invisible half. Dudamel has been electrically and passionately adamant that this community must be welcomed to his inaugural event, and the L.A. Phil, with the help of a Hispanic marketing firm, has reached out to many Latino households and distribution channels, offering tickets in advance of the official date. The classical music mavens who went ticketless may not have been happy, but the tenor of this afternoon's gathering audience is exactly what the young maestro must have hoped for. People exchange effusive greetings in Spanish, strains of salsa music emanate from car radios and boom boxes, and demand is high at the concession stands for tacos and burritos. There are large families trailing children of multiple ages, with toddlers on shoulders and babies on hips; there are teenaged couples holding hands, girls with flowers in their hair, men with their arms around each other's shoulders. It feels like a festival.

There is also, of course, a sizable contingent of non-Hispanic Angelenos—old and young and middle-aged, many jeans-clad, some runway-worthy. And there are probably a fair number of people like me, who have come from far away to witness this event because we are drawn by Dudamel's exhilarating brand of music-making and fascinated by his roots in El Sistema, Venezuela's national music education program.

On the plaza below the entrance, the L.A. Phil is offering canary-yellow tee shirts for sale, and they are selling like—well, like Dude Dogs. Black letters on the tee shirt say BIENVENIDO GUSTAVO! The same words are emblazoned across a long wall in a café near the plaza, where an impromptu mural is crammed with colorful pictures and scribbles. Paper and crayons and markers are laid out on the café tables, and clusters of children, mostly Latino, are busy creating additions to the enormous collage.

The children and their colorful creations are a reminder that today's celebration is more than a concert; it's a rally for music education. Dudamel has brought with him to Los Angeles a big idea about changing children's lives through music, an idea grounded in his own personal story as a member of El Sistema. Dudamel and the Philharmonic have insisted from the outset that tonight's Hollywood Bowl extravaganza must be a celebration of this big idea, as well as a star-studded symphonic event. And so the concert will feature not only the Philharmonic orchestra but also the fledgling musicians of Youth Orchestra Los Angeles (YOLA, for short), the El Sistema–inspired program that the L.A. Phil has initiated with Dudamel's guidance and support even before his official tenure here has begun. And the festival of opening acts during the afternoon is replete with children's ensembles.

At the entrance to the Bowl, I am handed a program as thick as a magazine, filled with proclamations and testimonials from the city of Los Angeles and the governor of California and with extensive bilingual program notes. On the back cover, a Rolex ad shows the Dude sporting a platinum watch and an urbane smile, his hair alarmingly tame. Seats in the Bowl are filling up fast. The vast scallop shell of seats is already in afternoon shadow, surrounded by still sunlit hills. It has the feel of old-fashioned entertainment in the grand style; wooden tables are unfolded among suites of seats, and the guacamole is flowing freely, along with wine and beer.

Onstage under the giant white-ribbed bandshell, children are playing music—many children, in many ensembles, some with celebrity mentors. A group from the Silverlake Conservatory plays and sings a Stevie Wonder medley; the young musicians range from lanky girls in sling-back heels to a very small boy wearing red suspenders. The rock musician who founded the conservatory, Flea, of Red Hot Chili Peppers fame, stands in the rhythm section and grinds away on his guitar. At the end of the set, Flea shouts into the microphone: "Thank you, everybody! Music education for the children!"

Herbie Hancock follows, playing "Maiden Voyage" with a student jazz band from the L.A. County High School for the Arts. Next up is a Mexican roots band featuring David Hidalgo and Taj Mahal, and many in the audience are on their feet, dancing and playing air congas. Jack Black is somehow onstage for a moment, with a prototypically Hollywood salute, just in case we've forgotten where we are: "So I'm kind of a big deal . . . but so's this Gustavo Dudamel guy. Dude's on fire."

The hills surrounding the Bowl are in shadow by now, with only their tips still glowing gold. Along with the programs, we have all been handed cardboard discs mounted on popsicle sticks, each with an eyeglass-shaped cutout through which everything looks rainbow-hued; seen through the glasses, the hilltops glow with a prismatic echt-Hollywood overlay of violet, emerald, and rose. The Bowl is brimming, overflowing with people; they are dancing, drinking, chatting, applauding, but there is an increasing sense of anticipation now. They want Gustavo. We all want Gustavo.

And still no Gustavo; but here is Deborah Borda, the president of the Los Angeles Philharmonic, onstage, and here is John Williams, the iconic *Star Wars* composer, who is the artistic chair of this event. Deborah Borda welcomes the crowd in the Bowl and adds a greeting to the crowd around the world, watching as the concert is streamed live from the L.A. Phil Web site. "There is a lot of magic here tonight," says John Williams.

A short video introduces the children's orchestra that YOLA has recently created, the EXPO Center Youth Orchestra, many of whose members have been playing instruments for less than two years. "YOLA is inspired by El Sistema, the Venezuelan music education program that engages hundreds of thousands of children each year," announces Deborah Borda's voice-over as the video shows images of small children cradling stringed instruments. There are whistles from the crowd at the mention of the Sistema, which has produced legions of accomplished young musicians since it was founded in Venezuela thirty-five years ago, but thanks to Dudamel's fame has suddenly become an overnight sensation in the United States. The video camera pans in on a member of the YOLA children's orchestra as she speaks of her trepidation about playing at the Hollywood Bowl. "It's scary to think about playing for eighteen hundred people!" she says, and a subtitle appears below her face: DON'T TELL HER IT'S EIGHTEEN THOUSAND!

After their video introduction, the children of the orchestra file onstage, dressed in black pants and brightly colored tee shirts of yellow and green, red and blue and purple, emblazoned with the "YOLA" insignia. There are a great many of them, and a range of ages—some look as young as seven or eight—and there is much calling and waving from the front-and-center section of the Bowl, known locally as "poolside," where donors usually hold court and where tonight the families of the young musicians are sitting. Deborah Borda reads a congratulatory letter from President Obama, and the children look very grave as they sit in their seats, clutching their instruments, listening to the presidential encomium and waiting for their conductor.

And finally he comes. He too wears black pants and a YOLA tee shirt; the only difference is that his tee shirt is black. He scurries through the violin section between the children, beaming, and shakes the hand of the concertmistress, a round-faced girl in a green tee shirt. The Los Angeles Philharmonic will have to wait: Gustavo Dudamel is making his official debut at the Hollywood Bowl not with a world-renowned symphony orchestra but with a group of children from South Central Los Angeles.

"Gustavo!" roars the Hollywood Bowl. "Gustavo!" He clasps his hands together and raises them to the audience. Then he turns to the children and lifts his baton, and the cellos and basses begin the opening strains of the "Ode to Joy."

The playing is stiff and timid at first; the winds join in, and then the brass, and there is a shaky entrance here and an iffy intonation there, but gradually they gain in confidence and volume. Dudamel conducts with the same vibrancy and concentration I have seen him give to the Israel Philharmonic at Carnegie Hall. He seems to be physically willing the children through the music, and their eyes are locked on him as they play. There is an L.A. Phil musician or two sitting with each section, helping to boost the children's sound and keep them on track; back among the double basses, a young boy with an Afro bends and sways in time with the balding musician next to him. *"Joyful, joyful, we adore thee . . ."* The second time through the chorus, the winds float a precise and lovely descant above the strings' melody, and the sustained notes of the brass are louder and stronger. And when the percussion comes in for the last chorus, the sound swells and lifts off, and there's no doubt that these children—scared, determined, struggling—are an orchestra.

At the end we are all on our feet, yelling as we applaud. The children's families, in their "poolside" ringside seats, are whistling, weeping, hugging one another. Dudamel doesn't turn around, and the stage-flanking video projections of his face show us that he's grinning at the kids, clapping at them, turning thumbs up. They stand wide-eyed and blinking, a little dazed under the stage lights.

He walks among them, bestowing hugs and kisses, and finally, from somewhere between the violas and the clarinets, he turns around to wave at the crowd.

It's conceivable that the musicians of the Los Angeles Philharmonic, backstage at this moment in their white jackets and black bow ties, are thinking that the YOLA orchestra is a very hard act to follow. But when they are massed on the stage of the Hollywood Bowl a few minutes later with a chorus two hundred strong behind them, and the maestro appears, his black tee shirt exchanged for a white jacket, the cries of "Gustavo!" and even "Venezuela!" erupt into a full-fledged, rock star–size ovation. Dudamel's smile as he takes his bow is subdued, almost shy; there is an echo of the YOLA children's sweetness in the face of this young man whose career has blossomed so unimaginably since his own days in a children's orchestra, not so many years ago. Then he turns to the orchestra. A few more lusty cries—"Gustavo-o-o!"—and the crowd is silent.

As the hushed opening strains of the Ninth Symphony fill the amphitheater, it occurs to me that something rare in modern symphonic history is happening: there are perhaps thousands of people here who are hearing this music for the very first time. I am almost envious: how thrilling to hear it new, as Beethoven's audiences heard it, and to experience it for the first time in this beautiful natural amphitheater! The use of the Ninth Symphony to symbolize and celebrate the brotherhood of man has become almost reflexive in the European and North American cultural history of the past two centuries. But here in this context, with a South American conductor, a chorus of white, African-American, Latino, and Asian singers, and thousands of Latino listeners, the symbolism is newly moving.

Dudamel is conducting from memory, as he usually does, and the wide video screens that flank the stage allow us to see what his players are seeing: his gestures at once grand and supple, his close attention to sonorous detail, the way his face registers every nuance of musical emotion as though it were his own heart's story. He mimes mystery, amusement, foreboding; he sneaks up on the players and surprises them; he seems to be asking them to dance. And the orchestra seems to comply. Here, in fact, is the radiance and passion and electricity its publicity department has been promising for months, here in the grandeur of this music and the rhapsodic connection between players and conductor. I have heard orchestra members say that working with Dudamel reawakens the feeling of pure delight that originally drew them to dedicate their lives to music-making, and it is clear that they are experiencing this intensely familiar work with a fresh sense of discovery and even adventure.

Dudamel has closely supervised the formidable task of amplification: each player has been individually miked, with an additional 120 microphones arrayed around the stage, all meticulously regulated by a team of audio engineers. The result of this electronic alchemy is a sound at once warm, bright, and transparent. After each movement there is applause—a strict taboo in the contemporary classical music world, but not all the members of this audience have been schooled in repressing their enthusiasms. "Wow!" they yell, and "Yeah!" and sometimes "Du-u-ude!" The moment each new movement begins, though, the audience is silent. As Dudamel leads the orchestra through the tranquil splendor of the Adagio, I glance at the children of the YOLA orchestra, who are now sitting down in front with their families, at the foot of the stage. I can see only the backs of their heads, but those heads are motionless.

The first full statement of the "Ode to Joy" theme, a few minutes into the final movement, is whispered so softly by the cellos and double basses that the whole audience seems to lean forward, straining to hear. The violins and winds enter, and Dudamel leads his orchestra through this most famous and beloved of all musical themes with tenderness and simplicity, reminding us that we heard it first, tonight, from children. Now the chorus stands, and the opening baritone solo begins. "*Freude!*" sings the baritone, and "*Freude!*" echoes the chorus. The German words are translated as subtitles on the video screens: "Joy! Joy!" The baritone proclaims,

*"Alle Menschen werden Brüder"*; the subtitle translates, "All men will become brothers."

And then the chorus repeats his words, and the subtitles are suddenly new: *"Todos los hombres se vuelven hermanos."* The crowd erupts in cheers. Has it ever happened before that 18,000 people have cheered a subtitle? The Spanish words on the screen bring the old German poem to abrupt and urgent life. The subtitles continue to alternate between English and Spanish, and when the chorus reaches the climactic line "And the cherub stands before God," the subtitle appears in Spanish:

*"Y el querubín se para ante Dios."*

*"Steht vor Gott!"* thunders the chorus. We can see that Dudamel is singing the German words with them. *"Vor Gott!"* He flings his arms wide, holding the entire chorus and orchestra in a long, climactic chord. Finally, he cuts off the chord and lifts his baton to continue—but the excitement in the audience is uncontainable, and although this is clearly not the end, applause breaks out.

With Schiller's *"Freude"* still echoing, the applause seems an outburst of sheer joy—in the majesty of the chord, in the immensity of the sound, and perhaps in that brief perfect confluence of God in many languages. The video camera pans on Dudamel, motionless, baton poised. The applause has shattered the exquisite timing of his dramatic pause. But he closes his eyes and doesn't quite suppress a smile. He is not merely tolerating the interruption; he relishes it—it's possible he even feels complicit in it. He waits, smiling, until the applause dies down, and when he gives the next downbeat to the bassoons, the audience's impetuous interruption seems to have been a necessary part of the music.

It is a brief moment, but it captures a great deal about what makes Dudamel so appealing as a conductor. His heart lies in musical joy, in the spontaneous feeling aroused by great music, and everything else—technical perfection, flawless execution, rigor and interpretation and ensemble, the multiple preoccupations of all great conductors—is in the service of expressing and communicating that joy. As the movement presses toward its epic conclusion, he seems to be not only conducting the orchestra and chorus but also, in the most literal sense of the word, conducting the audience, leading us into the ecstatic space opened up by this music. *"Abrazaos, o millones! Un beso para todo el mundo!"* proclaim the subtitles, and Dudamel mouths the words with the chorus: *"Diesen Kuss der ganzen Welt!"* The moon—did Dudamel supervise that too?—is full over the Hollywood Bowl. The chorus and the soloists sing of the almighty Father beyond the starry canopy, of the brotherhood of man, and, again and again, of joy. Dudamel tears into the supercharged last section of the movement; the famous hair takes on its own conducting life now, and the singers and orchestra seem nearly to levitate with energy. *"Alegría!"* trumpets the subtitle. *"Freude!"* sings the chorus. Dudamel punches home the last mighty chord, and as the audience bursts into cheers, he goes completely still for a moment, closing his eyes and wrinkling his nose like a child coming out of a dream.

And then he is with us, with the performers and with the clapping, stomping, whistling crowd; he steps down from the podium to take his bows. Many bows for the soloists, the singers, the orchestra; many curtain calls, and finally he lifts a microphone. "So," he says, "good evening."

He tries to go on, but the response is so uproarious that he is overwhelmed; again, there is a childlike quality to his abashed smile as he looks out into the crowd. The crowd gradually quiets, with one little girl's front-row cry lingering: "Gustav-o!"

"This is a very special moment for my life," says Dudamel in his heavily accented English. "It's wonderful to have all of these people here!" He gestures around the stadium, peering up into the darkness. "It's a lot!" he adds delightedly, as though he's just noticed. As he pays tribute to "this wonderful, this amazing orchestra," he seems to struggle for words, and pauses. Finally: *"Emocionadísimo,"* he says.

A great roar from the crowd, and he begins to laugh. *"Creo que algunos hablamos español aquí,"* he says, and then his words come rapidly in Spanish: we are here tonight, he says, for the music, and

Beethoven, and these children here—he gestures toward the front rows—who are our future. Then he switches back into English. "It's very important," he tells us, "to have our complete continent together. No South, no North, no Central . . . one America." He speaks slowly and fervently; it's clear that this idea is, for him, the meaning at the very core of the concert. "I'm very proud to be Venezuelan," he goes on. "Very proud to be South American. But *very* proud to be —American." He puts his hand on his heart. "This is the message of Beethoven," he concludes.

And now he slides back into Spanish again, announcing "*un pequeño regalo, muy cortito*" from the symphony. "*Es una sorpresa.*" He hops back onto the podium and gestures to the singers to rise, then turns once more to the crowd, to take care of those among us who are not lucky enough to be Latino tonight. "It's a surprise," he explains. "Enjoy!"

He puts down the microphone and lifts his baton. And as the singers and orchestra head once more into the final chorus of the symphony—"*Seid umschlungen, Millionen!* Be embraced, you millions! This kiss for the whole world!"—the top of the Hollywood Bowl seems to burst into flame. Well, of course. The only thing that could possibly top the glory of Beethoven's Ninth Symphony in this place, on this night, is Beethoven's Ninth Symphony with fireworks.

So we hear once more the magnificent canon that ends the symphony, this time with every triumphal chord and dramatic crescendo traced in sparkling bursts of light across the night sky. The fireworks are perfectly matched with the music: when the chorus sings in hushed tones of the "loving Father" beyond the stars, the fireworks are muted, a low glimmer above the edge of the Bowl; then, as the tempo quickens and the music intensifies, rockets streak across the sky and condense into a white-hot message: BIENVENIDO GUSTAVO!

I can't help but wonder about the purists in the crowd tonight—there must be some—who will object on principle to the cheapening of a great musical masterwork by a splashy pyrotechnical display. Are they managing to hold on to the aesthetic rigor of their position as the voices swell, the timpani pound, the colors race across the sky? It can't be easy. Because in fact the fireworks have much in common with Beethoven's music—both are gratuitous acts of beauty that move through time, with no purpose other than to delight, and then are gone. Creating fireworks is a matter of craft and artistry rather than of towering genius, of course; but like the music, they offer us a kind of delight that needs no framework of interpretation or even of language. As the symphony ends and the sky explodes, I'm fairly sure the purists are with the rest of us, cheering helplessly, laughing like children. And when the stage and sky go dark at last, and the crowd streams back down Highland Avenue, it seems to me that high art and popular culture have made peace tonight in a way I've never experienced before.

This is, of course, exactly the confluence the Los Angeles Philharmonic has dreamed of. And it seems to reside most simply and fully in the person of Dudamel himself, who combines boyish simplicity with the musical sophistication of a virtuoso conductor. As I follow the crowd toward the spangled lights of downtown Hollywood, I hear a small girl riding on her father's shoulders say, "Daddy, is Gustavo the king?"

The Los Angeles Philharmonic has been planning this musical coronation for a long time. Years before the RADIANTE GUSTAVO! banners began to fly, the city—in fact, the Hollywood Bowl—was the site of Dudamel's United States debut in 2005. Then twenty-four, Dudamel was a virtual unknown at the time among classical musicians in the United States—with the important exception of Esa-Pekka Salonen, the L.A. Phil's longtime music director, who had encountered him the previous year at the International Gustav Mahler Conducting Competition in Bamberg, Germany. Salonen and his fellow jurists awarded Dudamel first prize, and Salonen made a prompt transatlantic phone call to his boss, Philharmonic president Deborah Borda—a call that has since become part of the already highly burnished legend surrounding Dudamel's young career. "You have to see him," Salonen told Borda. "He is a conducting animal."

Dudamel was immediately invited to Los Angeles as a guest conductor with the Philharmonic at the Hollywood Bowl. Even that first concert was memorable: *Los Angeles Times* music critic Mark Swed reported that "with the opening bars . . . the party sitting next to me put aside its just-opened giant bag of Cheetos and forgot about it until intermission." He added, "The crowd clapped and whooped. That's not just rare but a downright wonder at the Bowl on the Philharmonic's classical programs."

As Dudamel's international career took off, with tours and guest-conducting appearances across the world, Deborah Borda was often in the audience—in Ottawa, in Düsseldorf, in Milan. It was while watching Dudamel rehearse with the orchestra of Milan's La Scala Opera, she tells me, that she became absolutely convinced that she wanted him to be the conductor of the L.A. Philharmonic. "The orchestra at La Scala is a wonderful orchestra, of course," she says. "But they are used to playing Verdi and Puccini, not coming out of the pit and playing a big symphonic work. Gustavo was conducting them in Mahler's Fifth Symphony, and at the beginning, I thought, oh, dear, this is serious. They sounded like an Italian marching band. But I sat and watched as he worked patiently and carefully with them. And by the end they sounded literally Viennese. It was miraculous. I knew then that he was just an incredible talent."

Dudamel was back in Los Angeles in 2007, this time bringing his Venezuelan youth orchestra, the Simón Bolívar Youth Orchestra of Venezuela, to play Beethoven's Fourth Symphony at Disney Hall. Again, the L.A. audience was wowed. "I haven't seen that kind of reaction from a crowd since I saw the Beatles at Dodger Stadium," wrote Swed in the *Los Angeles Times*. In April of that year, Borda offered Dudamel the directorship of the Los Angeles Philharmonic, and Dudamel accepted. In the normally drama-scarce orchestral world, the news created a sensation, since Dudamel was being courted by a number of major symphony orchestras—including the Chicago Symphony, where he happened to be guest-conducting when the announcement came that he had accepted the job in Los Angeles.

From that moment on, the Los Angeles Philharmonic planned a rollout of their new young star that was as masterfully crafted and meticulously timed as a pivotal crescendo in a Beethoven symphony. In a *60 Minutes* feature on Dudamel that year, Deborah Borda declared, "The atmosphere exists here for him to really change musical history. Gustavo has an ability to communicate what is passionate and vital about music in a very twenty-first century way." By the late summer of 2009, the city was, as one local wit had it, "Duded up": the banners were waving, the Web sites launched, the jalapeño-dressed Dude Dog on sale. Some of those free tickets to the Bowl concert were selling on eBay for hundreds of dollars. Not content to brand coffee mugs and tee shirts with the conductor's image, the L.A. Philharmonic released a classical music video game featuring Dudamel conducting Berlioz's *Symphonie Fantastique*—arguably the first video game ever produced by a symphony orchestra. "Bravo Gustavo" (quickly dubbed the "iDude") was designed to simulate the experience of orchestral conducting—a sort of "Guitar Hero" for hundred-piece orchestra and baton.

As his ascension to the podium in Los Angeles drew close, press coverage inflated steadily, with features in newspapers and TV news programs around the country. Internet postings commented on the intensity of the fanfare: "If he doesn't conduct the world's greatest concerts, end war in the Middle East, cure AIDS, and outdraw the Lakers, his first season will be considered an abject failure," wrote one blogger. *Times* critic Swed announced that he was planning to take "daily walks along the beach, where I'm determined to get the first shot of the new music director of the Los Angeles Philharmonic walking on water." The September issue of *Vogue* magazine featured a tuxedoed Gustavo giving the camera a smoldering look as he fastened a cufflink.

On the morning of his first official rehearsal with the orchestra, cameras clicked as though for a parade of Oscar nominees as Dudamel emerged from a car with his elegant wife, Eloisa Maturén. The day was one long photo opportunity, beginning with the young maestro embracing Borda and then ascending the stairs up to the garden terrace of the concert hall, greeting the orchestra musicians with embraces and fist bumps. His comments to reporters at the end of that first rehearsal were an apt combination of broken English, youthful ardor, and a touch of Valley-speak: "To feel coming from the musicians this first note—in my life, is so special. I think we will have a beautiful journey; we will go, like, to the stars."

At a press conference the next day, the young maestro demonstrated that even though starry-eyed, he was entirely clear about his central vision of Latino culture as part of a larger pan-American identity. When a reporter asked him what was on his iPod, he responded, "Oscar d'León and Pasión Vega, Juan Luis Guerra, Johnny Pacheco . . ."

"What about Americans?" interrupted the reporter. "You're in America now."

Dudamel smiled. "I am talking about Americans," he said.

The long crescendo has climaxed with the jubilation at the Hollywood Bowl. In the days that follow, public and critical reactions tend toward the rapturous. Mark Swed writes in the *Los Angeles Times* that the concert "reached possible record levels of exhilaration. . . . It felt like the greatest show on earth." One concertgoer blogs, "One wondered if Dudamel could be the next governor of California or the classical world's Evita Perón." Another writes that the new music director has "the talent of young Mozart and the vision of Barack Obama." And a third takes this thought to the logical next level: "I couldn't help but indulge a whimsical thought—Presidente Gustavo!"

For Deborah Borda, the event has been a culminating moment in a distinguished career in orchestra leadership. "I've produced many, many concerts, and there are three I will never forget," she tells me when I speak with her about the concert. "The first was the hundred fiftieth anniversary concert of the New York Philharmonic, which began with the orchestra playing the *Candide* Overture with an empty podium, as a tribute to Bernstein. The second was the opening of the Walt Disney Concert Hall here in L.A., in 2002. And the third, of course, was 'Bienvenido Gustavo.' It was really an epic event." She tells me that the live Webcast was watched by people in ninety countries around the world, on all seven continents.

For the young music teachers who worked for weeks and months to prepare the YOLA EXPO Center children's orchestra for its appearance with Dudamel, the evening was truly, as the maestro had told the audience, about the children. "When I first told the kids they would be playing in the Hollywood Bowl," says a violin teacher, "I got blank stares. No one knew what the Hollywood Bowl was."

The teachers tell me that some of the kids were real beginners, unsure until the last minute even of how to hold their instruments. "Cassandra held her bow right that night for the first time in her life," the violin teacher marvels. Dudamel, she says, never stopped smiling in rehearsals, and often told the children to make their instruments sound "happy."

Another teacher tells me about Ernesto, who is learning to play the cello, and whose mother struggles with a difficult home life and abusive husband. "The mother told me today that her husband mistreats her and she often feels absolutely worthless. And then she said, 'But I made him come to the concert, and now I can say to him, look at this!'" As she relates this story, the young cello teacher begins to cry. "She said to me, 'Now my husband can see that Ernesto and I, we are doing something wonderful, that we are worth something.'"

The Hollywood Bowl extravaganza on October 3 has been, in fact, only the first climax of the long publicity crescendo. The second and final climax happens five days later, at the official inaugural gala at the Walt Disney Concert Hall, where Dudamel, having succeeded in bringing high art to the masses, must now address the task of simultaneously wooing the Los Angeles glitterati and the classical music establishment. I can't stay for this concert: I need to return to my piano studio in New Jersey. But the celebrity media machine is pumping, and it is not hard to experience the excitement of the event from the East Coast, or from anywhere, for that matter, with an Internet connection.

It unfolds on Thursday evening, October 8, and like the Hollywood Bowl concert, it has been produced by the L.A. Phil with a high patina of showbiz glamour. There is a magenta carpet rolled out along First Avenue, a preconcert reception featuring flamenco music and a very sweet cocktail dubbed the "Pasión," a parade of celebrity attendees on the order of Sherry Lansing and Tom Hanks and Angela Bassett. "We found him first!" exults Quincy Jones to the crowd, referring to the fact that the Q Prize, awarded by Jones's foundation, was given to Dudamel last year. For Angelenos who can't afford the thousand-dollar ticket, the L.A. Phil has run a lottery offering free tickets to watch a simulcast video of the concert on eight plasma screens mounted on the Music Center Plaza; so while the 2,000 seats of Disney Hall fill with Hollywood royalty, a diverse and casually attired throng assembles on the plaza with blankets and sleeping bags, hot dogs and tacos, within earshot of the screeching buses on the city streets. Although the concert is not broadcast live, Deutsche Grammophon is filming it for a television screening and a DVD release.

The first half of the concert is devoted to a work by the preeminent American composer John Adams, who has been named to the new position of creative chair for the Philharmonic. "Cité Noir," commissioned especially for this event, is conceived as a paean to Hollywood's film noir tradition, with wailing saxophone and elaborate percussion evoking the darkly romantic jazz idiom of film scores of the 1940s and '50s. It is not an automatic crowd pleaser; its dense textures and jagged rhythms, as well as its thirty-minute length, probably pose a challenge for the audience in Disney Hall. But the evening's second and final work, Mahler's First Symphony, is received with unqualified euphoria. The audience in the hall and the audience on the plaza are simultaneously on their feet, delivering a standing ovation that goes on for a full twelve minutes. Dudamel never remounts the podium; he takes every curtain call from among the musicians, winding his way between the music stands and making sure that every player who has had a featured solo or moment rises for a bow. As he comes back again and again to acknowledge the cheers, a shower of purple and gold mylar confetti raining from the ceiling contributes a literal Tinseltown touch to the proceedings.

Back onstage for the tenth or fifteenth time, the maestro looks suddenly like a teenager who's stayed too long at a grown-up party. He makes a "bottoms-up" gesture to the audience, as though to say, "Let's all go have a drink, folks." And the celebrity crowd adjourns to Grand Avenue, which has been closed off to traffic and transformed into a flamboyant pseudo–Latin American street scene, with hot pink and orange tablecloths and performing acrobats dressed as tropical birds. Dudamel joins in the celebration, eating camarones and chimichurri and dancing with his wife. Asked by a *Los Angeles Times* reporter for a comment, the man who has just triumphed in a formidably difficult world premiere and explored the depths of a great symphonic masterwork smiles, shrugs, and says, "All this—it's a lot of fun."

The critics seem to have had a lot of fun too. Writes Mark Swed, "Dudamel can shape a musical phrase and put energy into it so that it seems to have a life of its own." The *New York Times* critic Anthony Tommasini concurs: "For all the sheer energy of the music-making, here was a probing, rigorous and richly characterized interpretation, which Mr. Dudamel conducted from memory." And the *Huffington Post* weighs in: "As with other great conductors, this young maestro senses, seizes on and communicates every scintilla of musical emotion in the great Mahler symphony."

Ever since Dudamel first came to prominence, he has been hailed in some quarters as "the next Leonard Bernstein." It is not an easy mantle to bear. But these reviews, and many like them, seem to justify the comparison. Dudamel does, in fact, display the same near-impossible combination of qualities that distinguished Bernstein: youthful ardor, unabashed charisma, expressive flamboyance, and singular musical intelligence. And there is something else, something almost intangible—a sense of humanness, of simplicity and even vulnerability, that evokes not only awe from audiences, but love. Dudamel, like Bernstein, has this quality. We could not help but love Lenny; we cannot help but love Gustavo.

"I first heard classical music," Gustavo Dudamel says to me, "when I was about three months old. My family lived in the city of Barquisimeto, and my father played the trombone. There are still pictures hanging on the wall of our house that show my father playing, and me, a tiny baby, staring up at him and smiling."

We are talking in Dudamel's office at the Los Angeles Philharmonic, a sun-filled space lined with shelves full of books and musical scores, with a grand piano hard by the leather couches. It is late afternoon; Dudamel is pausing for an espresso between a rehearsal and a performance. In person, in a striped tee shirt and jeans, he is even more relaxed and lithe than he looks on the podium, and his energy is just the same as it is onstage—high-spirited, effusive, and friendly. "You are writing a book about the Sistema, that is wonderful!" he has said to me in greeting. "Of course there must be a book!"

I ask him about the story, so frequently reported in the press, that as a small boy he liked to line up his toy action figures while playing cassettes of the great orchestras of Vienna and Berlin performing his favorite symphonies, and conduct the toys as though they were the orchestra. He smiles and nods. "Yes, it's true," he says. "I was always in love with conducting. But even earlier, as a baby, I would go to concerts where my father was playing, and so I would hear concert music live. And my mother loved music; she sang in the choir and was the librarian at the conservatory. To play music, to hear music, to be surrounded by music—it seemed as natural as breathing."

Barquisimeto, the fourth-largest city in Venezuela, is a bustling commercial and agricultural hub, but Dudamel describes it with affection as "the musical capital of Venezuela." His youthful parents—they were still in their teens when he was born in 1981—began his musical education early, sending him to the local El Sistema music program for lessons in singing, piano, flute. "It was a very beautiful atmosphere," he says. "It was in a little house, the former home of a piano teacher. Everybody played, everybody sang.

"Of course, since my father was a trombonist, I was infatuated with the trombone," he adds, "and was always waiting for my arms to grow long enough to play it. . . . Waiting, waiting, waiting. Finally, when I was nine, I gave up waiting and began to play the violin."

Dudamel studied the violin at a local conservatory established by the Sistema, the Jacinto Lara Conservatory, and quickly became the concertmaster of the youth orchestra in Barquisimeto. By the age of eleven or twelve, he was frequently the conductor as well. He tells me that he and his fellow orchestra members were often shown videos of the celebrated national children's orchestra of Venezuela in performances conducted by its founder, Maestro José Antonio Abreu. "I watched those videos and I thought, wow! They were incredible. And he was amazing—I had never seen conducting like that. I was a huge fan.

"And then one day the Maestro came to Barquisimeto to hear us play, and he said to me, 'You are very talented. I want to support you.' So I went to Caracas and became the concertmaster of the National Children's Orchestra. I was sixteen years old."

Even as he started out in the national orchestra as the first chair of the violin section, and studied with the Sistema's master violin teacher, José Francisco del Castillo, Dudamel had his heart set on conducting. "Watching Maestro Abreu conduct—that was the best possible school for conducting I could have had," he says. "And soon he said to me, 'Okay, you are my conducting pupil now.' And I worked with him every day, and when I was eighteen I became conductor of the orchestra."

Dudamel has been the conductor of the orchestra, which soon came to be known as the second Simón Bolívar Youth Orchestra (referred to within the Sistema as "Simón Bolívar B"), ever since. He has grown up with this ensemble, both literally and musically; ten years of rehearsing, performing, and touring with an orchestra of close friends and supportive peers have given him a safe, fertile environment within which to mature as a conductor. "I have known many of the players since we were children playing together," he says. "We all learned and grew together, as a family."

As the Simón Bolívar began to tour widely in Europe during the early 2000s, Dudamel attracted the attention of renowned conductors and orchestras across the continent. In 2004 he apprenticed with Daniel Barenboim at the Berlin State Opera; Barenboim described the young Venezuelan as the most exciting new conducting talent he had seen in years. Guest conductorships followed with the Israel Philharmonic Orchestra, the City of Birmingham Symphony Orchestra, even the august Vienna Philharmonic. An appearance with the Stuttgart Radio Symphony Orchestra commemorated the eightieth birthday of Pope Benedict XVI, with the pope himself in attendance.

As did Leonard Bernstein some decades before him, Dudamel attained his first permanent conductorship with a major symphony orchestra by pinch-hitting for an indisposed conductor. In 2005, Sweden's Gothenburg Symphony needed a last-minute replacement for a London concert, and Dudamel stepped in, winning instant acclaim and, shortly thereafter, the position of principal conductor. In 2007, just a few weeks after he brought his Simón Bolívar

Orchestra to Carnegie Hall for the first time, Dudamel appeared as guest conductor with the New York Philharmonic. Acutely aware of the honor of conducting "Bernstein's orchestra," he studied the markings in the great maestro's scores before his performances. The New York press and public received him ecstatically. "Once this kinetic young conductor took the podium," wrote *New York Times* critic Anthony Tommasini, "the comparisons with Bernstein were obvious. . . . He delivered teeming, impassioned and supremely confident performances. Clearly, the Philharmonic players were inspired by the boundless joy and intensity of his music-making."

Dudamel was thrilled when the New York Philharmonic offered him one of Bernstein's treasured batons to use. And Bernstein would very likely have relished the fact that the baton broke during the second concert, a casualty of Dudamel's emotive vigor on the podium. Barbara Haws, the Philharmonic's archivist, was able to reattach the pieces, and was quoted as appreciating the baton's "new historic dimension." The Bernstein family has embraced Dudamel as an heir to Bernstein's legacy, a visionary conductor who will keep alive their father's spirit of highly communicative, expressive music-making.

While the legacy of Bernstein has provided Dudamel with enduring inspiration, the mentorship of several great living conductors has been critical to his musical development, and he speaks of these men with gratitude bordering on wonder. "They all have different ways of approaching music," he tells me. "Barenboim is a very natural genius. And his baton technique is so clear—old-style in the very best way. And then there is Abbado . . . the hands of Claudio Abbado are magic. They move with such *cantabile*—it's amazing. And Simon Rattle has this incredible expressivity in his body and in his face."

Dudamel tells me that a sense of humility and immense respect for the music is common to all his mentors. "They are always going back to the score and looking for new things—even scores they have conducted hundreds of times!" An even more important similarity, he says, is their dedication to passing on their skills and knowledge to future generations. "They don't ever hold back," he says. "They want to give you everything they know, everything they feel. They are always thinking about building a future for the arts."

Dudamel speaks simply of his high-profile mentors and his rise to international stardom, as though this were a natural trajectory for a musician still in his twenties. I ask him how he accounts for what seems an exceptional level of success at such an early age. The famously expressive eyebrows go up, and he smiles. "It's the Sistema, of course," he says. "The Sistema has made everything possible for me."

How would he describe the special quality of the Sistema? "You know," he says, "it's about connection. In the Sistema everything is connected; the musical and the social aspects of playing music—they are never separated. Playing music together is connected with being a better citizen, with caring about other people, with working together. The orchestra, you know, it's a community. It's a little world, where you can create harmony. And of course, when you have this, connected with an artistic sensibility"—he spreads his hands wide—"anything is possible. Everything is possible."

Dudamel is certainly the living embodiment of this premise. As he enters his thirties, he is both principal conductor of a major North American symphony orchestra and music director of Venezuela's most famous orchestra. While his five-year conductorship of Sweden's Gothenburg Symphony ends in 2012, he will continue active guest engagements in Vienna, Berlin, and Paris, and at La Scala in Milan. A schedule that would seem punishing even for a seasoned maestro seems to be positively nourishing for Dudamel.

And the pull back to his Venezuelan roots seems strong and enduring. He tells me that just two months before his debut at the Hollywood Bowl, he was back in Caracas conducting another national youth orchestra, the Teresa Carreño Orchestra, in a free public concert in La Vega, an impoverished barrio, to celebrate the 442nd anniversary of the city. A crowd estimated at 50,000 people jammed the narrow streets and hung out of second- and third-floor windows, listening to teenagers play classical symphonic works. "It was beautiful," he says. "Like a miracle.

"Every time I go back to my country, I am surprised," he adds. "Amazing things, things that would seem impossible anywhere else, are happening there every day. That is what the Sistema is about—creating miracles."

# CHAPTER 2

# "*Mambo!*": A First Glimpse of El Sistema

THE CITY OF CARACAS LIES IN A LONG VALLEY SURROUNDED on all sides by lush green mountains—an almost Shangri-La kind of natural setting, hard to reconcile with the dense crazy-quilt of barrios that edge up the mountainsides in every direction. The barrios are makeshift structures of wood and tin strewn haphazardly across hillsides, often perched so precariously that they seem about to slide into one another—which happens all too frequently when earthquakes and landslides occur. Some neighborhoods lack even such basic amenities as running water; giant tangles of electrical wire represent residents' self-designed attempts to access the power grid. Gang graffiti alternate with street-corner shrines in the narrow streets.

I am with Jamie Bernstein in a car being driven up the side of a mountain through the twisting alleys of a barrio. There are children running and playing in the dusty sunshine, men selling coconuts at roadside stands, many stray dogs, a few chickens. The heat is dense: Venezuela is just north of the equator.

Jamie is in Caracas for a week to rehearse and perform a program of her father's music with the Caracas Symphony Youth Orchestra, one of El Sistema's most advanced ensembles. I have come along with her, as has her boyfriend, the composer Jeffrey Stock, to watch the process and to catch a glimpse of El Sistema in action; we are on our way now to see one of the city's many *núcleos*—the Sistema's word for its music learning centers—in a hillside barrio. Norma, our guide, tells us that the núcleo is called Los Chorros. "The name means 'waterfall,' " she says.

Norma Nuñez Loaiza works as a development assistant and producer for the foundation that administers the Sistema. Norma grew up playing the viola in the Sistema; she is young, voluble, and irrepressibly sunny. She tells us that for many years Los Chorros, despite its picturesque name, functioned as a detention center for juvenile delinquents and for abused and abandoned children. "But then changes in the laws caused many of the residents to be moved to provincial centers," she says, "and Maestro Abreu decided the Sistema would take over the facility. So the first students in the núcleo were the delinquent and abandoned kids who were left there." Los Chorros, transformed into a center for music education and performance, began to attract children from the neighboring barrios. Now it is filled every afternoon with hundreds of young people learning to sing and play music.

Some serious hairpin turns take us into the hills above the barrios, and we arrive at a rambling compound where several buildings are surrounded by ancient trees. There is a dilapidated playground and a weed-strewn soccer field, with the nets of the goals on both sides hanging in tatters from the frames.

Large letters on the side of the main building proclaim SISTEMA NACIONAL DE ORQUESTAS; a giant music staff emblazoned beneath the letters sports a bass clef and a flurry of eighth notes. A billboard in front of the building displays a portrait of Beethoven in smoky shades of blue, and a quote from the great man, in Spanish. Jamie, who grew up speaking both Spanish and English, translates: "The only experience of excellence that I know is kindness. L.V.B."

Norma leads us down the path and into the building, where an orchestra is waiting to perform for us. "There are four orchestras in this núcleo," she explains, "the prechildren's, children's, youth, and folk. You are going to hear the youth orchestra now." The orchestra room, its slatted windows open to the light and air, is so packed with children that we can barely enter: they are backed up against the walls, against the sides, their bow swipes narrowly missing one another. They are a variety of ages: a small, intent violinist sits with his feet swinging, not touching the ground; a trombone player is as tall as the conductor . . . who is very young himself, and is singing as he leads them in the majestic minor-key theme of the final movement of Dvorak's Ninth Symphony. The children play with great energy, and the sound is huge and impressively in tune. We ask how many years they have been playing together. "For one year," says the conductor.

They follow with a Venezuelan folk piece, full of canted rhythms and lively melodies—"a gift for you," the conductor tells us. In the quieter moments of the piece, we can hear music floating down the halls from other rooms—clarinets playing scales, violins playing a phrase over and over, a long low note on a trombone.

The young conductor is Lennar Acosta; he is the director of the entire núcleo, though he looks no older than some of the students. When the orchestra breaks for recess, he leads us down the music-filled hallways past small rehearsal rooms and smaller practice rooms, each with a captioned picture of a different Venezuelan composer taped to the door. Eleven hundred children come to the núcleo, he tells us, ranging in age from four to eighteen; they are here every day for three to four hours, studying music theory, taking lessons, and playing in orchestras and ensembles. Most of the children come from the barrios in the vicinity, though some travel by bus or with their parents from farther away. "For them it's a privilege to be here," he says. "Just the feeling of belonging to something like this. The kids understand that everything here—the instruments, the music stands, the teachers—everything is provided by the Sistema. All we ask of them is that they learn to be disciplined. To be respectful. And to be excellent."

He shows us the instrument workshop, where many of the núcleo's older children learn the skills of maintaining and repairing instruments—an ongoing imperative, given the tremendous need for instruments and the chronic shortage of new ones. As we walk back across the courtyard, the children we have just heard playing a symphony are now swarming on the playground and playing tag on the dusty field. A group of kids surrounds us. "*Cómo están?*" Jamie says, hugging them. "*Son músicos muy buenos!*" They are eager to talk to the visitors from New York. They have all been coming to the núcleo for about three years, they tell us; some have been playing for two years or less. They giggle and compete when Jamie asks them who their favorite composers are. "Beethoven!" "No, Mozart!" "No, Tchaikovsky!" "No, no, wait: Dudamel!"

Something close to consensus emerges: it's a tie between Beethoven, Tchaikovsky, and Dudamel. Still, there is a lingering dispute between the Mozart devotees and a small but lively Vivaldi faction. We ask them what they want to be when they grow up. "A music teacher in a núcleo," says Emanuel, the little boy whose feet do not touch the ground when he plays violin in the orchestra. The others nod their heads in agreement.

Emanuel tells us that he is eight years old, and that playing music is his favorite thing in life. His family's favorite thing, he says, is listening to him practice. Gabriela is fifteen, and a violist; she has been coming to the núcleo since she was twelve. Why does she like it? "Because of the beauty of the music," she says. "And because I'm always working with my friends, working in a team." She tells us that she has learned self-discipline here, which she never had before, and now dreams of being a musician or a dancer. Pacheco, who is fourteen, has been here for two years and has learned to play the bassoon.

He echoes Gabriela's words: he likes it here because he's working and playing with his friends. "I want to be a great bassoon player or a petroleum engineer," he declares matter-of-factly, as though the connections are obvious.

Within earshot of a rehearsal room where a wind ensemble is warming up, we talk with Lennar, the núcleo director, in his small office. A bulletin board on the wall is covered with photos of núcleo students from years past, and he shows us a photo of the núcleo's very first orchestra in 1998, the year it was founded. "It was made entirely of delinquents," he says, and then adds, pointing, "That's me. I was seventeen."

Lennar, whose face bears the scars of knife fights, came to Los Chorros before it was a núcleo, when it was still a center for the detention of juvenile delinquents. He was twelve. "I had been living in the streets," he says. "I was in extreme need for food and necessities . . . and I got in trouble with the law. So I was put here—not to be protected, but to be punished."

When the facility was turned over to the Sistema and became a núcleo, Lennar stayed. At first there were no instruments, and few teachers. "Teachers were afraid to come here, because we were delinquents," he tells us, "but Maestro Abreu engaged the members of the Simón Bolívar Youth Orchestra to come and teach us."

Then the instruments arrived. "I had never dreamed of playing an instrument," says Lennar. "I couldn't believe it when they put a clarinet in my hands."

Within a year of beginning to play the clarinet, Lennar auditioned for the Simón Bolívar Orchestra and was accepted. He continued his clarinet studies, and then, in a scarcely imaginable turn of events, the Sistema offered him a scholarship to go to Germany to learn the art and craft of building organs. He spent a year in Bonn, working as an apprentice with master organ-builders in their workshops.

In the course of the coming months, I will come to learn that this is a common thread in the rich fabric of Sistema stories: an artistic

need arises, an ambitious solution is imagined, an individual—
sometimes an unlikely one—is chosen and rises to the challenge.
But at this moment it is difficult to fathom the transformation
from Venezuelan street kid to musical artisan in Beethoven's birthplace. "So being sent to Los Chorros," says Jamie, "turned out to
be not a punishment but a reward."

"Yes," he says. "The music was my salvation. Completely."

Lennar brought his new skills home to Caracas and immediately
set to work, helping to build and install a pipe organ in the Sistema's
new performance building, the Center for Social Action Through
Music. "And then one day several years ago Maestro Abreu called
me," he tells us, "and he said, 'You must take over the direction of the
núcleo Los Chorros, where you came from. That is your responsibility now.' I was surprised, and didn't know how I would do it. I told
the Maestro I didn't think I could be artistic director. But he said,
'Yes, yes, you'll be able to do it. They need you there.' So I got some
instructional videos and started to study conducting."

When Lennar returned to Los Chorros as director, there were
three hundred students; now there are eleven hundred. Clearly, the
clarity of purpose that has enabled him to bring about this change
is rooted in his own experience. "The aim of the orchestra is to raise
and develop human beings and citizens," he says. "It's not always
easy. Sometimes it's very hard. There are many kids here who remind
me of myself at that age. . . . But it cannot be done separately from
making music. You have to work on both things in parallel: making
music and making citizens."

It is late afternoon when we say goodbye to Lennar, and parents
are beginning to arrive in the courtyard of the núcleo to pick up their
children. Pacheco, the future bassoonist—or possibly oil engineer—
introduces us to his mother. She is eager to tell us what the Sistema
has meant to her son. "Ever since he entered the program, everything
he does now, he does well. He's really growing! My other son missed
the chance to be in the Sistema, but now he has a daughter. And as
soon as my granddaughter is old enough, she'll be here." She uses the

same word we have just heard from Lennar. "They become citizens here," she says.

Other children come to say goodbye, with many hugs and entreaties to return. I ask Norma to let them know how much I enjoyed their playing and to convey my apologies for my poor Spanish. Emanuel gives me a wave. "Don't worry about it," he says, in English.

⌒

The Sarria núcleo has none of the dilapidated charm of Los Chorros. Located in a public school and operating in the afternoon hours when the school day is over, it is thoroughly urban in feel, a cheerless building in one of the poorest districts in Caracas. But when we step inside, we are met with the same pleasurable cacophony we heard at Los Chorros, with music coming from every direction and mingling in the hallways. Norma tells us that in this building there are four children's orchestras rehearsing every day, just as at Los Chorros, and two choirs.

In a large classroom with high transom windows and walls with peeling blue and white paint, a full orchestra of middle school–aged children is playing Tchaikovsky's *1812 Overture*. Like the children at Los Chorros, they play with a polish and expressiveness exceptional for a children's ensemble. The young woman conductor rehearses first the brass section, then the winds. Teaching assistants move among the children, demonstrating rhythms, correcting bow arms and fingerings. A small trumpet player beats time on her knees and whistles along with the wind section; an equally small boy with cymbals frowns in concentration, counting beats. There is a brief stir among the children as we are introduced, but they go right back to playing; by the time they finish with Tchaikovsky and launch into Bach's Sixth Brandenburg Concerto, they have forgotten about us.

"There are three economic levels of kids here, all from the

neighborhood," says the núcleo director, Rafael Elster, as he leads us down the hall to another ensemble. "The highest level, they live in the social projects near here. The second level, they live in small houses. And the lowest level is the *ranchos*—just huts, temporary structures without permanent walls or roofs." Rafael speaks rapidly, with a New York inflection to his accented English; after growing up in the Sistema, he spent a number of years studying trumpet at the City University of New York. "Like all núcleos, we are a no-exclusion program," he goes on. "Any child who wants to come can come. And so many want to come that we need to have several orchestras at different skill levels to accommodate them all."

He leads us into a smaller room, where five- and six-year-olds are playing violins and cellos. This room, like the first, has an obvious other life as a school classroom: there are tables folded against walls, and a chart displaying the "Sistema Dewey." "C—C—C—C—C—G," the children play, as the teacher claps a series of steady downbeats. "They are playing Vivaldi's 'Spring,' from *The Four Seasons*," says Rafael. "Because they are beginners, we have made them a very simple part. But they will be able to play in an orchestra along with the more advanced players when we have our concert. Because what we are really working on is their self-esteem. And when they play together with everyone, they feel they have a place. They feel valuable."

The paint in this room is peeling too; outside the window, a tangle of barbed wire hangs loose. "C—C—C—C—C—G," they play again. Feet tapping in time to the beat, they are entirely absorbed, and quite certain that they are playing not simply C's and G's but Vivaldi's "Spring."

I ask Rafael about the many assistants I have seen in every ensemble, moving quietly from one student to another, correcting mistakes and offering help. "We could not do this without them," he says. "Our process depends on many, many teachers. It's very labor-intensive. Most of them were Sistema students before, and after they have gone through the system, they stay on as paid teachers. They give lessons, they are section leaders, they assist and guide."

In a third room we listen to an energetic chorus of teenagers singing a Venezuelan *canción*, accompanied by a young keyboardist with long hair and a houndstooth necklace. In a fourth, another converted classroom with giant cardboard cutouts of fruits and vegetables on the walls, the núcleo's advanced youth orchestra is working on Mozart's Symphony No. 31. These young people, Rafael tells us, are between fifteen and eighteen. Some of the boys have earring studs and tattoos. They play the symphony with animation and an improbable sweetness, as though eighteenth-century Europe is perfectly transparent to them. Every pane of the classroom window is broken. The street outside must be filled with Mozart.

Rafael stands with us in the corridor outside the classroom as the conductor works with the string section on a complicated passage of triplets. He tells us that the Sarria núcleo started in 1989, when Maestro Abreu discovered that the large school in a crowded neighborhood was empty every afternoon and decided to install a núcleo here. There were forty-three students in the beginning; now there are over five hundred. "No exclusion," he repeats emphatically. "Classical music for hundreds of years has been excluding people. We are about changing that. We are the opposite of that! We say to everyone, 'You too can play classical music!'

"But we never forget that we are a social program first. The kids work in groups because we want them to learn to work in community. And the parents are always so astounded when they come to the concerts. Sometimes we don't let kids take their instruments home, for fear they'll get stolen or damaged, so many of the parents have never heard their kids play. They are in disbelief: 'That's *my* kid?!' " He gestures proudly around the bare hallways. "It's hard, what we're doing," he adds, "but it's not complicated. This is simply what happens when you give attention to kids, five hours a day, six days a week."

The strings have perfected the tricky Mozart passage. The whole orchestra starts up again, and the tempo is brisk and the sound enormous. "We're working on the future here," says Rafael. "Most of these kids won't be musicians. But they will be citizens."

∼

The government foundation that runs El Sistema has been known for a decade as "FESNOJIV" (pronounced "Fez-no-heev"), for "Fundación del Estado para el Sistema Nacional de las Orquestas Juveniles e Infantiles de Venezuela." (The name has recently been changed to "Fundación Musical Simón Bolívar," but this book will continue to use the acronym "FESNOJIV," as it is still widely known.) Our main connections there are Norma Nuñez and Rodrigo Guerrero, whose official title of deputy director for institutional development and international affairs seems to be only one of his many organizational hats; he is also a gifted translator, frequent official host to foreign visitors, inexhaustible information source, and diplomat at large. Rodrigo is as serious and unflappable as Norma is effervescent. And while Norma grew up playing music in a Caracas núcleo and spent years touring with the Simón Bolívar Orchestra, Rodrigo earned a degree in cultural management at the University of London and is not a musician. But they are equally immersed in El Sistema: for both, it is extended family, work, and life. "I started out twelve years ago as an office intern at FESNOJIV," says Rodrigo. "I was planning to be a journalist. But once I started working with the Sistema, I found I couldn't leave."

While Norma takes us on tours of núcleos—and, in between tours, introduces us to addictive local foods such as arepas, small stuffed pastries, and cachapas, corn pancakes folded around soft cheese—it is Rodrigo's task to educate us in the basic facts and figures of the Sistema. He tells us the fabled story of its founding in 1975 by Jose Antonio Abreu, whose professional profile happened to combine the two ambitions of young Pacheco at the Los Chorros núcleo; he was both a musician and a petroleum economist.

In a time and place when classical orchestras were by definition upper-class and European, he says, Abreu conceived the heretofore inconceivable idea of starting a youth orchestra made up entirely of Venezuelans. As the now-legendary story goes, only eleven young musicians showed up at the first rehearsal, which took place in an abandoned parking garage. In the thirty-five years since, the system has grown into a vast network of núcleos and youth orchestras spread across the entire nation; there are now close to 300 núcleos, Rodrigo tells us, and each núcleo is home to several orchestras. In a country with a population of just over 28 million, approximately 370,000 children and youths currently participate in El Sistema.

During my stay in Caracas, I hear other versions of these statistics, and they tend to vary slightly with the telling; I have the sense, however, that they are slippery not only because of a somewhat informal approach to recordkeeping but also because the Sistema is growing literally by the day. What is clear is that there are núcleos in the hills of the Andes, núcleos in inland cities and núcleos in seacoast towns, and that hundreds of thousands of children and young people across Venezuela are playing and singing classical music every day for hours, just as we have seen children play and sing at Los Chorros and Sarria. Every child, beginning at a very young age, is given an instrument, lessons, and a place in an orchestra; the youngest orchestras play simplified versions of orchestral masterworks, and these works are revisited at more and more advanced levels as children progress—with the result that Beethoven's Fifth Symphony and Tchaikovsky's *1812 Overture* are as well known among many Venezuelan children and families as the current reggaeton hits on pop radio.

The number of Sistema children who live in poverty is variously estimated as between 70 and 90 percent. For all children the program is completely free, providing instruments, teachers, uniforms, and often nutritional and social services as well. According to Patricia González, a representative of Executive Director Eduardo Méndez, FESNOJIV's total budget for 2010 was approximately $120 million. The great majority of that sum comes from the federal government; other sources include private donations and bank interest earnings. A report prepared by the Inter-American Development Bank, which has supported FESNOJIV with substantial loans, cites evidence that Sistema participants have better academic achievement records and fewer behavioral problems than Venezuelan youths who are not part of the Sistema. Venezuela's high school dropout rate for teenagers is over 26 percent, but for participants in El Sistema, the rate drops to 6.9 percent.

Many of the most successful graduates of the Sistema have gone on to prominent international careers in classical music. Edicson Ruiz, whose mother sent him to a Caracas núcleo when he was twelve to keep him away from street gangs and violence, displayed such prodigious talent on the double bass that he was winning international competitions after only three years of study; at the age of seventeen he became the youngest person ever to become a full-fledged member of the Berlin Philharmonic Orchestra. Violinist Alexis Cardenas, another Sistema prodigy, pursues a career as world-class concert soloist and active ambassador for traditional Venezuelan musical forms. Natalia Luis-Bassa, now a conductor in Britain, began her musical training as an oboist in the Sistema; flutist Pedro Eustache, one of the founding members of the first Simón Bolívar Orchestra, has won renown as a solo concert artist and as a world-music composer and inventor of instruments. The internationally known concert pianist Gabriela Montero made her debut at the age of eight with the Simón Bolívar Orchestra, conducted by Abreu himself. And many gifted young Sistema conductors—Christian Vasquez, Diego Matheuz, and Manuel Lopez, and their even younger compatriots Manuel Jurado, Rafael Payare, Diego Guzman, and Joshua Dos Santos—are gaining international prominence.

With the ascension of Gustavo Dudamel, the Sistema's most famous alumnus, to the directorship of the Los Angeles Philharmonic, there has been an explosion of interest among the media and the public far beyond the relatively rarefied world of classical music. A full-length documentary about El Sistema, directed by

Venezuelan filmmaker Alberto Arvelo and titled *Tocar y Luchar*—
To Play and to Struggle, the motto engraved on the medallions
all Sistema children wear in performance—came out in 2006, and
Arvelo followed with another documentary, *Let the Children Play*,
in 2009. During the same year, a European feature film, *El Sistema:
Music to Change Life*, electrified the film festival circuit and won
prizes from Chicago and Orlando to Greece and Switzerland. The
CBS News program *60 Minutes* profiled Dudamel in 2008 and again
in 2010; in the winter of 2010–11, he was a featured guest on the Tavis
Smiley and Jay Leno television shows. Articles in newspapers and
magazines, and bloggers in areas ranging from music to corporate
leadership, have expounded upon North America's belated discovery
that Venezuela, in the simple words of the FESNOJIV Web site, is
"bursting with orchestras."

Along with Dudamel's rise to fame has come a growing international awareness of his teacher and mentor José Antonio Abreu, the
founder of El Sistema, who continues to be its leader and inspirational force. Abreu's oratorical eloquence makes him endlessly quot-
able in articles and documentaries. "Poverty generates anonymity,"
he has said. "An orchestra means joy, motivation, teamwork, success.
Music creates happiness and hope in a community." Abreu does not
hesitate to claim that music and art have transformational potency in
the material world. "The huge spiritual world that music produces in
itself ends up overcoming material poverty," he says. And he insists
on the fundamentally civilizing nature of artistic endeavor. "To sing
and to play together means to intimately coexist," he has written.
"Music is immensely important in the awakening of sensibility and
in the forging of values."

Throughout the waning years of the twentieth century, pundits
were busy lamenting the decline of the audience for orchestral concerts and predicting the death of classical music at the hands of a
Western pop culture so aggressive that no musical tradition in the
world could withstand it. Now, suddenly, the media is filled with
images of wildly skilled and spirited children in a little-known corner

of a developing continent playing classical music as though their lives depended on it. Even more remarkable, it's clear that in fact their lives, in many cases, do depend on it. So heart-stirring is the news from Venezuela that an international pilgrimage of sorts has begun; Jamie, Jeffrey, and I are only the latest in a constant stream of musicians, teachers, policy-makers, and government officials from across the world, coming to see for themselves.

Norma says that now that we have seen two núcleos, we need to see the luthier. I have always understood a luthier to be a person, a maker of stringed instruments, but the word as used in Venezuela means a center for instrument-making and repair. Norma tells us that Maestro Abreu's intention is to establish instrument workshops all over Venezuela, a vast luthier network paralleling the orchestra network and supplying its instrumental needs—and staffed, of course, with Sistema graduates who have learned the skills of instrument-making. "The Maestro has seen the necessity for this for a long time," she says. "He saw that as the youth and children's orchestras continually expanded and multiplied, we would need our own source of instrument supply and repair." Abreu's goal is beginning to be realized, and there are now twelve luthier workshops across the country; the Caracas luthier is the pilot program and training center for them all.

We visit on a day of warm and steady rain. Like the núcleos we have seen, the luthier is a kind of "found space," established in a setting intended for other purposes. This building also serves as a school, a community center, and a warehouse for storing educational materials. But the luthier has taken over a dozen or so small rooms, and they are oases of quiet, meticulous craftsmanship in the midst of various kinds of commotion.

Norma introduces us to Maestro Luis Alaluna, the founder and leader of the luthier, who has trained three or four generations of instrument technicians since its inception in 1982. He shows us into a room filled with worktables and tools and the smell of wood shavings, where young technicians are at the painstaking business of creating stringed instruments by hand. It is startling to realize that there is no element of mass production or economies of scale here, even though the Sistema's need for instruments is enormous, and growing exponentially. "Culture for the poor must never be poor culture," Abreu has famously said, and clearly this applies to the instruments as well as the music of the Sistema.

"From the very beginning," says Maestro Alaluna, "Maestro Abreu insisted that Sistema children must play instruments of high quality." He shows us a room full of stringed instruments of all sizes, including tiny cellos and tinier violins, in various states of disrepair. Since it's impossible to make new ones fast enough to meet the need, he tells us, "We repair whenever and however we can." One double bass has a neck that is snapped in two, and several young technicians are bending over it like nurses. "The big instruments, they are the most fragile," says Maestro Alaluna.

This work so essential to music-making is mostly silent; as we walk from room to room, there are only the soft sounds of scraping and sanding by hand, and the occasional plink of a string. Norma translates as Maestro Alaluna speaks of the training process. "We take young people from the ages of fourteen to twenty-four, who are drawn to this work, and we give them all the training they need. It is all absolutely free, paid for by the Sistema—even their work clothes. And then when they are trained, we employ them to go to núcleos throughout the country to teach what they have learned and to create regional luthier centers."

One room is devoted to the art and craft of building cuatros, the traditional Venezuelan folk instrument that looks like a small four-stringed guitar; a teacher is working with a student on a delicate design of inlaid wood around the sound hole of a new cuatro. In another room are enough small harps to populate an entire Rococo painting of cherubim. "We are teaching young people to build harps," says the Maestro. "The Sistema is going to begin a program for very young children to play the harp." Norma tells us that Rodrigo's father, a lawyer who is also a trained harpist, supervises the harp curriculum for the entire Sistema.

In a room with windows wide open to the downpour outside, a young man is building a guitar. The box of the guitar is constructed of oak, he tells us, and the soundboard is made of pine. It will take him three months to finish. "This is the first guitar of this young *chico*," Maestro Alaluna says proudly. "He is a very fine musician, and now he is learning how the instrument is made."

Jamie asks the young man if he will play for us. He puts down the oaken box he is sanding and picks up a finished guitar. "A Venezuelan folk tune," he says to us in English, and he begins to play—a handful of chords and a wandering melody, sometimes barely audible above the thrumming rain. The tune is gentle and melancholy and he lets it take its time. We are still, listening to the tune and the rain, sharing at least for a moment the feeling that pervades this place—the feeling that there is no beauty or virtue in rushing the process of making a perfect stringed instrument by hand, or in hastening to end a tune. When it does end, with a chord trailing into silence, we applaud, and the young man smiles and begins again to sand his oaken box.

∿

The Center for Social Action Through Music is the heart of the Sistema in Caracas, and it is not a found space. It is a grand, architecturally ambitious new building on a busy street in the middle of the city, completed just a few years ago, and designed by Venezuelan architect Tomás Lugo to be the centerpiece of Sistema rehearsal and performance activity. Its modernist aesthetic is at once spare and fanciful; the stark lines of the gray concrete and steel edifice are interrupted by a shimmering fall of yellow and white metal strands suspended above the courtyard like a bright, sculpted rain shower—the last work of kinetic artist Jesús Soto. The tiled floor in the lobby, an intricately irregular pattern of colored stripes designed by the artist Carlos Cruz-Díez, crackles with syncopated rhythmic energy. The Center is distinguished by the work of many great Venezuelan artists, Rodrigo tells us, but it is Maestro Abreu whose seminal ideas have dominated its creation at every level, from the original concept to the design of the doorknobs.

We arrive at the Center on a sunny afternoon; the cobblestone courtyard, protected from the street by metal barricades and gates, is bustling with young people carrying instrument cases. Jamie is here to rehearse the all-Bernstein concert, for which she is providing an introduction and narration. While the rehearsal gets underway, I am treated to a tour of the Center by Rodrigo, whose rapid-fire commentary is both smoothly professional and energized by a familial sort of pride. "Every single detail of this building has been designed for musical purposes," he says. "Maestro Abreu instructed the architect that all the spaces should be designed to be used for rehearsing, performing, and recording. Even the offices are equipped with good acoustics, so that a rehearsal can break out at any moment."

He leads me up and down the Center's ten floors, three of them below ground; many of the stairwells and hallways on the upper floors are open to the warm air, and the park in the back feels like a natural extension of the building. Music is, in fact, breaking out everywhere—in a jewel box of a rehearsal room completely paneled with Venezuelan wood; in another rehearsal room where natural light is pouring through windows etched with fanciful colored designs; up and down hallways lined with practice rooms, every one of them occupied. The Center includes six concert halls of varying sizes, and Rodrigo explains that while they are primarily for use by the Sistema's youth orchestras in Caracas, they are also used by visiting orchestras from all over the country, and that in fact the halls' superb acoustics draw orchestras from across the world to make recordings there. "The point," says Rodrigo, "is to have orchestras constantly rotating through the building, rehearsing and performing. And all the rehearsal and performance spaces are wired and interactive, so that every room has the capacity for recording and broadcasting to remote sites."

A glass-enclosed library on the top floor houses the Sistema's vast video and audio archives as well as a computer lab and a trove of musical scores. "Every performance here needs to be archived," says Rodrigo—a statement I will remember over the course of the week, as I observe not only every performance but also many rehearsals being recorded on video. "And the archives need to be totally available to everyone," he tells me. "Maestro Abreu is eager to encourage music students to pursue musicology and related academic disciplines as well as performance, and this is an incredible resource."

The Center's technological and aesthetic sophistication would be impressive anywhere in the world. Here, in this particular place and context, its message is unmistakable: the students of El Sistema, no matter how poor the barrios they come from, deserve the very highest level of artistry and technology. Nowhere is this message more dramatic than in the back of the building, where a sleek state-of-the-art band shell, the Concha Acústica, opens onto Parque Los Caobos, an unkempt and largely deserted public park of dirt and gnarled trees. "Maestro Abreu plans to revitalize the park from within the Center, and sees it as becoming an active part of the Center," says Rodrigo. "In fact, we're going to change where some of the trees are," he adds, as though it's understood that the Sistema is a force of nature. The band shell will be inaugurated next week, he adds, when Dudamel will be in town to lead the Simón Bolívar Orchestra in a free public performance of Beethoven's Ninth. "Gustavo said, 'Why not start with the greatest?'"

The view from the balcony at the top of the Center takes in the whole cultural collage that is the city of Caracas: a cathedral, a mosque, a Maronite Christian church, and a synagogue; museums and university buildings and a primary school; car-jammed streets and a metro station; a barrio with rubble-strewn courtyards and clotheslines hung with drying laundry. Huge logos for Pepsi and Nescafé dominate the skyline, with the dusky green slopes of Ávila Mountain behind them in the distance. "Maestro Abreu decided the Center should be right here in the heart of the existing culture," says Rodrigo. "His vision is to turn this whole area into a city of music, where musicians will be rehearsing and performing constantly. And we will invite the best teachers in the world to come here, so that no one will have to go abroad to study."

Against the cluttered urban backdrop, it is a stretch to imagine that Caracas could become to the twenty-first century what Vienna was, musically speaking, to the eighteenth and nineteenth. But Maestro Abreu and the leadership of FESNOJIV clearly have ambitions of such scope in mind. The five-year plan for this neighborhood is to construct an "international cultural complex" on a vast scale, with the Center for Social Action as its centerpiece. To guide the development of this complex, the prestigious international architectural firm ADJKM has been chosen through a competition sponsored jointly by FESNOJIV and the Andean Development Corporation, a financial institution whose mission is to "support sustainable development and regional integration in Latin America." The planned complex is modernist in design, with buildings draped in veils of vertical louvers, and grand in conception, with a large new conservatory anchoring the space and a modular, multiuse concert hall suspended over the park.

Rodrigo points out that the Center and the forthcoming building project will continue to bring valuable economic benefits to the city, in the form of a wide array of jobs—for builders, contractors, architects, and engineers as well as musicians, teachers, artists, and the considerable infrastructure of service and maintenance people. "And Maestro Abreu is committed to building six more centers, all across the country, that will be just like this one—centers for rehearsing, performing, teaching, centers that will be a powerful inspiration and symbol to the núcleos around them—and that will provide many jobs for many people."

As we head downstairs to look in on Jamie's rehearsal with the orchestra, Rodrigo is reeling off statistics on the rapid growth of the Sistema—seventeen new núcleos formed last year, twenty-four this year, and a goal of reaching a million children in five years—when his cell phone rings; he answers it and speaks rapidly for several minutes. "The Maestro," he tells me when he hangs up, and then continues with the sentence interrupted by the phone call, exactly where he had left off.

I am struck by how completely Rodrigo has absorbed the vision and mission of Maestro Abreu, without subordinating his own identity. His devotion to the ideals of the Sistema goes beyond professional loyalty and is deeper than hero worship; it is passionate and personal, and it grounds his life. We have seen this in Norma as well, and in the directors of the núcleos we have visited: a clear and defining internal alignment with Abreu's principles and worldview. The vision they share is remarkably consistent, and yet there is no sense of a party line; it seems, rather, to be a lived community of shared values.

And about those doorknobs. They are designed to work by pushing on the knob—so that if, for example, one is carrying an instrument and a music stand, one can open the door to a rehearsal room by simply backing up against the doorknob. "The Maestro's idea," says Rodrigo.

He backs up, demonstrating, and opens a door to the concert hall where Jamie is rehearsing with the youth orchestra. I have witnessed Jamie's lively engagement with young Venezuelans several times already, on our núcleo visits; but I am not prepared for the feeling I get, upon entering the hall, that Leonard Bernstein in the form of a petite blonde woman is on the stage with the Caracas Symphony Youth Orchestra. They are working on the Symphonic Dances from *West Side Story*, and Jamie is talking to them about the music with the kind of expansive charm her father once employed to captivate me, along with the rest of the Western world, in his televised concerts for young people. She explains that the first notes of the Prologue, which evoke the famous theme of the Jets gang, are not only "coooool jazz," but are also related to the call of the shofar, the ancient instrument used in Jewish worship. She goes on to describe the plot of the musical, in Spanish and with much gesturing. The teenaged orchestra members listen raptly. When the conductor, a young man named Dietrich Paredes with chiseled features and the nimble body of a dancer, lifts his baton and launches them into the work, their energy is both intense and controlled. Jamie sits on a stool near the podium, swaying back and forth with the music, singing along.

Rodrigo tells me that this concert hall, the building's largest and main performance space, is a point of special pride at the Center. The walls are lined with wooden acoustical panels, glossy and grace-ful as sculptures, irregularly patterned and all moveable to suit the specific needs of each concert; they stretch to a stratospherically high ceiling, where the tech booths float. The steeply raked seats are upholstered with bright stripes of purple, green, orange, blue, yellow and red, echoing the colors of the floor tiles in the entrance hall. Box seating is cantilevered out from the walls on either side, but it's asymmetrical; one side does not match the other.

The stage itself, bathed in a warm glow of light, is wide and deep enough to accommodate the kind of two-hundred-plus-piece orches-tra in which the Sistema specializes. Its floor is of gleaming Ven-ezuelan wood, donated by the great Italian conductor and longtime Sistema champion Claudio Abbado. At the back of the stage is a majestic pipe organ, the visual centerpiece of the hall—the organ Lennar Acosta helped to build and install. It is set like a vast jewel above the stage, its light blond wood surrounded on all sides by its silver pipes and framed by chocolate brown wood panels. The entire hall has the feel of a musical fantasia—playful, kinetic, and beautiful.

The orchestra's rehearsal of the Prologue has run into a problem: at one point in the score, the music's evocation of the aggressive rhythms and sonorities of urban street life is supposed to climax with the shrill sound of a blown whistle—an ordinary whistle, the kind used by cops on street corners. But there is no whistle to be had today: it seems that so many youth orchestras in Caracas are playing the Symphonic Dances from *West Side Story* at this moment that the Center has run out of whistles. Dietrich assures Jamie that a whistle will be found in time for Sunday's performance.

He moves on to rehearse an orchestral version of the *West Side Story* song "America," and Jamie tells them that she plans to use a word game to help the audience at Sunday's concert understand the complicated rhythms of the song's melody: *"I like to be in Amer-i-ca, Okay by me in Amer-i-ca . . ."*

"I'm going to have children from the audience come onstage," she says. "They'll represent syllables of the words 'plátano' and 'mango.' And so we will construct the rhythm '1-2-3, 1-2-3, 1-2, 1-2, 1-2' by chanting '*Plátano plátano mango mango mango.*'" The orchestra members burst into laughter and applause. There seems to be a visceral connection between Bernstein's music and El Sistema: the spirit of this music, with its combination of swagger and lyricism, feels akin to the youthful, exuberant spirit of the Sistema itself—and seems to have captured its heart, if the whistle shortage is any indication. "The first time I heard Bernstein's music," Norma has told me, "I completely got goose bumps."

Jamie has said that she and her family see the Sistema as the realization of her father's lifelong dream of educating young people in a love for classical music. As she raises her fists in the air to join the orchestra members in shouting *"Mambo!"* there is a clear convergence of Bernsteinian and Venezuelan energies. At the end of the rehearsal, Dietrich bows to her and kisses her hand, and the orchestra gives her a standing ovation, complete with drum rolls and wolf whistles.

A few moments later, walking with Rodrigo and Jamie toward the lobby of the Center, I catch a glimpse of a scene that is just as surprising, in its own way, as the phenomenon of two hundred teenagers playing a symphonic masterwork with ardor and finesse. It is lunchtime for these teenagers, and lunch is courtesy of the Sistema; they are sitting in a wide, airy hallway space around big circular tables with linen tablecloths, helping themselves to steaming hot food from silver serving dishes. No brown bag lunches here: again, the message is that the young musicians of the Sistema deserve not only to play great music in a spectacular concert hall, but to dine graciously together as well. Chattering away as they eat, they seem relaxed and at home in this space. And after lunch they will pack up their instruments and hurry through the bright-tiled lobby, across the sun-washed cobblestones of the Center's courtyard, and out into the teeming city on the other side of the barricade of metal gates, to go home.

On Sunday, the day of the concert, Jamie and Jeffrey Stock and I arrive to find that the courtyard itself is teeming—filled with children of all ages and their parents, waiting in line to get tickets. Norma and Rodrigo tell us that the Sistema has provided free buses to bring children and families here from all over Caracas and its suburbs. When the concert hall doors open, the crowd pours in, filling every seat. With the glorious organ hovering over the stage and the bright Day-Glo colors of the seats, the parents in their Sunday finery, and the children full of boisterous morning energy, the hall feels like a whimsical intersection of church and circus tent.

Jamie takes up her position on the stool stage right of the conductor, and the hall quiets. The first piece on the program, a dance episode from Bernstein's *On the Town*, is one I have not heard in rehearsal. Dietrich, the conductor, gives a decisive downbeat, and the music begins with a jazzy solo clarinet riff over piano chords. Five or six notes in, Dietrich stops the music.

There is a moment of dead silence, and then he lifts his baton and begins the piece again. Again, the clarinet solo, a repeated note with the bluesy flick of a grace note attached . . . again, the music stops. A third try. And a third stop.

The audience is very still. Jeffrey Stock, sitting next to me, whispers that the clarinet player is adding an extra beat each time. Dietrich begins once more, and this time the rhythm is swiftly corrected and the piece is launched.

And from here on the concert goes like gangbusters. Sitting on her stool, Jamie dances in place as the orchestra brings her father's music to life, and between pieces she regales the audience with commentaries in Spanish. "Listen to the theme of 'Cool,' " she says, "these four long-drawn-out notes sound so ominous, don't they?" She asks Dietrich to have the orchestra play a fragment of the theme, four slow notes played by a muted trumpet over a soft swing beat on a single snare drum. The effect is unsettling, even spooky, and Jamie holds up a rubber band to illustrate the suspense in the music, stretching it slowly between her two hands during the slow four-note theme and snapping it abruptly as the theme breaks off at the fourth note. The audience gets it, and the performers are laughing as they play. I cannot help but notice, though, that the first clarinetist sits with his head bowed; he has not played since the beginning of the concert.

"America" is the grand finale. "Who wants to be a plátano?" Jamie asks the audience. "Who wants to be a mango?" A small phalanx of children comes running to the stage, eager to hold up the signs and chant the syllables. After much "choose-me" hand-waving, twelve children are in place onstage; the orchestra plays *"I like to be in Amer-i-ca,"* the children on the stage hold up their signs, and the children in the audience yell, *"Plá-ta-no plá-ta-no man-go man-go man-go."*

The crowd responds with huge enthusiasm—for the skill and spirit of the young musicians and conductor, and for the composer's daughter who has traveled a continent to bring her father's music alive for them, in their own language. After the concert she is greeted like visiting royalty by Maestro Abreu, who has been in attendance in one of the boxes, and he tucks her arm under his and escorts her out to the courtyard of the Center, where a Caracas noon is in full blaze. The crowd swarms around them; mothers thrust babies into Abreu's arms and take photographs with their cell phones.

"Everywhere he goes," Rodrigo tells me, "people want him to touch their children. It's like a blessing."

The Maestro, a small, slight man no taller than Jamie, stops repeatedly and beams for the cameras. Children are pressing in to hug Jamie as well; she too is a kind of talisman. "I wanted to be a plátano!" they tell her, or "Next time, can I be a mango?"

And Abreu is already busy making plans. "You will come again soon, yes?" he says to Jamie. "We will do more concerts! A tour! All over Venezuela!"

Abreu has arranged for a luncheon at an elegant hotel in honor of Jamie and the concert, and has invited a number of principal players from the orchestra. As we sit down to eat, there is sympathetic talk of the first clarinet player, whose mortification about his program-opening blunder was evidently so great that he disappeared after the concert and cannot be found. We are well into the second course when Dietrich appears with his arm around the clarinet player, whose face is streaked with tears.

The musicians begin to applaud as they walk in, and one by one each member of the orchestra stands up and hugs the clarinetist. Jamie hugs him too, although he can't bring himself to look at her. And then Dietrich sits the clarinet player next to him, and the clarinet player is suddenly very hungry, and everyone has lunch.

On our last night in Caracas, we attend a standing-room-only concert of the Simón Bolívar Youth Orchestra, with Dudamel conducting and the great pianist Emanuel Ax soloing in Beethoven's Fourth Piano Concerto. FESNOJIV throws a gala reception afterward, at a restaurant halfway up a mountain with panoramic views of the city lights, where Dudamel and his young musicians celebrate with friends and guests. The party is noisy and festive, but at the quiet heart of it is Maestro Abreu, seated at the end of a long dinner table and constantly surrounded by friends and admirers. To each of them he gives a few moments of pure, concentrated attention, as though there is no one else in the room.

Watching him, I realize that the journey that began with my curiosity about Gustavo Dudamel has led me to José Antonio Abreu. There has been hardly a conversation during my visit in which the Maestro's name was not invoked, a núcleo visit where his guiding hand was not somehow evident, or a concert where his diminutive figure was not present in the front row or in a box seat. Virtually everyone I have met, from FESNOJIV officials to small children, has been able—and inclined—to quote Abreu; his words and ideas are the very language of the Sistema.

And the "creation" story—those eleven young musicians brought together by the Maestro in an abandoned urban garage—has been a recurrent theme among our guides and many of the people we have spoken with. It is a fascinating fable, but short on details, and I wonder if it is apocryphal. Who were those musicians? Why did they come together? And how, exactly, did Abreu transform them into the world's most memorable youth orchestra, and the foundation of a nationwide musical miracle?

I turn to Rodrigo, who has come with us to the party, and ask him about the story. Is it really true that everything began with eleven music students in a parking garage?

"To hear the whole story," he tells me, "you need to come back. You have to talk to the people who were there, who were part of it at the beginning, before it was even a 'system'—before anyone could imagine what it would become.

"And you'll find those people here," he adds. "Almost all of them. They are still with us, still working with the Sistema in some way."

It's impressive, I tell him, that so many people have remained with the Sistema for all of its thirty-five years. "Look at me," he responds. "When I began to work with FESNOJIV, I thought I would only be here for a little while. But the Sistema isn't like a job you do for a while and then move on . . . it is a way of life. And once you have lived it, it's difficult to live any other way."

# CHAPTER 3

# To Play and to Struggle:
# The Evolution of El Sistema

"When I was nine years old, I wanted more than anything to study piano," says José Antonio Abreu in his sonorous, meticulous Spanish. "I was living in the city of Barquisimeto, where my family had moved from Trujillo when I was very young. And there was a music school there, founded and run by Franciscan nuns. My teacher was Doralisa Jiménez de Medina." He says this reverently, as though naming a saint. "She had been trained by Sister Marta, who was a very brilliant pianist before she became a nun. Sister Marta taught my teacher everything she had learned when she studied piano in Paris."

We are sitting, the Maestro and I, in the Caracas offices of FES-NOJIV, which occupy several floors of a concrete high-rise called the Parque Central, in downtown Caracas. The building itself is resolutely uninspiring, and the elevators have a habit of stopping at every floor whether or not they are asked to. But the office walls are crowded with bright collages of photos—literally thousands of snapshots, taken over the course of thirty-five years, featuring children playing clarinets and violins and trumpets and double basses, children of all ages and in every conceivable kind of ensemble. I have come back to Venezuela, as Rodrigo advised, to explore the roots of the Sistema story, and this is clearly the place to begin.

The Maestro sits at the end of a long table in a conference room across from his private office. Bolivia Bottome, FESNOJIV's director of institutional development and international affairs, is at the Maestro's right hand—a place she frequently occupies, both literally and figuratively. She translates his words for me, her English as elegant and nuanced as his Spanish. Abreu is enveloped in a heavy gray overcoat; this room is highly air-conditioned, but I have noticed that the overcoat goes everywhere, even in semitropical Caracas. He peers at me through thick glasses with his habitual expression of calm but hyperalert intensity.

I ask him about his first childhood experiences with music. "My earliest musical memories are of my piano lessons," he says. "I have a very strong recollection of my teacher's beautiful technique. Her scales were exceptional, and her touch on the keys"—he gestures with his fingertips—"perfect. And she had the gift of adapting her teaching to each student. I loved Mozart particularly, so she started me on a Mozart sonata almost as soon as I could play a scale.

"She was not a woman of wealth," he goes on. "But her students were mostly poor and middle-class—I was one of fifty students—and she charged us very little, maybe twelve bolívares a month, which was about fifty cents a month. And those who couldn't pay even that much came for free. The loneliest children looked forward to lessons the most: it was their time to feel the happiness, and the possibility to expand, that they could never feel at home."

How did it happen, I ask, that he had such a vivid sense of his teacher's other pupils? "Ah, you see," says Abreu, "Doralisa had seven pianos. She was always getting people to donate their old pianos to her. So sometimes there were seven of us there at the same time, and she would go from student to student, and adapt her teachings to each student."

I ask the Maestro how it was possible for several students to be playing at the same time, without general cacophony. "My teacher arranged many of the great musical classics especially for us," he says. "She made two-piano arrangements of all the great sonatas, so two of us could play them together. And of symphonies, she made arrangements for three, four, five pianos—I remember the *Jupiter* Symphony arranged for seven pianos! And every part was written specifically for the technical ability of each student. It was a great happiness for us."

*Una gran felicidad.* We are quiet for a moment, the Maestro and Bolivia and I, contemplating the image of Doralisa Jiménez de Medina, steeped in Parisian classical pianism, bestowing a symphonic masterwork upon seven children at seven pianos in a town on the central Venezuelan plateau, all those years ago.

"Did your teacher hold recitals?" I ask.

He smiles. "We performed all the time. We performed because it was someone's birthday, or because it was some holiday. We performed on Friday because it was Friday and on Saturday because it was Saturday. Only later did I come to understand that she invented all those occasions, as a way to help us lose stage fright and relax in performing. So we were always playing for each other and for other people, always enjoying it."

Here, in Abreu's earliest music lessons, lie the basic principles of El Sistema: the joy in playing music together as a community, even on a traditionally solo instrument; the commitment to free lessons for children whose families cannot afford to pay for them; the insistence on performance as an integral and ongoing part of the learning process. It is clear, I say to the Maestro, that the spirit of this remarkable woman is alive in the vision of childhood, music, and community that has guided his life's work.

"Absolutely," responds Abreu. "The way that I learned piano

marked me forever. I never had the pressure of a severe, hard music master on my back. My teacher taught me the feeling of music as part of community life and as a fountain of joy. And when I left Barquisimeto in my teens, and went to pursue my education in Caracas, that feeling is what I took with me."

⟍⟍⟋

Caracas in the late 1950s and early 1960s was flush with oil money and pulsing with modernization. The population surged with new arrivals from the countryside, looking for work; the city was expanding upward with skyscrapers and outward with new housing developments. The oil boom brought foreign businesspeople and tourists who further fueled the economy and energized the social scene. And cultural life was beginning to take on a cosmopolitan sheen. "It was a special time in Caracas," says María Guinand, the eminent Venezuelan choral conductor and leader of the Schola Cantorum. "After the Second World War, we had had a very fertile immigration of Germans and Italians, Basques and Catalans. . . . They contributed to the panorama of culture in the city. Musically, many composers were making new and distinctly Venezuelan music. And choirs were being born in different areas of society."

For young Venezuelans who aspired to be classical musicians, however, the atmosphere was distinctly less vibrant. There were few conservatories in the country where the serious study of music could be pursued, and admission to those was very difficult to secure. As a result, the classical music world of Venezuela was dominated by professional orchestras in Caracas and the western city of Maracaibo that were made up almost entirely of musicians from Europe and North America, playing European symphonic works for the country's upper-class elite. The flourishing economy created by the oil boom meant high salaries for orchestra players; musicians all over the world knew that lucrative orchestra jobs could be had in

Venezuela. But for Venezuelan musicians, there were few opportunities to pursue their art.

"Other Latin American countries had highly developed orchestral cultures," Abreu has said. "The orchestras in Argentina, Brazil, Mexico—and even small countries like Uruguay—were wonderful. But we did not have this in Venezuela."

When the eighteen-year-old Abreu arrived in Caracas, then, he found a city feverish with economic growth but inhospitable to young instrumental musicians. His response to this complex reality reflected the combination of musical ambition and economic pragmatism that would characterize and propel his entire career. He enrolled in the national conservatory to study piano, organ, and harpsichord, as well as composition with the nationally renowned Vicente Emilio Sojo, the founder of the modern Venezuelan compositional movement—"like a Venezuelan Villa-Lobos," in Abreu's words. At the same time, he began the study of economics at the Andrés Bello Catholic University, a Jesuit institution. By the time he was twenty-five, in 1964, he had earned a Ph.D. in petroleum economics from the university and a degree in composition and organ performance from the conservatory. His musical accomplishments were recognized with the award of the Symphonic Music National Prize in 1967; during the same period, he broadened his academic credentials with postgraduate work in economics at the University of Michigan.

At the beginning of the 1970s, Abreu was well on the way to carving out an impressive career in academia and in the political arena. He held professorships in economics and planning at several universities, and served in the Venezuelan Congress as one of its youngest deputies. While he continued an active musical life, playing the organ in churches and piano in informal ensembles with friends, his professional destiny seemed to lie in economics and politics.

But Abreu never forgot the contrast between the communal joy of his early music education and the arduous, often solitary experience of conservatory training. And he never ceased to be disturbed by the near-impossibility, for young Venezuelan musicians, of finding orchestral jobs and opportunities to play together. A story still circulates within the Sistema about a Venezuelan student who graduated from the Caracas conservatory in the early 1970s with a performance major in bassoon. Upon receiving his degree, the young bassoonist took his instrument to the courtyard of the old building that housed the conservatory, poured gasoline on it, and set it on fire. "Why not?" he announced as a crowd gathered. "I will never be able to play this bassoon in a symphony orchestra in my country."

Says Valdemar Rodríguez, the Sistema's deputy executive director, "This incident made a lasting impression on Maestro Abreu. He vowed to find some way, somehow, that Venezuelan musicians could actually do something with the music they learn and they love."

⌒

"From my very first days at the conservatory," Abreu tells me, "I felt as though I had come up against a big wall. It was completely different from the kind of musical learning I had experienced with my piano teacher. Students at the conservatory studied and practiced alone . . . it was a very hard and arid way of studying. I was a violinist as well as a pianist. And I wanted to play. But the possibilities for playing were extremely limited." Abreu uses the word *limitadísima*, to which English can't quite do justice. "One had to study alone for many years . . . and even then, the possibility of playing in an orchestra—it was like a myth.

"So I did not follow that traditional line. I assembled some kids to play together, which is what we all wanted to do. We rehearsed anywhere we could—sometimes in an ice-cream shop when the owner would give us permission, sometimes in someone's house. And we would play anything, whatever music we could get our hands on. We especially loved the music of the Baroque—Bach, Handel, Corelli."

I ask him if the professors at the conservatory were supportive of these impromptu musicales. "There were some great professors who understood us and gave us support," he says. "But others did not. So I started discreetly recruiting teachers I thought could be on our side. One of the first to help us was Angel Sauce [pronounced "sow-seh"], who had been a pupil of Sojo before me. And eventually we had twelve professors, ten Venezuelans and two foreigners, who were willing to support us.

"I decided that what we needed from them was not theory, but very practical workshops about specific pieces we wanted to play. We had no way to pay the professors, of course. They helped us for free, just because they cared about us and about what we were doing. And there was no name for this, academically, and no course credit. We were just a group of Caracas music students who were trying to find a chance for orchestral experience."

Abreu's manner of speaking is so calm, and Bolivia's translating voice so urbane, that it requires an effort to comprehend the radical nature of the experiment he is describing, and to imagine the conviction and courage it must have taken to embark upon the creation, in essence, of a counterconservatory in that tradition-bound place and time. "You understand," he says, "this is the prehistory of the Sistema. A group of music students learning to play parts of specific works, and a group of very good teachers willing to work with them, helping them read and learn the parts."

To give these players opportunities to perform, Abreu organized the "Festival Bach," a series of weekly concerts at the Ateneo de Caracas and occasionally in nearby cities. Each week they played an entirely new program; frequently, the Maestro would decide to feature one specific performer at the next performance, and would give the prospective soloist a week's notice—sometimes less—to prepare an entire concerto. For young musicians who had never performed before, the stress was sometimes acute. But they learned to perform frequently and fluently—and to rejoin the ensemble, with little fanfare, when their solos were over. And their audiences learned that young Venezuelan musicians were capable of exceptional music-making.

After some years, Abreu tells me, he decided to expand and formalize his experiment by attempting the creation of a youth orchestra. "I found an abandoned garage space in Caracas," he says, "not large, but big enough for an orchestra to rehearse. And I managed to find a donation of music stands."

Ah, here it is—the famous founding myth of the Sistema— the "eleven young people in a garage in 1975" legend so frequently reported and repeated by the media. Abreu speaks slowly and carefully, as though to dispel the mythical aspect of the story. "I called many young music students to come to a rehearsal in the garage," he says. "But only eleven showed up. It was a disheartening prospect. And I knew that this was a moment of truth: either something momentous had to happen, or it was over. I said this to the eleven students. I told them this could be a historic moment. And I asked them to come with me on this journey.

"Twenty-five young music students came the next day. The day after that, there were forty-six. We recruited students from the music schools in Caracas, which did not have orchestras. Some came with their own instruments; others, who did not have instruments, came with borrowed ones. Within a month we had seventy-five young musicians."

What he had, in fact, was an orchestra—a youth orchestra in a country where there had never been one before; an all-Venezuelan orchestra in a culture where orchestra players were, almost by definition, non-Venezuelan; a spontaneous, self-invented volunteer orchestra with no budget, no institutional affiliation, and no name. In an unaccountable collective act of faith, the young members of this orchestra continued to assemble and rehearse together day after day, for many hours a day, in an empty urban garage. How could such an orchestra possibly survive?

To answer this question, Abreu relied on two great lessons he had learned from Doralisa de Medina. One was the idea of students working together and teaching one another, a practice he and his friends had honed in the Bach Festival ensembles, where young emerging professionals were constantly teaching and coaching the less experienced music students. And the other idea was the essential role of performance in sustaining ensemble. "I decided we must perform in public," Abreu tells me. "That would motivate us to stay together, to continue."

Some of his new recruits, he discovered, could barely play their instruments. So he developed a method of "teaching over the orchestra parts," meaning that less skilled players would develop facility on their instruments through the process of learning their parts in an orchestral score. With sometimes twelve hours a day of rehearsal under the vigilant baton of the Maestro, the learning curve of the individual players and the orchestra as a whole was steep; and on April 30, 1975, within four months of its formation, the orchestra gave its first public concert in Caracas. They played works by Bach and Vivaldi; they played the Overture to Mozart's *Magic Flute* and Tchaikovsky's *Romeo and Juliet*. Frank Di Polo, who is now president of the Juan José Landaeta Society, a support organization for FESNOJIV, played a violin solo; Abreu's sister Beatriz was at the organ. The concert was attended by a large audience, including several government ministers and officials, and the orchestra received a standing ovation.

Abreu lost no time creating the next performance opportunity. When the president of Mexico, Luis Echeverría Álvarez, came to visit Caracas, Abreu used his governmental connections to arrange a free concert, and conducted his orchestra in a performance for the visiting Mexican dignitary at the ministry of Foreign Affairs. "It was very prestigious to play there, at the ministry," Abreu says, "and all the musicians were very proud! And the Mexican president was so impressed with us that he invited us on the spot to come to Mexico. Of course, I said yes immediately, but I had no notion of how we could pay for such a trip. And then my friend at the Ministry of Culture said, 'I will provide you with an airplane from the Army.'"

The seventy-five young musicians flew in a military plane to

Mexico City, where they played four concerts, including one in the ornate neoclassical Palacio de Bellas Artes. In addition to works by Mozart, Abreu's first musical love, and several pieces by Venezuelan composers, they played the complex, polyrhythmic Toccata for Percussion by the world-renowned Mexican composer Carlos Chávez. They were astonished when the composer himself came backstage at intermission. "He said he was amazed at what he had heard, and that he would like to come to Venezuela to work with us," recalls Abreu. "I said of course, perhaps he could come next year. And he said, 'No, no, I mean tomorrow.'"

Carlos Chávez came to Caracas and spent three months working with this unorthodox ensemble of inexperienced but determined young musicians, not only on his own music but also on masterworks such as Beethoven's *Eroica* Symphony. By then in his late seventies, Chávez was an iconic figure in Latin America, a composer of international stature as well as the conductor of Mexico's National Symphony Orchestra and director of its conservatory. He worked with Abreu's recruits as he would have rehearsed the most seasoned professional musicians, refining and polishing every musical detail. By this time the orchestra had graduated from the garage to a rehearsal space on the top floor of an industrial building—with no elevator. "Every day he went up more than a hundred steps to this attic, with no air conditioning," says Abreu, "and worked with us from nine to nine, twelve hours a day, with so much passion and love for the kids! I was surprised to find so much love."

Abreu pauses a moment, then adds, "In spite of our difficulties, we encountered love and goodwill at every step along the way—people who understood the spirit of what we were doing, and wanted to help. That is why we were able to thrive."

Frank Di Polo, who now serves as director of FESNOJIV's support foundation, was twelve years old when he first met the eighteen-year-old Abreu in Caracas in 1957. A child prodigy on the viola, Frank was already playing in the chamber orchestra of the university; Abreu conducted the ensemble from time to time. "We have been lifelong friends ever since," Frank tells me.

Frank is a ubiquitous figure in the Sistema, accompanying every tour and, between trips, roaming the concert halls of the Center with a camera at the ready; it's tricky to find him at rest, but I am finally able to interview him during the intermission of a concert in Caracas. He speaks of Abreu with an informal familiarity that eludes even close associates of the Maestro; they have a clear brotherly bond, made all the stronger by Frank's marriage to Abreu's sister Beatriz. Frank tells me that at the age of fifteen, he won a scholarship to the Eastman School of Music in the United States, and when he returned to Caracas several years later, he became the first-chair violist of the professional Venezuela Symphony Orchestra—one of the very few Venezuelan members of the orchestra.

"But José Antonio and I, we were still playing together all the time," he recalls. "Playing here, playing there, wherever we could in Caracas. And then one day he said to me, 'Frank, I'm getting some kids together for a youth orchestra. Can you help me?'

"And I said, 'Of course! Let's go.'"

Frank Di Polo came to that very first gathering of eleven students in the parking garage, and from then on, he helped Abreu begin to build the orchestra, driving around Caracas in an old Chevrolet—which he still drives, and which was dilapidated even then—recruiting every young musician he knew, and some he didn't know. I tell him that I have seen the Chevrolet's cameo appearance in the recent documentary film *El Sistema: Music to Change Life*. In an interview that is one of the highlights of that film, Frank says that in the early stages of the youth orchestra, "We never stopped to think, ah, yes, creating a Sistema—that's what we're doing."

I ask him now what, in fact, they were thinking about when they began. "We were just getting an orchestra together," he says. "We wanted Venezuelans to have the chance to play symphonic music.

So we would drive around, and we would say, 'Hey, do you want to play in our orchestra?' "

No one said no. They came to one rehearsal out of curiosity, came to the next with excitement, told their friends. At first, Frank says, rehearsals were held on Friday, Saturday, and Sunday. "And then it was Thursday, Friday, Saturday, and Sunday. And then it was every day." Because Abreu had professorial and political duties to attend to on weekdays, rehearsals during the week could not begin before evening, and sometimes went until midnight. On Saturdays and Sundays, they would often last ten or twelve hours.

Frank is a jaunty character, with long hair and an easy grin; he plays a mean jazz trumpet in addition to the viola and might be described as the "hip cat" among the Sistema founders. As he speaks to me about the birth of the orchestra, there is no mention of personal or professional sacrifice. Only later do I learn that when he realized the enormous commitment of time and energy that building the new orchestra would require, he resigned his position as principal violist with the Venezuela Symphony Orchestra. "Frank said goodbye to the symphony orchestra, just like that," remembers David Ascanio, a concert pianist who has taught for many years at the Sistema's central conservatory in Caracas, the Simón Bolívar Conservatory. "It was incredible. He was first viola in the professional symphony, but he said, 'I have to leave. I will accompany José Antonio to the end.' No other members of the symphony dared to do that."

David Ascanio was another of the many people whose love for Abreu led him to respond, "Of course, let's go!" to the Maestro's quixotic proposal. Like Frank, David has known Abreu since his youth, and tells me that he remembers his first encounters with Abreu in the early 1970s as pivotal and even transformative in his life. "I met him when I was fifteen," he says. "I won't ever forget that small man with such intense eyes, asking me to play for him. I started to play the Bach Partita Number Two, and then stopped—I was a little intimidated, I think. And he said, 'Go on! Play the whole thing!' And when I finished, he said, 'I want to help you. I want to contribute to your musical education.'

"This was really like a touch of God for me. Because I wanted to study music at a university, but there was no possibility for that in Venezuela. So I studied with Maestro Abreu, and he taught me—not only about piano, but everything about music: history, aesthetics, mythology. He would surround the music I was playing with books and art. When we studied the *Jupiter* Symphony, for example, he would talk about what was happening in history when Mozart composed it."

David Ascanio went to New York in his late teens and earned his bachelor's and master's degrees at Juilliard, studying piano performance with Adele Marcus. "And when I came back to Venezuela, in 1975, Maestro Abreu said to me, 'There is no youth orchestra here—so we are going to make one.' And of course I told him I would help him." David borrowed his father's old Mercedes—the early Sistema seems to have had several automotive mascots—and became Abreu's impromptu chauffeur, in addition to rounding up instruments, music stands, and orchestral parts wherever they could be found. "We never had enough," he says. "Because more people were joining the orchestra every single day, every single week."

David Ascanio's brother Ulyses was a guitarist "with Jimi Hendrix hair," who only wanted to play rock music. "I said to him, 'You must come to the orchestra!' He didn't have any interest, but finally I persuaded him to come—and he immediately got out his violin and came again the next day, and the next. And now he is the conductor of one of the best Sistema youth orchestras in Venezuela."

Frank Di Polo recalls that even in those first weeks, word of the new orchestra traveled fast. "My wife Beatriz, the Maestro's sister, was playing in a small chamber orchestra in Trujillo, in the Andes," he says, "and José Antonio called her and said, 'Can you come, and bring the others with you?' And soon people all over the country heard we were starting a national youth orchestra. We had to rent a house and put some mattresses on the floor, for people who came from far away. Because they were coming from everywhere!"

He flings out his arms to convey the idea of a national musical pilgrimage. This image is reinforced by David Ascanio's description, which has an almost biblical quality. "The news about the orchestra was spreading so fast," he says, "and people were coming and coming with their instruments from everywhere in the country! They were like people in a big desert, you know, with a thirst for water. And Maestro Abreu had not only water—in that moment he had holy water, I can tell you."

I ask whether Abreu auditioned the players before inviting them to join. "No, no, no," David responds. "No auditions, no questions, nothing! If you wanted to play, you were welcome. 'You play violin? Okay, here's your chair, sit here,' he would say. It didn't matter how much or how little you knew. Because part of joining the orchestra was teaching the others, and learning from the others. One of the Maestro's fundamental ideas has always been that even if you know nothing but A, B, and C, you have the power to teach A, B, and C to others. And not only the power—but also the responsibility. And not only that! You yourself will learn by teaching. And you will break through to D, E, and F.

"So people came, and word spread. A cellist would join, and then he would call his cousin in Barquisimeto or Trujillo. 'Hey, it's true! We're making an orchestra! Bring your oboe and come!' And they kept coming."

They kept coming—from the music schools of Caracas, from the mountains of Trujillo and the plains of Barquisimeto, from the countryside and from the seacoast. Many were still in their teens; some had never been away from home before. They came to play, and they played constantly—in the parking garage, in the industrial attic, on weekends and late into the night. "Sound," says David. "More than anything else, José Antonio was obsessed with working on the sheer beauty of the orchestra's sound. In rehearsals, he would say, 'I want *this sound!*' And they would play the same passage over and over and over, trying to get at what he wanted, until he would finally say, 'That's it! *That's* the sound!' "

Seeking the muse of sonority, Abreu's orchestra learned to play Tchaikovsky's *1812 Overture*, Handel's *Water Music*, the symphonies of Mozart and Beethoven. Some of the players had been dedicated for years to developing their musicianship; others struggled with instrumental technique even as they strove to learn the art of ensemble playing. It was an integral part of every rehearsal that players whose skills were more developed helped those who were less advanced.

"What really kept all of us there, I wonder?" says David Ascanio. "It was not the promise of a better musical career. It was certainly not, in that moment, a promise of a scholarship or a grant. And it was certainly not the idea of creating a huge 'system.' No: it was the opportunity for each of us to really make music, in capital letters, in the highest possible way.

"From Abreu's energy we could feel the message behind the music—the spiritual fountain from which it comes. And that was really what it was about, for us. To serve that spirit as we could, in that moment. That is what kept us in the orchestra."

The Schola Cantorum, Venezuela's internationally famous choral ensemble, was founded in the late 1960s by Alberto Grau, a young composer whose impulse to organize fellow singers for the sheer pleasure of communal music-making was resonant with Abreu's orchestral ideals. Grau's wife and colleague María Guinand, who is now director of the Schola Cantorum, remembers the formidable resistance encountered by Abreu in the process of creating his orchestra. "It was very, very hard at the beginning," she tells me. "Most musicians of the older generation did not like what José Antonio was doing. To mix less skilled musicians with skilled ones, and to have them simply learning by doing—they thought this couldn't possibly be a good orchestra. It couldn't possibly be a real symphony orchestra."

David Ascanio's recollections echo those of María Guinand. "The resistance he had to overcome from the older professional people of the conservatory and in the symphony orchestra—it was a huge thing. I believed in him, and I did everything I could. But I truly did not know how he was going to do it."

Frank Di Polo is more succinct. "They thought he was a crazy man," he says.

Faced with the solid skepticism of the Venezuelan musical establishment, Abreu made an almost unimaginably bold move: he decided to take his orchestra, less than a year after its first rehearsal, to the International Festival of Youth Orchestras in Aberdeen, Scotland in 1976. The Aberdeen festival, then in its fourth season, already had a reputation for attracting top-notch youth ensembles from across the world; Latin America, however, had never been represented among the participants.

"It was so exciting!" says David Ascanio. "We had never crossed an ocean before, any of us. We felt like Christopher Columbus in that airplane with José Antonio! We knew what people said: that we were a bunch of young people following a crazy man. But we said, 'We don't care! We're following him!'"

Carlos Chávez, the orchestra's famous mentor and teacher, came to Scotland with them, and conducted their performance of several European masterworks—Tchaikovsky's Sixth Symphony, Wagner's *Meistersinger* Overture—as well as his own Toccata for Percussion, which they had so painstakingly perfected under his guidance. The Orquesta Nacional Juvenil de Venezuela was competing against well-established youth orchestras from fourteen different countries, including Germany, France, England, Japan, and the United States. It is entirely possible that of the 1,400 or so musicians in attendance at the festival, only one—José Antonio himself—was not utterly astounded when the musicians from Venezuela won most of the principal chairs in the specially chosen festival orchestra.

"It was incredible!" says Frank Di Polo. "They were auditioning individual musicians from each orchestra to create a select festival orchestra, which would play in the Royal Albert Hall with Van Cliburn. I was chosen to be concertmaster of that orchestra. And there were at least twenty other people from Venezuela chosen for that orchestra—more than from any other country!"

David Ascanio remembers with relish that the Venezuelans not only outperformed but also out-partied everyone at the festival. "At night, all the musicians would go to a place where there was live music and dancing," he says. "On the first night, the British authorities closed it down at ten o'clock. The next night, we Venezuelans wanted to keep dancing, so they kept it open until ten-fifteen. And the next night it was ten-thirty, and the next night, eleven. . . . We stayed out dancing every night. But we would always be at rehearsals at eight in the morning."

He gives me a deadpan shrug. "In Venezuela," he says, "we seem to have an incredible stamina for parties."

How was it possible that an inexperienced and entirely unorthodox association of Venezuelan musicians could take a celebrated international festival by storm? David's detail is somehow illuminating. The high-spirited energy with which they danced together late into the night was not so different from the passion they devoted to learning symphonies, teaching one another, searching for sonic splendor, creating themselves as an orchestra. And just as no one could tell them it was too late to stay out dancing, no one in the entire musical establishment of Venezuela, or for that matter in the world, could tell them that it was impossible for a group of Venezuelan kids to make great symphonic music.

⌒

"When we came home from Aberdeen," says Abreu, "we had won the attention and respect of the international musical community. And it was then that I was able to persuade the Venezuelan government to take responsibility for the orchestra."

He tells me that the government had taken notice of his orchestra even before the trip to Scotland, when the national press had quoted Carlos Chávez's enthusiastic accolades about his concert with them in the Municipal Theater of Caracas. "At that moment, the government realized something was happening," he says. "But after the festival, they were convinced."

The president of Venezuela at the time was Carlos Andrés Pérez, who was leading an era of government expansion fueled by the growth of the oil industry. "Perez asked me, 'What can I do for you? How can I help?'" says Abreu. "I told him that I needed the state to take financial responsibility for the orchestra, to consider it a state project. Most important, I told him I needed support not as an artistic project, but as a program of youth development through music. There was a Ministry of Youth at that time, and I knew that was the ideal place for us."

Abreu relates this story as though this was an obvious choice, a matter of course, rather than the stroke of genius that has made it possible for the Sistema to accomplish a longevity and success unique in the world's history of government music programs. I ask him how he had known, even then, that his orchestra would best be protected and supported as a social project rather than an artistic one. "It was always clear to me," he says. "In the Ministry of Youth we were together with all the programs that were just for children and young people, especially those dedicated to the lower- and middle-income families. It was a totally different priority from the one you find in the world of music. But it was my priority.

"The Ministry of Culture would not have been the right place for us," he adds. "Within all of Latin America, the ministries of culture upheld a very elitist idea of art, as something for a privileged minority. That is why, from the very beginning, I wanted the official acknowledgement of the state that this is a social program."

This careful positioning ensured that the government would view the program as a linchpin, even if an unorthodox one, in the nationwide fight against poverty, instead of as a transmitter of elite culture. President Pérez agreed to Abreu's request, and a budget for the youth orchestra was established within the Ministry of Youth. Government support brought the orchestra both a crucial source of funding and an official performance space they could call home. The Teresa Carreño Cultural Complex, a large center for theater and ballet as well as orchestral music, was then in the process of construction; one of the first buildings to reach completion was the José Felix Ribas Concert Hall. The youth orchestra, by this time renamed the Simón Bolívar Youth Orchestra of Venezuela, began to give concerts in the new hall, their performances sometimes punctuated by the sounds of drills and hammers as construction continued on the rest of the site.

And performance-hungry young musicians continued to make their way across Venezuela to join the new youth orchestra in Caracas. As the orchestra grew, so did its leader's understanding of what he was creating—not only an artistic institution, but a vehicle with tremendous potential for changing the social and emotional lives of young people and their families. Abreu tells me of his amazement at observing, over and over again, that when a young person joined the orchestra, personal change happened on several levels: not only would the young musician grow in spirit, confidence, and the capacity for self-discipline, but also—and perhaps even more important— his family would be energized by pride and the determination to support him. In Abreu's words, aided by the precision of Bolivia's translation, "The family would create a kind of 'lock of support' around the young player. So family ties were actually strengthened.

"And within the orchestra, the feeling of community grew with every rehearsal. I realized that the orchestra was actually a model of community, because it taught both solidarity and social discipline."

Abreu leans forward and says, in Spanish enunciated so slowly and clearly that I understand it as though he is speaking English:

"To me, an orchestra is first and foremost a way to encourage better human development within children. That is why I always said, and I say today, that this is not an artistic program but a human development program through music. It is very important to be clear about this. Because everything that happened then, and everything that has happened since then, has been a direct consequence of this concept."

Here is the seminal development at the heart of the Sistema story: the transmutation of Abreu's initial musical mission into a humanistic vision of social transformation through music. David Ascanio witnessed the change firsthand. "When kids came from the provinces to join the orchestra," he says, "the Maestro was astonished to see that some of them had spent all their money on the bus ticket to Caracas, and had no money left to go home. He realized, 'My God, these rehearsals represent a big sacrifice for kids and the families. They must really want this! So I want to help them.' And he did help them, often with his own money—for travel, food, everything. And he saw the result. He saw these kids who had nothing, spending hours and hours every day making music, contacting their inner being. And he saw that to practice an instrument, to play in an orchestra, gave them a dignity and integrity that they could feel, even if they couldn't name it. And he said to himself, 'That's it—that's my goal.' "

David snaps his fingers to illustrate the moment of revelation. "You know," he continues, "it's not just a *bonita* idea—'Isn't it sweet, the children playing music?'—I mean, sure, that's beautiful. But his vision is much bigger than that. It's about the orchestra giving a sense of life to young people, in the deepest possible way."

Very quickly, says Abreu, he realized that his idea was bigger than a single orchestra—even a single enormous orchestra. "I understood," he tells me, "that youth orchestras needed to be everywhere." Since he himself could not be everywhere, he conceived the idea of starting centers in other cities where youth orchestras could be born and nurtured. Within a year of returning from Scotland, Abreu had launched the formation of two such centers, or núcleos, in the central industrial cities of Maracay and Barquisimeto. Many more núcleos sprouted across Venezuela over the following years: in Trujillo, in Maracaibo, in Mérida and Maturín, in port cities and mountain towns. By the early 1980s there were more than fifty núcleos across the country, including several in Caracas, where children received training in instrumental, choral, and general musical skills and played together in orchestral ensembles.

"For many years, even while I was developing the national youth orchestra, I traveled the country of Venezuela, state by state and province by province," Abreu recollects. "I looked for any place a núcleo might begin. Sometimes I would find an old house to rehearse in. Sometimes, a band conductor who could teach. Or a retired professor who had a talent for helping kids play. Anything could be the seed where a núcleo could begin to grow."

Abreu says that the rapid and public success of the first youth orchestra was the key to national growth, because it served as a highly visible and engaging model. "Our success, and the fact that the government supported us," he declares, "allowed me to show the remainder of the country that an orchestra could be an instrument for social change."

To create and direct the emerging núcleos across the country, Abreu needed to enlist people who understood the essential goal of social transformation through musical community. And who better than the young people with whom he had forged that goal? With the creative vigor of artists and the energy of missionaries, members of the Simón Bolívar Orchestra went into the provinces, sometimes returning to their hometowns, to spread the word. They started núcleos and began the process of orchestra-building in local communities, even while commuting back and forth to Caracas for rehearsals and performances of their own orchestra.

"My older brother Francisco was one of the original members of Abreu's first orchestra," says Sam Marchan, a Venezuelan violist who now lives in New York and teaches at the Sistema-inspired Harmony Program. "We lived in Mérida, and Francisco went to Caracas to study. He joined the orchestra at the very beginning, in 1975. I saw through his eyes all the fascination and the struggle—it was something absolutely unique in Venezuela, a chance for young musicians to be artists. When they went to Aberdeen and won all those accolades, and my brother came home afterwards with his pictures and stories, it was incredibly exciting.

"And then when Dr. Abreu decided to expand the program, he sent many of his musicians to the provinces. He said to my brother, 'I think it's time for you to go home to Mérida and start a núcleo.' So that's what Francisco did. And when I was old enough, I started to play in my brother's núcleo."

Another orchestra member who was given the charge to start a provincial orchestra was Gregory Carreño, the father of current Simón Bolívar Orchestra concertmaster Alejandro Carreño. "My father was a singer and a clarinet player living in the city of Maracay," Alejandro tells me, "and when Maestro Abreu began the first youth orchestra, my father went to Caracas to be a part of it. And then after a while the Maestro asked my father to go to Trujillo and take charge of a núcleo there that was just beginning, founded by the Maestro's sister Beatriz. So my father went to Trujillo, and he was director of the núcleo there for many years."

Abreu used the same exceptional powers of persuasion to recruit teachers for the núcleos, however and wherever he could. Local musicians and music students were engaged as teachers, and their work was supplemented by regular visits from professional musicians in Caracas, both Venezuelan and foreign, who were flown or driven to provincial núcleos on a sometimes weekly basis. Luis Rossi, an Argentinian clarinetist who has been a master teacher in the Sistema for thirty years, tells me that in 1980 he left a prestigious job with a professional symphony in Santiago, Chile, when a friend told him about Abreu and his new orchestra.

"I came to Caracas and began to play with the youth orchestra," he says, "and then the Maestro began sending me into the provinces to teach. Every Monday, I took an early morning plane to Maturín, where there was a new núcleo, and I would spend the day teaching there and take a plane back at night. In the beginning, the núcleo was in the back yard of a house—I would be in one corner of the yard, and a trombone lesson in another corner. It was incredibly hot, and I taught all day without stopping. I think that was how it was everywhere—people teaching for many hours, anywhere they could."

That was how it was for Paul Goldberg, an American cellist who came to Venezuela in 1981, lured by a prestigious job with the mostly foreign Philharmonic Orchestra of Caracas. "After I came, I heard about Maestro Abreu's program," he tells me, "and I heard they were hiring professional musicians to teach. They would pick you up in a plane and fly you out to the provinces for the day, and pay you for it. So I began going regularly to two or three provincial núcleos a week, teaching orchestral skills and basic musicianship to kids. The núcleos were very simple—they were anywhere there was space to teach and play."

Luis Rossi remembers that Abreu's mission seemed far-fetched and improbable, even to those enrolled in trying to realize it. "Everybody said it was an impossible dream. And even those of us who admired him and followed him, we couldn't really tell about the future. But he had such a clear vision! It was all about reaching the poorest people, the people who did not have any other chances in society. I would say to him, 'How do you expect me to teach these students to play a Tchaikovsky symphony? I'm still trying to teach them to play a scale!' And he would say, 'I don't know how you'll do it. But what I do know is that in this country, young people are very talented. So you'll do it.' End of discussion." Luis laughs and shakes his head. "And I did it. Because I wanted to be a part of this. I could feel how important it was."

Paul Goldberg felt a similar imperative. "Of course, I loved being in Caracas and playing with the Philharmonic—it was a great orchestra, with great players, mostly from the States. And the money was just flowing. We could bring in opera stars from the Met, anyone we wanted. But somehow I found that the teaching work at the núcleos was more compelling to me. So I left the orchestra and left Caracas, and took a full-time teaching job in the Venezuelan interior. I taught for about a year, going back and forth between several different núcleos, giving lessons, helping to build an orchestra. It was hard work but incredibly satisfying—the kids were so disciplined, so eager to learn. My friends in Caracas thought I was crazy to give up the good job, the restaurants, and the nightlife of the city. But I never regretted it."

When Paul came back to the States, he got a degree in public administration, and he has been working in that field ever since. "How to engage the public sector in civic life—that is what interests me the most," he says. "And that is what I learned from Maestro Abreu."

As núcleos spread across the country and Abreu's orchestral network began to take on aspects of a "system," the issue of engaging both the public and private sectors for funding purposes was a constant and urgent preoccupation. In 1979, the Venezuelan government formalized its commitment to the program by creating a state foundation, the Foundation for the National Youth Symphony, which provided public financial support and also a vehicle for private contributions. But the explosive growth of the Sistema meant that financial need always outran available resources. Abreu met this challenge by encouraging núcleos to solicit financial support from municipal and provincial governments as well from the federal government. "We were always taking our youth orchestras into the local state legislatures," remembers Paul Goldberg, "and playing for council members and municipal leaders. That was key to getting local support."

From the very beginning, Abreu's guiding principle for seeking support seems to have been "Show, then ask." An impromptu band of musical enthusiasts playing Corelli in a Caracas ice-cream shop could never have won the support of the Venezuelan state. But a youth orchestra acclaimed by Latin America's leading composer and celebrated in an international festival gave him a powerful case to make. And always, the most powerful of all possible arguments for support was the experience of hearing and seeing a youth orchestra play. "That is how the Maestro convinced so many people," says David Ascanio. "He would say to everyone, 'Just come to the concert, then decide if you want to support it.' And of course, what happened, every time? The energy of the concerts was so unique, so original—so unimaginable, really—that people would say, 'I don't know what this bunch of kids is going to do, but I know I have to help them.'"

One of the great perennial debates in the field of arts education has always been about access versus excellence—whether it is more important to extend arts education as widely as possible or to achieve a high level of artistic skill among a smaller elite. Abreu, it seems, has never subscribed to this dichotomy. From the Sistema's earliest years, the Maestro's vision has embraced both unlimited access and a superior level of artistry, and he has pursued both goals with equal zeal. He has often been quoted as saying, "Culture for the poor must never be poor culture," and he says it more than once during my interview with him. He tells me about a group of musicians from the United States who visited a provincial núcleo and expressed surprise at the high quality of the instruments even the smallest children were playing. "What they didn't understand," he says, "is that the poorer the community, the more you must aim for the highest level of artistic excellence."

Thus even as núcleos were rapidly spreading across the country, exponentially increasing the number of young people who had access to orchestral playing, there was also a constant focus on providing more advanced players opportunities to develop musical excellence. The process of teaching and learning technical skills and musicianship had always been an informal but integral part of the Simón Bolívar Orchestra; in the early 1980s, that process was formalized by the creation of a Sistema conservatory, the Simón Bolívar Conservatory, with a professional faculty dedicated to intensive musical training for talented young musicians.

"José Antonio and I worked together to establish the first music conservatory for the orchestra," says María Guinand, who was the conservatory's first director. "There were instrumental lessons, and there were lessons in harmony and in solfège, musical language. And often the same teachers were teaching everything—the violin teacher would also lead classes in solfège."

In its early stages, says FESNOJIV deputy director Valdemar Rodríguez, the conservatory was located in a rented house. "It was an actual house, you know, with a living room and kitchen and bedrooms," he says. "And we had lessons going on in every room."

Soon after the conservatory began, David Ascanio started a chamber music program there. "We started twenty-two chamber groups," David says, "string quartets, woodwind quintets, everything. I worked with them all. So I had to learn every instrument— what a great gift to me that was! I will always be grateful for it. And I believe that this was the first time Venezuelans had ever played chamber music together."

~

At the same time that María Guinand and David Ascanio were at the forefront of Sistema initiatives to create avenues and standards of musical excellence for advanced players, other Sistema teachers were concentrating on developing pedagogical principles and practices for very early childhood education. In particular, a young violinist in the Simón Bolívar Orchestra was fascinated by the challenge of preparing young children to play in orchestra settings. Susan Siman, who had come to Caracas from the large western city of Maracaibo at the age of eighteen to join the orchestra, tells me that after a few years of playing in the orchestra along with her husband, violinist Ruben Cova, she heard that núcleos in Caracas were looking for teachers. "I was interested in teaching young kids—I already had a couple of my own—and I asked about it," she says. "I was told, 'Well, you know, some are in dangerous areas, and the pay isn't really that good.' . . . But I thought, Why not? I wanted to try. So I started teaching several afternoons a week, beginning at the núcleo Los Teques. I would go right from there to orchestra rehearsals in the evenings."

Susan's husband began to teach as well, and they worked together at the Montalbán núcleo in Caracas; she spent fifteen years at Montalbán, the last eight as the núcleo director. Her distinction as a violin teacher attracted an increasing number of exceptional young students, including Alejandro Carreño and a young violinist and conductor named Gustavo Dudamel. But more and more, she was drawn to the particular puzzle of early childhood music learning. "I thought to myself, I'm a mom! I could use what I have learned as a mom, in my work with the littlest children of the núcleo."

Susan says that she was most fascinated by the question, "What do we need to do to prepare a very young child to play successfully in an orchestra?" Her experience as both mother and teacher convinced her that the answer lay in developing a complex variety of skills—social, emotional, and physical, as well as musical. "We didn't have one strict method," she says. "We were open to everything—Suzuki, Kodály, many things. We encouraged the development of fine motor skills by making wooden and papier-mâché replicas of instruments that the kids could learn to 'play' before they had the capacity to play real instruments. And this also taught them how to love and care for an instrument."

The early childhood classes at Montalbán flourished under Susan's direction and became her "lab," she says, where she could freely experiment and keep records of her results. And she began to train a cadre of teachers who would move on to núcleos across Venezuela and bring a new level of sophistication and creativity to the task of preparing very young children for orchestral playing. "I loved playing in the Simón Bolívar," she says, "and I did it for many years. But I also really wanted to make a difference in the lives of children. So I kept asking myself: How can I lift myself up within the Sistema? And how can I really make a contribution to its future?"

Frank Di Polo says that the superior quality of training for very young children is one of the most important and valuable elements of the Sistema. "Developing ways of teaching music to children who are one and two and three years old," he says, "that is one of our highest achievements. It is a big part of what the Sistema is all about."

⌒

One of the many aspects of Abreu's genius, then and now, is his uncanny ability to perceive people's potential talents—often, talents they did not know they had—and to catalyze and enlist them in the service of the Sistema. Again and again, when I ask people for their reminiscences, the story that emerges is a variation on this theme, which I first heard from Lennar Acosta: "I told the Maestro I couldn't possibly do that, but he insisted—and I discovered I could."

"A friend of mine had told me about José Antonio," says Lydie Pérez, an assistant director of FESNOJIV, when I meet with her in the office she has occupied since the organization's inception. "I was young, forty years old, and I had moved to Venezuela from France, and my friend said there was a young musician who wanted to make a foundation for a youth orchestra." Lydie, now seventy-five, has a halo of strawberry-blond hair and speaks in a delightful if occasionally impenetrable linguistic salad of French, Spanish, and English. "So I spoke with Dr. Abreu, and he said he needed help raising money for his orchestra. I told him, 'I know nothing about music! Nothing! And I've just been offered a great job in publicity, which is the field I love.' And he said, 'No, no, I would like you to come and work with me. Leave the music to me; I need your help with the money and the paperwork.'"

Lydie Pérez was up against what every musician in the youth orchestra had already discovered: the difficulty of saying no to José Antonio Abreu. "So I went to work with him as he was beginning to build his orchestra. I was so ignorant that he had to make me a chart of the sections of the orchestra. But I learned."

In addition to assisting Abreu with administrative tasks, she began to serve as surrogate mother and caretaker for the members of the orchestra, especially those who had left their homes and families far behind. "We rented a big house for the kids from out of town to sleep in, and we had someone to cook for them," she says. "In the beginning, I was anything they needed me to be . . . nurse, chaperone, secretary. Frank, David—they were my kids. And ever since then I have gone with the orchestra everywhere, whenever they traveled. I still do. And I am seventy-five."

The walls of Lydie's office are covered with collages of thousands of snapshots of musicians from every year of the orchestra's development, all the way back to the earliest years. Many of the photos were taken, and many of the collages composed, by Frank Di Polo, who over the years has somehow been able to add the role of semi-official Sistema photographer and videographer to his vast responsibilities as performer and administrator. Lydie points to one photo after another, effortlessly recalling names and events from twenty or thirty years ago. Then she pulls from her desk drawer a piece of loose-leaf notebook paper covered with dense, wavy notations in black ink. "These are the February birthdays," she says. "I have a list like this for every month. I keep records of the birthdays of all the musicians who have ever played in the orchestra, and I always call every single one of them to say happy birthday."

I ask how it felt to be involved with the orchestra at its very beginning. "You know," she says, "even in the earliest days, José Antonio was saying, 'I promise you will all be going around the world.' And maybe we secretly thought—he's a little crazy. Maybe we didn't always believe him. But we always, always followed him."

Among the people who followed Abreu and, in the process, discovered personal capacities and talents they had never known they had, none has a more emblematic story than Bolivia Bottome, FESNOJIV's director for institutional development and international affairs, who for many years has traveled the world both as Abreu's close associate and as an eloquent spokesperson for the Sistema. Bolivia was raised in Caracas by an American father and a Francophile Venezuelan mother; beneath her customary poise is an adventurous spirit, which I discover when she takes me for a ride in her four-wheel-drive Jeep in the mountains outside Caracas. As she negotiates hairpin turns with casual élan and a truck driver's nerve, she recounts the story of her involvement with the Sistema.

"'The very first time I met José Antonio, I was fifteen," she tells me. "My father's cousin was running for political office, and I went with my mother to some of the campaign activities. And at one of them, José Antonio was presenting a workshop on oratorical skills— how to speak in public. He was a master orator from the very beginning, you know. And then later, when I was attending the University of Caracas, I began to sing in a choir for fun, and sometimes at parties after choir rehearsals I would see José Antonio, who was a good friend of the choir director. I learned then what an incredible musician he is . . . he could play anything you asked him to play on the piano, absolutely anything!"

Bolivia earned a degree in psychology at the university, married, and began to raise a family; for a number of years she lost track of the young man who had so impressed her with his oratorical and musical virtuosity. "And then one day in 1981, I saw him on the street, and he gave me a big hello and asked me what I was doing. I told him I was in transition between one job and another, and he said, 'Well then, you must come and work with me.'

" 'What could I possibly do with the Sistema?' I asked him. I didn't feel qualified; I loved music, but I wasn't a musician. But he was very insistent. And so I began to work with him, on things like organizing a music curriculum."

In 1983, Abreu was appointed minister of culture by the Venezuelan government, a position that gave him the opportunity to reconceive the traditional elitist model of Latin American cultural ministries in a more progressive, education-oriented image. One of his first acts as minister was to initiate the creation of a university-level institute of music, so that young musicians ambitious to pursue professional careers would not have to go abroad, as Frank Di Polo, David Ascanio, and so many others had done, for their higher education. Bolivia worked with Abreu on the proposal for this initiative, helping to get it approved despite strong resistance from some university faculty who objected to the idea of an institute for a "non-academic" field.

"When we finally got the approval," Bolivia tells me, "the Maestro said, 'Okay, we're going to start the institute and you're going to be the director.' I said, 'I *am*?!' I knew nothing about directing a music institute! But he told me I would be able to do it, and he would give me every kind of support I would need.

"And he was right. We opened the Instituto de Estudios Musicales in an old house near the conservatory. We offered actual university degrees in all the areas of musical study, not only performance, but also aesthetics, musicology, music pedagogy, composition. María Guinand was in charge of all the musical and academic aspects. She was wonderful to work with. And I was the director of the institute for ten years."

Bolivia shifts her Jeep into a higher gear and guns the engine as the winding road up the mountain becomes steeper. "And then one day José Antonio called me and said, 'We are going to start a TV program that features musical performances of the Simón Bolívar Orchestra and other ensembles, and we need someone to be the presenter on the program, interviewing the musicians and introducing the musical works. And you are going to do it.' And I said, 'I *am?!*' "

Bolivia worked for eight years on the new television program, *Objective: Music,* which was nationally broadcast and highly successful. And in the late 1980s, when Abreu needed someone to represent the Sistema abroad in a diplomatic capacity, he tapped her for this role as well. "He said to me, 'We are making an agreement with the Bolivian government to help create a youth orchestra there, and you are going to go and meet with the officials and sign the papers.' And I said . . . " Bolivia smiles without finishing the sentence.

We have reached the top of the mountain, and the Jeep embarks upon a descent down a road that feels even more dizzyingly precarious than the upward climb. In the distance, a range of faded green mountains shimmers in the heat; there is a drought in the countryside, and a constant smell of burning wood fires. "A few years ago I left the Sistema for a while to take care of my father, who was ill," Bolivia continues. "But I never lost touch with José Antonio. And then last year he called me and asked if I would come back to FESNOJIV as director of international relations. And of course I said yes." She is quiet for a moment and then adds, "I have never said no."

Like so many other personal stories that make up the history of the Sistema, Bolivia's is a story of courage—the courage to continue saying "yes" to a cause that inspired her, even though, with each new and daunting challenge, she was unconvinced that she could succeed. She adjusts her sunglasses and peers at the road ahead, which dips sharply toward the valley and then rises again. "I love to drive downhill really fast," says FESNOJIV's gracious and genteel director of international relations as she presses hard on the accelerator. "Whooo! Here we go!"

Throughout the 1980s, even as he oversaw the expansion of núcleos across the country, built government alliances and pursued private fundraising, created an orchestral conservatory and a state institute for music, and took on the responsibilities of the Cultural Ministry, Abreu continued to conduct the Simón Bolívar Youth Orchestra. But he was eager to find a replacement. "I conducted the orchestra because initially there was no one else; it was my responsibility," he tells me. "But by nature, I'm not a conductor. Ideally, I wanted to promote the orchestra, not conduct it."

Abreu found a crucial colleague in the world-renowned Mexican conductor Eduardo Mata. After seventeen years at the helm of the Dallas Symphony, Mata was seeking to explore and record difficult and relatively unknown music by Latin American composers. The Simón Bolívar Youth Orchestra was perfect for his purposes; they were dynamic and enthusiastic, with a tireless appetite for long hours of rehearsal and a vast proficiency with the intricacies of Latin rhythms—strengths they had begun to develop in part through the guidance of Mata's teacher, Carlos Chávez. Maestro Mata led the orchestra in their first recording ventures during the early 1990s. "In Eduardo Mata," Abreu tells me, "I identified the person who could help me, who could lead the orchestra so that I could dedicate myself to managing."

Throughout the last twenty years, as Abreu has dedicated himself to managing the growth and development of the Sistema, he has continually reimagined the twin goals of access and excellence on an ever-greater scale. His political and diplomatic acuity have enabled him to gain the backing and material support of seven consecutive Venezuelan governments, ranging across the political spectrum from center-right to the current leftist presidency of Hugo Chávez. Abreu works vigorously to ensure the continuation of this support, frequently bringing government officials to youth orchestra concerts, even as he is careful to keep the Sistema separate from partisan politics.

In the years since the state foundation that administers the Sistema was formalized as FESNOJIV, in 1996, additional support has come from sources other than the Venezuelan government, including UNICEF, the National Telephone Company of Venezuela, and the World Bank. The Inter-American Development Bank has acknowledged the program's social impact with a series of substantial loans. Upon the award of an IDB loan of $150 million in 2007, a *New York Times* article by journalist Arthur Lubow reported that "weighing such benefits as a falloff in school dropout rates and a decline in crime, the bank calculated that every dollar invested in the Sistema was reaping about $1.68 in social dividends."

As the work of the Sistema has grown more and more widely recognized across Venezuela, and has gained increasing renown for its transformative effects on the lives of young people, the impetus to create new núcleos has come more and more from provincial cities and towns themselves, rather than from FESNOJIV. In Rodrigo Guerrero's words, "Communities have come to see the Sistema not only as something they'd like to have, but as a necessity. They have seen the tangible results of what it can do." He adds, "Thirty-five years ago, the Maestro and his friends drove around and said, 'Who wants to play music?' Now, it's the opposite: everyone all over the country comes to us and says, 'We want to play!'"

In 2001, Eduardo Méndez, now the executive director of FESNOJIV, was appointed the national director of núcleos, to help guide and coordinate this growth. Eduardo tells me that as a rule, all núcleo expenses relating to human resources and salaries are covered by FESNOJIV, as are some operational expenses and support for special seminars and concerts; but each núcleo is responsible for working out cooperative arrangements with local and regional governments and private sources to cover all other expenses, including buildings, facilities, and instruments.

There is a constant stream of new applications, he says, from new youth orchestra programs across the country that want to become affiliated with the Sistema. "We can't always accommodate them right away," he adds, "but even if we have to postpone them for a while, we try never to say no."

In recent years, the Sistema has continued and expanded its efforts to reach marginalized populations. A number of pioneering núcleos have made a priority of mainstreaming children with special needs, creating ways for blind, deaf, and handicapped young people to participate fully in orchestral and choral performance. And an initiative to establish núcleos in prisons was launched in 2007. At several prisons in the Andes and on the western coast, and at a women's prison in Los Teques, inmates gather regularly in orchestras and smaller ensembles to play Venezuelan folk music and symphonic masterworks.

Even as núcleos have proliferated, they have continued to expand internally and to develop multiple layers and stages of pedagogy. By the last decade, most núcleos had established two or three orchestras each, at varying skill levels, and many had formed early childhood programs, folk ensembles, and choirs as well. For more advanced students, some núcleos developed their own informal conservatories. "Sometimes, the local conservatories take place in a courtyard or under a mango tree," says Valdemar Rodríguez, "so you can't have lessons when it rains."

The steady expansion of the núcleo system to include hundreds of thousands of children across the country seems only to have intensified Abreu's ambition to pursue musical excellence in tandem with pedagogical growth. "I decided to create an academy for each of the different instruments, to unify teaching across the country in each instrument," he tells me. "In this way, the Sistema truly began to take on the quality of a system. The very first maestros of each instrument established the basic pedagogy. For example, all the string teaching in the Sistema derives from the teachings of the first master string teacher, José Francisco del Castillo. Ever since the beginning, the string teachers have been his students, or the students of his students.

"And it's the same with the other instruments. The beauty of the academies is that if a violin student moves from Mérida to Barquisimeto, for example, or a trumpet student moves from Trujillo to Caracas, that student's studies can carry on with continuity, with no interruption." Abreu adds that national academies also reinforce the feeling of group identity among players of the same instrument. "It's one of the central elements of the Sistema," he says, "group identity within an orchestra, and also group identity with others who play the same instrument."

Along with the academies have come other unifying traditions. Annual festivals take place for each instrument: Frank Di Polo runs a countrywide viola festival each year, and Valdemar Rodríguez a clarinet festival. These festivals seem to be mega-recitals that morph into conventions, bringing students, teachers, and enthusiasts together to engage in marathon bouts of music-making, with scores of soloists exploring every corner of the repertoire. "The best students come from all over the country to the festivals, and so do the best teachers," says Luis Rossi, the Argentinian clarinetist who was the Sistema's first master clarinet teacher. Luis, who now maintains a clarinet-making studio in Santiago and makes instruments for world-famous musicians including Paquito D'Rivera, continues to teach at the Sistema's Simón Bolívar Conservatory and helps with the clarinet festival each year. "There is nothing like this anywhere else in the world," he says of the festivals. "I mean, where else are you going to find several full orchestras ready to accompany dozens of soloists? This doesn't exist anywhere else! It's completely unique here."

He adds that the level of playing at the festivals is "incredibly high. The repertoire of the clarinet program in Venezuela is at least as high as it is at the Paris Conservatoire. Of this I have no doubt."

The Simón Bolívar Conservatory has continued to expand and thrive, with jazz and folk music programs now complementing the rigorous curriculum of classical studies. "Our conservatory is similar in some ways to the conservatories in the States," says Valdemar Rodríguez, "with the one important difference that ours is very, very flexible. We are constantly in the process of changing and growing."

There is another important difference, eloquently encapsulated in a description on FESNOJIV's Web site. "The Simón Bolívar Conservatory of Music," it explains, "operates under a different concept than traditional conservatories: the collective practice of music is an essential part of its teaching program."

In the area of formal higher education, Abreu has consolidated the Institute for Music with institutes for other performing arts, such as drama and dance, forming a comprehensive National University of the Arts. And under the guidance of María Guinand, who was so influential in creating pedagogical structures for the conservatory and the institute, a master's degree in music has recently been established at one of the Caracas universities. "Students who complete their studies at the conservatory or the institute, and want to earn an advanced degree, no longer have to leave the country to do so," María tells me. "They can do it here at home."

According to Rodrigo and other Sistema spokespeople, plans for the future include an increased emphasis in two major areas: composition and choral work. While Venezuela has since the mid-twentieth century been home to a thriving school of contemporary composition, Sistema pedagogy has thus far focused more on performing than on creating music. In the words of Alexis Cardenas, the violin virtuoso who came up through the Sistema, "We have excellent orchestras, directors, and soloists. Now we have to go on to something else: a sonic 'imaginarium.' We need new composers to carry on our musical traditions."

As for choral music, singing together has long been an integral part of the work and mission of the Sistema, and many núcleos have multiple choirs at various age and skill levels, just as they have multiple orchestras. But the primary focus has undeniably been on orchestral work. Abreu and his colleagues are eager to see the Sistema develop an intensified focus upon the choral sphere.

According to María Guinand, such an evolution will find natural support in Venezuelan vocal traditions. "The rich panorama of choral life here has developed throughout all layers and classes of society," she says. María, whose cosmopolitan education is evident in the British flavor of her accented English, speaks of the philosophical and spiritual kinship between the Sistema and her choral organization, the Schola Cantorum. "You know, the Schola began just a few years before the Sistema did," she tells me. "And the beginnings were very similar. My husband, Alberto Grau, a composer and choral conductor who had gone to the conservatory with Maestro Abreu, simply gathered a group of young musicians and said, 'Do you want to sing?' And there was no place at the conservatory for such a thing."

Abreu and Grau became close friends and frequent collaborators, she adds, and shared a pedagogical emphasis upon learning by doing and upon the primacy of ensemble. Like the Simón Bolívar Orchestra, the Schola Cantorum gained international recognition very early in its existence, winning first prize in Italy's Guido d'Arezzo Competition in 1974, and went on to garner increasing worldwide acclaim. María Guinand has been its principal conductor for many years. "We are a private foundation," María says, "not public like the Sistema. So we have our own path. But we are always working in close alliance with the Sistema. And to see the Sistema make a wide and deep space for choral life—that will be a very beautiful thing."

"There is one simple reason that the Sistema is so successful," Gustavo Dudamel says to me when we speak about his musical roots in Venezuela. "It is the Maestro. He is the soul of it—not only the creator, but also the soul. From the very beginning, he has had the capacity to know everyone's needs, to take care of everyone. He gives this care not only to the people closest to him, but to everybody! He knows the little boy in San Juan de los Morros, six years old, playing the violin. He knows the little girl in Mérida, beginning the clarinet." Dudamel spreads his arms wide as if to embrace a great orchestra. "He has time for everybody," he says. "I don't understand how it is possible, but it is very beautiful."

He adds that because of Abreu's example, the Sistema as a whole is imbued with an ethic of caring and mutual support. "He has passed it on to all of us," he says. "We are his sons and daughters; we have his blood in our veins." Since many of the young people in the Sistema now are the children or students of people who grew up in the Sistema, the tradition has been passed down from one generation to another. "It's in our DNA," he says.

Dudamel adds that he himself experienced this legacy first in the núcleo at Barquisimeto where he began his musical training. "And that núcleo," he explains, "had an especially beautiful atmosphere. Because it was located in the house where Maestro Abreu took piano lessons when he was a child."

The house, I ask, of Doralisa de Medina? Yes, he says, that little house was the núcleo of Barquisimeto until a new, larger one was built in the 1990s. The symbolic resonance of this coincidence is powerful: Dudamel became a musician in exactly the same place where Abreu had the formative experiences of joy in musical community that would later lead to the creation of the Sistema. "Yes," agrees Dudamel, "the DNA goes all the way back to Doralisa."

When I ask Dudamel what was most memorable about studying with Abreu, he struggles for a moment to find the words he wants. "All the time he is teaching you music, he is also teaching you social values," he says finally. "It is always about music. And it is also always about love. He's an amazing teacher, an amazing human being. And a genius."

The missionary zeal with which Abreu sustains this devotion and commitment to those around him, while at the same time constantly continuing to build and expand the Sistema in Venezuela and across the world, comes at a certain personal cost. It's widely known that the Maestro's passion for his work consumes his life, often taking the place of less lofty concerns like sleeping and eating. Bolivia tells me that he often simply forgets to eat. "I remember one time, at a fancy dinner with people from other Latin American countries, fettuccine Alfredo was served, and I was so pleased—because that is one of the few foods he really enjoys! José Antonio will actually eat a good meal tonight, I thought. But as luck would have it, he was sitting next to a representative of the Sistema program in Colombia. And of course all he wanted to do was talk about this program. And the fettuccine just stayed on the plate."

Unsurprisingly, given the single-minded nature of his dedication, Abreu expects a high level of dedication from those with whom he works closely. I am told by his colleagues that often the phone will ring in the middle of the night; it's José Antonio, brimming with a new idea that can't wait until morning. At a soirée hosted by a Caracas bank in support of the Sistema, I watched an entire table full of young FESNOJIV employees sit down to dine, lift their forks—and then put them down again when someone's cell phone rang with an urgent call from the Maestro. In an instant they were gone, leaving their own plates of untouched pasta.

His associates acknowledge that he is a stern taskmaster. But they also describe him as consistently inspiring. "When you watch how much he gives to others, and how much he gives to the world," says Rodrigo, "you want to try to follow his example. Our lives may be busy, but they are also filled with meaning and purpose."

Bolivia tells me that Abreu finds a primary source of spiritual strength in his Jesuit Catholic faith. She recalls that on a recent trip to Korea to receive the Seoul Peace Prize, the Maestro wanted to go to mass on Sunday morning. "I found out that the only Catholic church in the area was going to be doing many baptisms that morning. I told José Antonio, 'This is going to be very, very long.' But he wasn't fazed. So we spent a very long morning listening to a high mass—in Korean. And José Antonio was delighted.

"He doesn't speak about this part of his life very much," she adds, "because for him it is a personal matter. But he is deeply spiritual. And his faith sustains him."

During the late 1990s and early 2000s, as the Simón Bolívar Youth Orchestra of Venezuela embarked upon increasingly ambitious European tours and began to attract widespread acclaim, the international classical music community gradually became aware of the quiet miracle long under way in Venezuela—and of the man who had created and shaped it. The world-renowned conductors who were fascinated by the Sistema and stirred by working with its orchestras, including Simon Rattle, Daniel Barenboim, and Claudio Abbado, recognized the importance and impact of Abreu's work. "José Antonio Abreu is a Nelson Mandela, a revolutionary," Rattle has said. "He saves lives with a system that accounts for thousands of young people who now live in music."

In November 1995, UNESCO appointed Abreu as a special delegate for the development and promotion of the Venezuelan youth orchestra model across the world; in 1998 the organization formally awarded him the title of Ambassador for Peace. A number of international tributes followed: In 2001, Sweden gave Abreu its Right Livelihood Award, often called the alternative Nobel Prize, for "outstanding vision and work on behalf of our planet and its people," and in 2002, Italy honored him with its Life and Music award for the promotion of classical music and the transformation of young lives. In the United States, Abreu was first formally recognized in 2004 with a ceremony at Lincoln Center awarding him the World Culture Open Peace Prize for Arts and Culture and celebrating him as "a beacon of hope in a troubled world."

Four years later, in 2008, awareness of his work increased dramatically among the arts community in the United States when he appeared as guest speaker at the National Performing Arts Convention in Denver, Colorado. For many artists and arts administrators in the United States, this was a first introduction to the Maestro and El Sistema. "His speech was unforgettable," says Jesse Rosen, president of the League of American Orchestras, which cosponsored the convention. "He elevated people's aspirations about what it means to be an artist."

Accolades came thick and fast thereafter; suddenly, it seemed, the world was avid for Abreu's vision of hope. In the fall of 2008, Spain's prestigious Prince of Asturias award was given to El Sistema "for having combined, within a single project, the highest artistic quality and a profound ethical conviction applied for the improvement of our social reality." Abreu was pleased that the award was given to the Sistema as a whole, and insisted that all the players from the original Simón Bolívar Orchestra come with him to Spain in the spring of 2009 to receive it. Lydie Pérez, the orchestra's unofficial mother figure, has tears in her eyes when she describes the awards ceremony to me. "I think it was my most moving experience in all my years with the orchestra," she says. "It felt like a family reunion."

In the fall of the same year, Abreu was awarded the $50,000 Glenn Gould Prize, Canada's most exclusive arts award, for "making a marked impact on an entire generation of youth through music." The Q foundation, in partnership with the Harvard School of Public Health, bestowed the second annual Q Prize upon both the Maestro and Dudamel for social leadership on behalf of children; the awards were presented by composer and producer Quincy Jones, whose foundation funds the prize. A few months later Abreu and Dudamel were given the Latin Grammy's Doctorate Honoris Causa award, in Las Vegas; from there Abreu flew directly to Stockholm, where King Carl XVI Gustav was on hand to present him with the Polar Music Prize for exceptional musical achievement. Germany's Frankfurt Music Prize, Holland's Erasmus Prize, and the Seoul Peace Prize, all given in recognition of Abreu's transformative work with young people, followed in short order.

In the United States, Abreu was honored with a flurry of awards from various cities and universities, culminating in February 2009 with the award of the TED Prize, which brought his work and mission to a new level of international attention. The TED organization, a nonprofit group focused on "Ideas Worth Spreading," grants each prize recipient the opportunity to make a highly publicized wish, and guarantees a commitment of financial and promotional resources to help bring the wish to reality. Abreu's wish, transmitted in a live Web cast from Caracas, was for the formation of a fellowship program in the United States to provide intensive training in El Sistema's principles and practices for young musicians who are devoted to both art and social change. With TED's help and support, the program was inaugurated the following fall at the New England Conservatory in Boston. It was designated, over the Maestro's objections, the Abreu Fellowship.

⌒

In my interview with Abreu, he never mentions the profusion of international awards and honors that have come his way in recent years. But he glows with pride as he speaks about the profound effect that world acclaim for Dudamel and the Simón Bolívar Orchestra has had upon the young people of the Sistema. "Venezuela has not traditionally been a country with a very intense feeling of national identity," he tells me. "But as the orchestra travels abroad and receives recognition from great musicians everywhere, this brings a tremendous sense of national pride and belonging—not only for the orchestra members, but for all the students of the Sistema. It is so exciting for them to discover the unity of belonging to something great."

Abreu tells me that the new Center for Social Action Through Music has provided a concrete symbol of that pride. "When we first talked about creating an artistic center, someone offered to donate a big house in Caracas," he says, "but I knew that we needed something absolutely first-rate, a beautiful and exciting new building of our own. And it is important that it is in the middle of Caracas, with the city for its front yard. I dream of making all of Caracas a city of music, so that every family can share the joy. I dream of four concerts a day, every day!"

His eyes shine behind his thick glasses. "You understand," he goes on, "that there will be beautiful centers like this in every one of the provinces. And the Sistema will keep expanding until we reach our goal of free and full access to music for every child in the country."

Once again, I am struck by the simplicity and matter-of-factness with which he articulates his mission. I ask him how he can be so confident that it will happen. "It will happen, because of our young people," he answers without hesitation. "These youngsters who are leading núcleos, leading orchestras, everywhere in Venezuela—they see themselves as not only orchestra conductors but also as community leaders. They are brilliant directors—*directores brillantísimos*—but every one of them feels that it's just as much of an honor to conduct a meeting of neighbors in the community as it is to conduct an orchestra. So they are social leaders and musical leaders at the same time. They are working all the time with families as well as with kids. In Guarenas, for example, even though it can be thirty degrees centigrade [eight-six degrees Farenheit] inside the núcleo, the parents are there working with their kids, listening to their kids rehearse and perform.

"And this is what you will find everywhere," he says emphatically. "Always, the life of the community is around the orchestra."

I think about the struggling communities in the inner cities of my own country, and I picture, for a moment, the possibility of such communities finding their power and voice through the synergistic vitality of youth orchestras. I ask the Maestro if he thinks the Sistema can succeed in the United States.

"Of course," he responds. "It's going to be a very big success! You have such amazing resources. You already have so many excellent teachers, excellent instruments, excellent buildings—everything we never had! And we will learn from you. Your experience will change us; you will enrich us, as much as our experience enriches you."

He beams. "*Magnífico!*" he concludes, rubbing his hands together, and I understand that we have come to the end of the interview.

But not quite. He tells me he has something to give me, and asks me to wait a moment while he goes to his office across the hall. Bolivia and I wait at the long conference table, mystified. He returns with a piece of paper. "I want you to have this," he says. "Because it is where the story begins." He hands me a Xerox copy of a faded black-and-white photograph, a small picture of a middle-aged woman with dark eyes, strong features, and an expression of composed intensity very similar to that of the Maestro.

"One of the great ladies of Venezuela," he says. "Doralisa."

# CHAPTER 4

# Dancing with Cellos:
# The Simón Bolívar
# Youth Orchestra of Venezuela

I F YOU ARE APPEARING AT THE JOHN F. KENNEDY CENTER for the Performing Arts, that monumental marble sheet cake perched over a bend in the Potomac River in Washington, you find your way to the stage door not, as is customary elsewhere, by ducking down some windy alley, but by entering the vast and resplendent Hall of Nations—red-carpeted, golden-pillared, its 63-foot ceiling hung with flags from a hundred nations. In the past year, as in every year, many of the great performing artists of the world have walked into this hall and through the stage door under the billowing flags: Yo-Yo Ma, Midori, Renée Fleming, Emanuel Ax, Pinchas Zukerman, the pop diva Roberta Flack, the great baritone Thomas Hampson.

On a wet afternoon in April 2009 so dense with cherry blossoms that the very rain seems pink, I sit on a bench in the Hall of Nations and watch a decidedly different sort of arrival at the Kennedy Center stage door. A bus pulls up along the esplanade and discharges a steady stream of young people, as noisy as high school kids on a field trip. Another bus follows, then another . . . and then another. There seem to be hundreds of young people. In fact, there *are* hundreds of young people. It is the Simón Bolívar Youth Orchestra of Venezuela.

One by one and two by two, they burst through the great glass doors into the Hall of Nations and stop, startled by its grandeur. They hold up cell phones and snap photos of the flags rippling like bright sails, the walls of gleaming marble, the swath of scarlet carpet vast as a soccer field. A young woman with braids clutches a violin case and holds hands with a young man in an orange shirt carrying a French horn. Two fellows hauling double basses give each other high fives. The young people chat and giggle, ooh and aah, just like any group of young tourists visiting the Kennedy Center . . . but unlike other groups of young tourists, they are there to give a concert that is the hottest ticket in town and has been sold out for weeks.

They sold out in Houston the previous weekend too, and in Carnegie Hall the previous season. In the past few years, they have been rapturously received in Berlin, in Tel Aviv, at the London Proms, at the Lucerne Festival. How is it that an ensemble whose oldest members are in their twenties has achieved such international acclaim? In part, no doubt, it's the sheer brilliance of their playing; for virtuosity and artistry they are reputed to be the equal of many a distinguished professional orchestra. But their fame is also partly due to the unique story of their origins.

The Simón Bolívar is the crown jewel of the Sistema. Like many of the hundreds of thousands of children who take part in the Sistema each year, its members are likely to have begun daily music lessons and membership in musical ensembles when they were as young as four or five. When they reached their teens, each of these young people triumphed in the intensely competitive process by which the best Sistema musicians in the country are chosen to be part of the Simón Bolívar Youth Orchestra. In Venezuela, this is something like making the Olympic soccer team.

Often, they have risen to this achievement against long odds.

Many of their parents are poor, some jobless; some have peers who are involved in gangs, dealing drugs, or in jail. Some have lost parents at an early age, to violent crime or the depredations of poverty. To be playing at the Kennedy Center for a packed house is the fulfillment of a dream that many young people in such circumstances would not be able even to imagine.

But here they are, nearly two hundred of them, and it is time for their rehearsal. They pocket their cell phones and hurry past the security guard and through the stage door. The hall is, very briefly, quiet enough for the flapping of the flags to be audible; then it begins to fill again with people shaking their umbrellas dry as they pass through on their way to the entrance to the concert hall. Such is the current cachet of the Simón Bolívar that even its rehearsal is the hottest ticket in town.

The main concert hall of the Kennedy Center is conceived on the same grand scale as the entrance hall: acres of burnished wood gleam under colossal Swedish chandeliers, and the 2,442 seats not only span four massive tiers, but spill across the back and sides of the stage as well. As the open rehearsal begins, it seems to me that every seat is filled, and that there is a wide demographic universe of people who want to hear Venezuelan youths play symphonic classics: there are families with small children, intense college students clutching BlackBerrys, seniors in rain boots and plastic scarves. A low hum of chatter continues as we wait for their conductor to make his appearance, and then gradually begins to subside; it's probably dawning on others, as it is on me, that in fact he's been onstage all along. He's crouched between the first and second violins, pointing to their scores and talking intently; he's wading among the wind players, shaking hands, hugging; he's downstage right, conferring with the stage manager. Short and slight and sweatshirt-clad, Gustavo Dudamel is easy to confuse with the orchestra members. He has been conducting this orchestra since he was eighteen—nearly a third of his life.

There is a stool on the podium, and no music stand. Dudamel

perches on the stool and faces the audience. "Hello," he says, and the hall goes instantly quiet. "It's a great honor to be here." His thick accent makes English sound like a Romance language. "We are part of the huge orchestra system founded by Maestro José Antonio Abreu. And we have a crazy program today—not only crazy but a lot of fun." For the conductor of an open rehearsal to chat up his audience is rare in my experience; most conductors, and in fact most musicians, tend to proceed through such rehearsals as if the audience is not there. "We're going to play now one of the most important pieces of modern times, *Le Sacre du Printemps*," says Dudamel. "It was written a hundred years ago, but it is still modern. The premiere was a huge scandal, because . . . but wait." He leans forward as if to confide in all 2,442 of us. "Just let the music speak to you," he says. "It is about . . . everything."

He turns to the orchestra, slides off his stool, and raises his baton. Instruments poised, they don't take their eyes off him; they seem to be holding their breaths. His wrist dips slightly and the bassoon keens the opening phrase; this famously reedy, mournful tune sounds full, almost opulent, under his floating baton. As the French horn enters, then the bass clarinet, now the English horn, cognitive dissonance begins to set in: the sound of the orchestra is impeccably blended and ravishingly beautiful, but the players, many of them, still have the look of kids. That sumptuous, golden French horn tone is being produced by a girl in a yellow shirt and a pony-tail. The player of the plangent bassoon line is a boy in a Hard Rock Café hat.

The cellos begin their pizzicato pulse, and then the whole orchestra is in motion. Dudamel sways, dips, dances; all two hundred players dip and sway in their seats, reflecting his movements like a many-sided mirror. The layers of sound thicken; the piccolo clarinets deliver their angular call, like the song of some brutal and beautiful bird. I wait for the second theme, a simple folk melody delivered by the trumpets; when it comes, the hard luster of the trumpet sound is so sharp I can feel it in my spine. The melody rises and falls, falls and rises; when it's played by more seasoned orchestras it is suffused with yearning, but this young trumpet section gives it an intensity that is brash and muscular as well as lyrical. "*Más! Más!*" Dudamel calls to them, and they give him more, so that even in this tender tune we can hear intimations of the ultimate rite of spring that is to come.

Fernando, one of the trumpet players, is far from brash and muscular; a thin, boyish fellow, he wears glasses and has a shy smile. He is twenty-one, born and raised in Caracas, the son of a violinist. "I started in the Sistema when I was four," he tells me when I meet him during a rehearsal break. "I took piano lessons and recorder lessons. I was pretty bad." He looks embarrassed, as though most four-year-old piano players are pretty good. "My uncle played trumpet, you know, pop music, in dance bands. When I was eleven, I told my father I wanted to play the trumpet."

Fernando began to study the trumpet and to play in one of the Sistema's youth orchestras in Caracas; at the age of sixteen he was admitted into the Simón Bolívar orchestra, and he has traveled the world with the orchestra for five years. I ask him about his favorite pieces of music. "Mahler Two," he says. "Beethoven Five. Tchaikovsky Four. And maybe this one." He gestures with his head in the direction of the hall where he has just blazed through the trumpet lines of *The Rite of Spring*. "You can express everything with this music," he adds, echoing Dudamel's declaration to the audience.

"But you know," he goes on, and now he speaks with the intensity I heard in his playing, "we don't play just to interpret the music—we play with an underlying social purpose. And that's the most important, right? To let the world know that using music we can rescue children, purify the soul. That's our real work, to show the world this."

It is startling to hear a twenty-one-year old use such broadly visionary terms. But many of the Simón Bolívar players speak comfortably and even eloquently of the world-changing power of music;

their words echo those of their mentors, Abreu and Dudamel, but are clearly grounded in their own lived experience. Fernando tells me that he intends to make a career as a music teacher in the Sistema. "When children are playing music together," he says, "all the differences in class, in race, everything—they disappear. They don't exist anymore. For a child, it gives the message that unity and harmony in the world are possible, that war is not necessary." Coming from this thin, fervent young man whose radiant trumpet sound is still ringing in my ears, the idea that children playing symphonies together can prevent war does not seem entirely illogical.

The song of the trumpets disappears, pulled under by a churning wash of orchestral sound. The turbulence thickens, and then a new melody is tossed up—another birdcall, this one piercing and crystalline. The call is so bright and clear that it's hard to believe a single piccolo is playing it. And now the strings burst forth with their famously dissonant repeated chord, pounding out the syncopated accents. Dudamel conducts like he's wielding a pile driver. He stops them suddenly: "You need to growl more!" he says. "More ferocious!" He growls at them. They giggle, but when they play it again the music has an undeniable ferocity, a sound at once cruel and magnificent. I notice that whenever Dudamel stops the orchestra, he starts them again by calling out a measure number. Not only has he memorized the score, as is his usual practice—he has memorized all the measure numbers he uses in rehearsal.

The piccolo's tune comes again, a sound spun fine as a silver thread. Dudamel drops the pile driver and is on tiptoe, back to dancing. The piccolo seems to flirt with him, its call teasing and skittering across the top of the restless orchestra. Whoever is playing the piccolo line understands that there can be ferocity in spun silver.

Luisa is the piccolo player. She is twenty-two, with delicate features, her long dark hair pulled back with a barrette. She tells me she grew up in the center of Venezuela, in the state of Aragua, and began to play the flute in a children's orchestra there at the age of nine. "My grandmother made sure I joined the Sistema," she says. "She always said I didn't know how to dance, and she wanted me to learn rhythm."

Clearly, Luisa learned rhythm. Like Fernando, she won entrance to the Simón Bolívar Orchestra when she was sixteen. I ask her about her most memorable concerts. "So many," she says. "When we played in Berlin, it was very moving. We were all crying when we left the concert."

"Because you were moved by the music?" I ask.

"No, because of the—" She searches for the word. "Because of the achievement. The honor. And the first time we played the London Proms, I had, you know, goose bumps."

I ask her about the Sistema, and like Fernando she becomes instantly voluble. "It opens up opportunities for a new life for children who would not have that any other way. And it teaches a child the meaning of discipline, and responsibility with conscience . . . if you learn that when you're very young, you keep it through your whole life."

"What did it mean to you personally?" I ask.

Luisa is quiet for a moment. "It saved my life," she says finally. "I lost my mother and my grandmother in the same year, when I was still a child. Without the Sistema I would have been . . . totally lost."

The orchestra manager is calling for the rehearsal to resume. I thank Luisa and shake her hand; she gives me a little hug goodbye and heads for the stage door at a run.

From the glinting piccolo solo in the "Dance of the Adolescents" all the way to the end of the piece, *The Rite of Spring* moves between episodes of dark lyricism and outbursts of wild and intricate chaos. The musicians of the Simón Bolívar—some still adolescents—throw themselves at this music full-throttle, driven by their whirling dervish of a maestro. By now I've adjusted to the startling disconnect between the youthfulness of the players and the splendor of their playing, but I continue to be impressed by the sheer kinetic energy happening on stage. The heat source, of course, is Dudamel himself, and the musicians match him; they play with a huge physicality, the violinists swaying dramatically forward and back, the wind players bobbing and dipping. When he stops them, his instructions are usually brief. "Kill it!" he says to a timpanist at a particularly clamorous juncture. "Singing, singing," he beseeches the oboes. And once or twice the instruction is simply "Aaaahhhhh!" They seem to know exactly what he means.

The Rite of Spring hurtles to its apocalyptic end with a violence that leaves me momentarily breathless. The musicians, however, are breathing fine; as soon as Dudamel has finished his brief concluding remarks, they are stretching, fidgeting, whispering to each other. As they wander offstage, the red-coated ushers of the Kennedy Center, who tend to guard the concert hall as if it were the Pentagon, move through the aisles shooing us out. No one wants to go. But the ushers are merciless, and so we begin to wander out too—except for a very excited young couple with an infant, who perform an improbable end run around a couple of ushers and rush the stage, holding up the baby and calling for Dudamel, who reaches down and grabs him. Baby and maestro smile, their dimples matching; photos are snapped, high fives are exchanged, the baby gets a kiss, and the young family leaves with The Rite of Spring still thundering, no doubt, in their ears.

⁓

When I go back to the Kennedy Center that evening for the concert, the rain has stopped and a cold breeze is blowing off the Potomac.

According to the Center's publicity, the Grand Foyer that serves as the lobby for all performance venues is 630 feet long, making it "one of the largest rooms in the world." The Belgian mirrors lining the hall are purported to be 58 feet high, and each of the Orrefors chandeliers from Sweden weighs, literally and precisely, a ton.

Vast as it is, the lobby feels crowded tonight. Double-breasted suits and elegant silver coifs are in abundance; clearly, Washington's art patrons are out in full force, and when they take their places in the concert hall, every seat, as at the rehearsal, is filled. On the stage the orchestra members are already in place, resplendent in black gowns and suits, warming up. The girls have flowers in their hair. The boys have found their combs.

The lights dim, but not before I spot Maestro José Antonio Abreu himself in the box closest to stage right. Despite his advancing age, enormous responsibilities, and very full schedule as El Sistema's global ambassador, he continues to tour with the orchestra whenever he can. A Kennedy Center official appears onstage to announce that there are many eminent diplomats in attendance tonight, as befits the international stature of this wonderful young orchestra—for whom the Center has had to enlarge its already enormous stage. Then Dudamel enters, walking through the orchestra instead of in front of it, emerging from between the first and second violins to hop onto the podium. The applause is polite.

First on the program is Ravel's *Daphnis and Chloe* Suite No. 2, a much-loved post-Romantic work whose opening moments come as close to a visual depiction of a sunrise as an auditory art form possibly can. Tonight the sun comes up blazing, the music reflecting and reverberating like light through the great hall. *Daphnis and Chloe* originated as the score for a ballet about the love affair of a goatherd and a shepherdess in pastoral Greece, and the young musicians wring sensuality from every note. The entire string section sways in synchronized motion, like a meadow combed by the wind. In the final movement, the "Danse Générale," the whole orchestra is roiling, driven by an insistent snare drum to an explosive and abrupt close. During the explosion of cheers that follows, Dudamel steps down from the podium and backs into the orchestra, taking his bows from somewhere among the violins.

A work by the Venezuelan composer Evencio Castellanos follows. The music brims with Latin folk melodies and dance rhythms; one would conclude that these young people play it with such relish because it's in their heritage, their very bones, since childhood— had they not just played a masterpiece of French Impressionism as though they had all grown up under the plane trees of the Tuileries. More wild applause, and during intermission, a potent audience buzz. A distinguished gentleman with a mahagony cane is talking on his cell phone: "Honey, you won't believe what I just heard. . . ." In line at the ladies' room, silk-clad matrons compete energetically as to who's known longest, and most, about this incredible ensemble.

Intermission ends, and the Simón Bolívar Youth Orchestra of Venezuela tears into *The Rite of Spring.* All the growls and exhortations of Dudamel's rehearsal are completely absorbed into their playing, and there is no doubt that the music is about everything: terror and beauty, love and lust, hunger and death and life. As in rehearsal, Dudamel is the literal physical embodiment of this "everything." Simply to watch him conduct is to understand something about the mysterious and protean panorama of human experience unfolding in the music.

At the end there is silence, as though the audience can't bear to disturb the violent majesty of the final chord. Then, gradually, a roar gathers and bursts from the crowd, and they are on their feet. The musicians take their bows with Dudamel almost hidden among them. One by one, he pulls all the soloists up to the front to be acknowledged. The applause refuses to end, and Dudamel takes two, three, four curtain calls.

Then the stage goes dark, the players abruptly invisible. When the lights come back up, all two hundred musicians are wearing jackets of yellow, blue, and red, with a semicircle pattern of white stars— it's the Venezuelan flag. The audience roars again, and Dudamel, similarly flag-bedecked, mounts the podium for the encores. If you are the young members of the Simón Bolívar Orchestra, receiving a standing ovation at the Kennedy Center, how do you trump your incandescent performances of two of the great masterworks of the twentieth century?

Simple, it turns out: you dance.

The encores are two more Latin pieces, and the musicians, playing, leap to their feet. Playing, the trumpet players swing their instruments back and forth and then spin them around their fingers between phrases. Playing, the cellists twirl their instruments as though they are dance partners; the horn players execute a synchronized salsa sort of move, turning in circles one after the other. Entire sections stamp their feet and shout to punctuate the music. The percussionists toss their sticks in the air, catch them, and keep playing.

If the audience was wound up before, it is now close to frenzy; the combination of the spirited abandon of the dancing with the impeccable polish of the music is almost unbearably exciting. I don't know how, or why, we're all staying in our seats. Onstage they're dancing in pairs, dancing in sections; finally the whole orchestra is dancing. Dudamel has long since stopped conducting and is among them, dancing too.

At the end of the second encore they are panting and beaming as they take their bows again. They turn and face the box where Maestro Abreu sits, and wave and clap and blow him kisses. The excitement in the concert hall is at fever pitch. But the young musicians are not quite finished. Now they take off their jackets and fling them into the crowd. They fling them into the orchestra, into the boxes; some of the boys have impressive pitching arms and manage to reach the fourth tier. Pinstriped and bejeweled patrons of the arts scramble over one another to catch the jackets like baseball fans diving for a fly ball.

And then it really is over. If you are a member of the Simón Bolívar Youth Orchestra and have just taken Washington by storm, you hasten out through the Hall of Nations to the huge buses waiting on the plaza, and you go back to your hotel to party, no doubt, until morning. As for the audience members, among the many images of this evening I won't forget is the sight of an elderly woman in pearl earrings and high heels, her mink stole folded carefully over her arm as she follows her trench-coated husband through the Grand Foyer and out into the Washington night, dressed proudly in the Venezuelan flag.

It is not until I reencounter the Simón Bolívar Orchestra in Venezuela, and speak with more of its present and past members, that I learn that the Kennedy Center concert was in fact a return engagement for some of the players, who had first performed there as members of a National Children's Orchestra formed by Abreu in the 1990s. I discover further that there have been—and still are—several incarnations of the Simón Bolívar Orchestra throughout the years, as original players have matured and young virtuosi have developed within the ranks of the Sistema. Venezuelan violinist and master teacher Susan Siman, whose personal story is intertwined with that of the orchestra and the Sistema over many years, tells me much of this story.

Susan is the daughter of Spaniards who emigrated to Los Angeles and then to Maracaibo, Venezuela, where her father, a trumpet player, won a job in the all-foreign professional orchestra. She grew up in Maracaibo and began to play the violin at an early age. "I first heard of José Antonio Abreu and what he was doing when I was twelve years old," she says. "He was going to city after city, creating youth orchestras across the whole country. His message was that it's very important for young people to play classical music together, because it is a beautiful way to connect with one another and with excellence. Even at the age of twelve, I could sense something important was happening!"

Susan is a warm, energetic woman who speaks in gusts of infectious enthusiasm. She tells me that Abreu guided the formation of a Sistema youth orchestra in Maracaibo, and she began to play in the orchestra. "The Maestro gave us Beethoven's Fifth, and at first we couldn't play it," she says. "He gave us Mozart's *Eine Kleine Nachtmusik*, and we couldn't play that either! But he worked with our director and gave her a lot of guidance. He believed in us. And we began to get better. I played in that youth orchestra for six years, and I formed my musical identity there."

In 1983, when she was eighteen, Susan married the concertmaster of the Maracaibo youth orchestra, Rubén Cova, and the couple came to Caracas to audition for the Simón Bolívar Orchestra. "My husband didn't pass the audition on the first try, but I did," she tells me with a wry smile.

"He got in on the second try," she adds quickly.

The orchestra Susan Siman and her husband joined was already, eight years after its inception, a national institution; the strength and solidity of the support Abreu had won from the government meant that its members could be paid salaries and receive benefits. These members included many of the original group who had rehearsed in the parking garage, traveled to Mexico City, and triumphed at Aberdeen, along with younger virtuosi who, like Susan Siman, joined after they had already experienced the formative power of the Sistema's teaching in its fast-growing network of núcleos. Among the new recruits were Eduardo Méndez, a violinist who joined the orchestra at a very early age and is now executive director for the Sistema, and Luis Rossi's clarinet student Valdemar Rodríguez, who gave up an engineering career to enter the orchestra, and later to become the Sistema's deputy executive director.

Susan Siman describes life in the Simón Bolívar Orchestra during the 1980s and early 1990s as exciting but challenging. "We would study at the conservatory during the day," she says, "and many of us would work as teachers in the núcleos during the afternoon. And at night we would rehearse, sometimes four or five hours. We did it with no question. It was a joy for us—but it was also very, very hard work."

Without exception, members of the orchestra from that time speak of being shaped and influenced by Abreu's vision of artistry within community and by his single-minded devotion to the orchestra. "When the Maestro was conducting," says Susan, "we learned more than orchestral technique. It was a process of creating music and creating family at the same time."

Many also speak of the depth of Abreu's musicianship. "When he conducted, it was very, very intense—different from anything I ever heard before," says Luis Rossi, who recalls soloing with the orchestra in Rossini's Variations for Clarinet. "His ideas were always surprising—so different and so good. He made me think about music in new ways. His mind was very, very developed, and his ideas were always very good—he is a truly great musician. And more than that, he was always so friendly, so respectful, so easy to communicate with, and so receptive to other people's ideas."

David Ascanio tells me that Abreu's capacity for absorbing and understanding music is unique in his experience. "I once saw a young composer bring him a new orchestral score," he says. "The Maestro looked through the score for a few minutes, then went to the piano and played through it flawlessly, making comments about it as he played. It was unbelievable—he could play any piece of music he saw, instantly."

Many former orchestra members also speak of Abreu's vast general knowledge of the arts and of politics and history. Cellist Roberto Zambrano, who has since become one of the Sistema's most dedicated núcleo directors, tells me that the experience of playing in the orchestra was an education in the fullest sense. "Maestro Abreu gave us so much," he says. "He taught us not only about music, but about culture, history, the arts in general."

David Ascanio remembers that one of the orchestra's early tours included a trip to Venice, and as they rode into town from the train station on *vaporetti*, the Venetian floating buses, Abreu borrowed a megaphone. "He was pointing out the sights, explaining the history of Venice and of each building we passed," says David. "It was unbelievable how much he knew. The gondoliers were all crowding around our *vaporetti*—they probably learned a lot if they could understand Spanish!" For that visit, he adds, Abreu somehow persuaded the city fathers to close the San Marco Cathedral and the Ducal Palace to the public, so that the orchestra could give private concerts for the government and nobility. "Can you imagine?" he asks. "The two most famous buildings in Venice—closed down for a bunch of kids from Venezuela."

⁓

In retrospect, one of the most surprising aspects of the story of the Simón Bolívar Orchestra is that its founder and beloved leader did not remain its principal conductor. From the orchestra's very beginnings, when Carlos Chávez took the podium at the international convention of youth orchestras in Aberdeen, Abreu's priorities have been clear: to dedicate himself to the development of the Sistema as a whole, and to foster the musical growth of the national youth orchestra by exposing it to the world's great conductors. An ideal opportunity for such growth came in the early 1990s, when Eduardo Mata conducted the Simón Bolívar in a series of recordings for the Dorian label—recordings that testify to the young but maturing orchestra's already-signature sound, rhythmic precision, and explosive energy.

Classical music producer David Walters, who supervised the recordings for Dorian, tells me that he remembers being impressed by the young players' combination of virtuosity and high spirits. "The level of musicianship was just amazing," he says. "And their attitude was incredible. The particular pressure of recording sessions was unfamiliar to them, but they were always upbeat, always happy to do one more take."

Conductor Eduardo Mata was particularly excited by the

orchestra's ability to meet the arduous demands of contemporary Latin American works. "They were willing to rehearse forever," says David Walters. "One reason Mata was so interested in working with them was that they were completely game to spend the long hours necessary to master the complex rhythms of those new pieces. He could never have gotten that with a North American orchestra."

Also striking, he says, was the sense of close camaraderie and community among orchestra members. "They were mostly from poor families, and there was a very strong feeling of family," he tells me. "They were all really good friends. I never felt a sense of jealousies or animosities."

Not only did orchestra members seem to love each other; they also loved a good joke. "They were very spirited, and they loved to laugh," David Walters recollects. "I remember that one time, the entire viola section came to a recording session wearing gorilla masks. We were in the control room and we turned on the video monitor, and there they were, playing away gorgeously, with their masks on. Maestro Mata enjoyed the joke for about two seconds, and then that was that.

"But they were always joking. They all had nicknames for each other, and they came up with instant nicknames for us too—I was 'Superman' and my associate engineer was 'RoboCop.' Maestro Mata was 'The Sun King.' And they were so friendly to us, inviting us to their parties and into their homes. During the rainy season one of the cellists offered to take us out to the jungle to chase alligators. Sport, you know?"

David says that Abreu came often to rehearsals and recording sessions when Maestro Mata conducted. "Whenever he came, the orchestra members would all crowd around him and try for a chance to talk with him," he adds. "They had a kind of reverence for him."

What David remembers most distinctly, he tells me, is the sheer beauty of the music-making he heard among the young Venezuelans. "Once I heard a guitar quartet playing in a stairwell, in the building where we were recording," he says. "I don't know whether they were members of another orchestra or a visiting ensemble without a rehearsal room. And I didn't know the piece they were playing. The other engineers and I were going out for lunch, and we didn't have time to stop and listen—it was one of those moments you can't quite fully appreciate in the moment you experience it. But they were playing with such beautiful timbre and pitch, such perfect ensemble—such an intensity of listening and awareness and sensitivity. When I remembered it later, I understood that in that Caracas stairwell I had encountered beauty in its purest form."

Eduardo Mata died in 1995 when the small private plane he was piloting crashed in the Mexican desert. Executives at the Dorian label, including David Walters and Brian Levine, its president, recognized the value of the work Mata had begun with the orchestra and continued to record them with other conductors. At the same time, Abreu came to a crucial realization: some of the members of the Simón Bolívar Youth Orchestra of Venezuela were no longer quite so youthful. It was time to begin creating the next generation.

"The Maestro came to some of us in the orchestra and asked for our help," relates Susan Siman. "He told us he wanted to create a new, younger national orchestra, and he wanted to call it the National Children's Orchestra." Abreu knew that the groundswell of youth and children's orchestras in Sistema núcleos throughout the country was developing the talents and skills of children of all ages, and he was convinced that the time was right for a new national ensemble of musicians even younger than the first generation had been when they began.

"So a group of us orchestra members, the ones who were most experienced as teachers, went out into the provinces to all the núcleos, looking for the most talented, most advanced young musicians," says Susan. "We were seeking kids who were young but mature enough to do the kind of hard work that would be required of them." She and her colleagues talked to dozens of núcleo directors and listened to hundreds of children, and chose five or six from each núcleo to come to Caracas for auditions. Some were as young as nine or ten. "Usually, the parents were not able to come with them," Susan adds, "but they understood the value of this opportunity for their children. So we arranged for accommodations for the kids, and we took care of them—like counselors, nurses, substitute parents really—while they were auditioning. My husband and I were parents ourselves, so we knew what the children needed."

From the very beginning the young people chosen for the National Children's Orchestra felt a close connection with one another. "It is the Sistema way," she tells me. "It is an orchestra, but it is also a community. And in a very real sense, it is a family."

Among the children who left home and came to Caracas to become part of the National Children's Orchestra family was a young teenager named Gustavo Dudamel. It did not take long for Abreu to realize that in this slight, intense violinist he had found the future leader of his orchestra, and daily conducting lessons began almost immediately.

Dudamel recalls the lessons with awe. "I remember thinking that the knowledge of Maestro Abreu is infinite," he tells me. "It's impossible to say how big it is. His memory for details! His ability to memorize a score! I was very inspired by this."

He was equally inspired, and sometimes daunted, by the Maestro's discipline. "He's really strong," he says. "Sometimes I would say, 'Maestro, I'm tired!' And it was always 'No, no, we have to keep working.'"

Like many of the new orchestra members, Dudamel was living away from home for the first time. "I was eating really badly, and I had some stomach problems," he remembers. "Maestro Abreu took me to the doctor. And then he called me every morning. 'Are you eating breakfast? Did you sleep enough?' "

He adds, "But you know, it wasn't only me he was taking care of. It is hard to imagine . . . but he has this kind of space for everyone."

In his signature fashion, Abreu made sure that the new orchestra gave its first international performance almost immediately after it was formed. In 1996, he took the orchestra—called the National Children's Orchestra of Venezuela—to play at the Kennedy Center in Washington. Alejandro Carreño, another of Susan Siman's violin students recruited for the orchestra, has vivid memories of the trip. "Some of us were only nine or ten years old," he says. "We were so little, we didn't really understand where we were, but we were very excited! We had our tiny cameras and we were taking pictures of the street, the stairways, everything!"

Alejandro, who at twenty-five is now the concertmaster of the Simón Bolívar Orchestra, tells me that many members of that National Children's Orchestra in the 1990s went on to become members of the current Simón Bolívar Orchestra. "So when we went back to the Kennedy Center in 2009, as the Simón Bolívar, it was wonderful to share those beautiful memories of when we were small."

Alejandro is tall and handsome, with long hair pulled back into a neat ponytail. In concert, when his childhood friend Gustavo steps off the podium to shake his hand, the concertmaster towers over the conductor. He towers even more dramatically over his wife Verónica Balda de Carreño, also a violoinist in the orchestra, who is petite even in her very elegant, very high heels. When I ask Alejandro and Verónica to tell me their personal stories, Alejandro wants to begin with hers, and he helps her with translation. She tells me that she comes from a family of musicians who came from Argentina to live in Maracaibo and play in the professional orchestra there—the same reason Susan Siman's parents had moved to that city a generation earlier. "My father and my grandfather were both great masters of the violin," says Verónica, "so it was a natural instrument for me. At a very young age, I began to play violin in the núcleo at Maracaibo. And when I was ten, I auditioned for the National Children's Orchestra, and I got in. That was in 1995. And that is how Alejandro and I met—as ten-year-old violinists in the Children's Orchestra."

"Playing in that orchestra was an incredible experience," adds Alejandro. "For all of us, it was the first time that we could share and experience the cultures of kids from different cities, different provinces."

I remember Maestro Abreu's observation that in Venezuela, regional cultural identities have traditionally been much stronger and more well-defined than national identity. Alejandro tells me that for him and Verónica, and for many other children, the experience of playing in the national orchestra gave them their first real sense of national belonging. "I came from Trujillo, Verónica came from Maracaibo. But when you are sharing music with people from all over the country, now you are truly Venezuelan. The spirit of the whole country becomes your own spirit. You learn how to love each city, each town. Because when you make friends with someone, and that person talks with love about his own town, you learn how to love that town. And when you go there, it's like you are home."

"So really," adds Verónica, "anywhere we go in Venezuela, we are home."

For Alejandro, the Sistema itself has also been a kind of home throughout his life. "I've known Maestro Abreu since before I was born," he says, with no sense of exaggeration. His father, clarinetist and conductor Gregory Carreño, was one of the original band of musicians who gathered with Abreu to invent themselves as a youth orchestra in the Caracas garage in 1975. When the youth orchestra movement began its spread into the provinces, Abreu asked Gregory Carreño to go to the city of Trujillo and take charge of developing the núcleo there.

"That was where he met my mother," says Alejandro. "And they married and started to raise a family. When I was very young, in the mid-nineties, Maestro Abreu formed the National Children's Orchestra. My father was the conductor of that orchestra. He would go to Caracas to work with them and would bring back videos of their performances. I saw all those little kids my age, playing in such a fantastic way, and I said, 'I have to be there!' So I started to learn to play the violin, and I worked very hard, and after nine months I auditioned and got in. And there I met Verónica, I met Gustavo, I met all my friends—my whole world. I was ten years old."

When Alejandro was a teenager, his father Gregory was badly injured in a car accident; for days it was not clear whether he would survive. Abreu visited him every day to pray by his side and was tirelessly supportive throughout the long rehabilitation process that followed the accident. Today, many years later, Gregory Carreño uses a wheelchair but continues to be a central figure in the Sistema, as regional coordinator of the núcleos in the state of Miranda and conductor of the orchestra there.

"The Maestro was incredible when we were in crisis," says Alejandro. "But he has also been there for me in many less dramatic ways. I can remember being a child and going to talk to him when I was upset after a schoolyard fight. 'Maestro, that kid hit me again!' From his perspective, of course, this was not a big problem; but he understood that for me, for a child, it was very real. And he helped me with it. He does that at every level, at every age—I am always amazed at his capacity to understand and to help people. That's why he is so beloved."

⁓

At the age of fourteen, Alejandro asked Maestro Abreu if he could audition for the Simón Bolívar Orchestra. "It's not the right time," was the response. "You're not ready yet." A year later, in 1998, the Maestro decided it was the right time both for Alejandro and for

Gustavo; he summoned them to his office, gave them audition materials, and told them they had two weeks to practice. "So we practiced
like crazy, and we auditioned, and we got in," says Alejandro. "Gustavo became conductor very quickly after that. Verónica got in too,
and then there was a big wave of kids from the National Children's
Orchestra coming into the Simón Bolívar. It was beautiful—we kept
playing together, traveling together, living our lives together."

For Abreu, the practical problem caused by the swelling ranks
and increasingly disparate ages of the Simón Bolívar members
became an opportunity to re-create the ensemble as two separate
performing entities. The first generation of members was designated
the Simón Bolívar A; the younger, newer members, who had been
recently brought in from the new National Children's Orchestra,
now constituted the Simón Bolívar B. "We are all one orchestra,
really," explains Alejandro, "but we don't often perform as one—it's
hard to fit four hundred people on a stage! So the A orchestra, which
is made up of many of our teachers, doesn't tour so much."

It is the B orchestra that tours extensively and that the world
knows as the Simón Bolívar Youth Orchestra of Venezuela. When
I speak with members of this ensemble on my visit to Caracas, I
am consistently impressed by the way orchestral music-making
and social connectedness are inseparable in their experience. There
seems to be no distinction between these two aspects of life; to make
music together is to be part of a community. At dinner one night
with some orchestra members, I ask Dani, a French horn player,
how long he has played with the orchestra. "We have been playing
in the orchestra for about eight years," he responds. His spontaneous impulse is to answer not only about himself as an individual but
also about the double bass player to his left, the flutist to his right,
the cello player across the table.

When I ask about competitive feelings among members of the
orchestra, Dani and his friends seem to have trouble grasping the
question. I try again: when a solo part comes up in an orchestral
piece, do they feel competitive about the chance to play it? "When

one of us gets a solo, the others are happy about it," I am told. "We know he couldn't have accomplished it without us. And we know that we will play it too, one day!"

For anyone who has experienced the brutally competitive world that is the inevitable norm for young classical musicians in the United States, it's impossible to avoid an initial "too-good-to-be-true" reaction to such sentiments. But after talking to many musicians of the Simón Bolívar, and hearing the same feelings expressed again and again with unmistakable genuineness and spontenaity, I have to conclude that it's a mistake to underestimate the capacity of the Sistema to shape the way these young people feel about and relate to one another. Competitiveness is an element of the human condition. But the Sistema's alternative model of cooperative interdependence seems to be so deeply satisfying that it is sometimes able to trump even such elemental emotions.

"When you are part of the Sistema, it is always with you," Alejandro tells me. "If you have a problem, the feeling is not 'Oh, that's your problem, go take care of it.' No—if you have a problem, it's everybody's problem."

It seems equally true that if some are celebrating, everybody celebrates. The whole orchestra attended the wedding of Alejandro and Verónica in Trujillo—and they were even in on the proposal, which happened, according to orchestra lore, during a rehearsal. And the marriage of Dudamel to his longtime girlfriend, ballet dancer and journalist Eloisa Maturén, at a Caracas cathedral in 2006 was a celebratory wedding-cum-concert; both the Simón Bolívar Orchestra and the Schola Cantorum performed, and at the reception, the groom played tangos on the violin, accompanied by a Latin ensemble conducted by Frank Di Polo.

"This feeling of caring for one another comes straight from Maestro Abreu," says Alejandro. "In a way, he is everywhere. But not in a magical sense—he's everywhere because he cares about every single person.

"For us, music is never solitary," he adds. "It's not a matter of practicing in a room by yourself for years, until you are ready to play together. We play together from the beginning, and we learn together. And we grow up together, sharing so many different experiences." He gestures as though bowing across a violin and then sweeps his arm outward in a circle. "When you are with your instrument, and you are playing together with your friends, you're just where you should be. You are sharing something that goes very deep, and without words. Words have a limit, but the feeling in the music —there are no words for that."

As did their seniors in the Simón Bolívar A ensemble, the members of the Simón Bolívar B combine the capacity for collective musical sharing with an irrepressible spirit of mischief. While I am in Caracas, the orchestra performs the Suite for Soprano and Orchestra from Alban Berg's opera *Lulu*, a highly dramatic Expressionist work that reaches its climax in a bloodcurdling scream from the soprano. I am told that, in one of the rehearsals, the soprano was absent—so when they came to the climactic moment, every orchestra member screamed, bloodcurdlingly, and precisely on cue.

During the last decade, since the Simón Bolívar B ensemble was formed and Dudamel became its musical director in 1999, the orchestra has toured more and more widely and frequently, performing regularly throughout Latin America and in major European cities like Berlin, Vienna, and Paris, and extending its reach to London, the United States, Canada, Scandinavia, Russia, and Japan. Everywhere they have gone, their distinctive quality of unrestrained gusto combined with prodigious artistry has enraptured audiences and captured the attention of famous musicians, many of whom have been drawn to Caracas to work with them.

Simon Rattle said of this experience, "The orchestra is clearly the most important thing in the world to all of these young people. And that comes through loud and clear in their music."

Claudio Abbado has called the orchestra and the Sistema "the most important project in the music world in our time." And Plácido Domingo, after hearing the orchestra for the first time, said, "I did not expect to walk into heaven and hear celestial voices. The truth is, I have never felt so moved, not only because of the emotion but also, I must say, because of the quality."

Both the quality and the emotional depth of the orchestra under Dudamel's baton have been captured in a series of recordings by the German label Deutsche Grammophon, which has picked up where Dorian left off. These include symphonic masterworks by Beethoven, Tchaikovsky, and Mahler; Stravinsky's *Rite of Spring*; and a number of contemporary Latin American works. Several orchestra members tell me that it was a particular thrill to record Beethoven's *Eroica* Symphony in a live performance at the Beethovenhalle in Bonn, the composer's birthplace.

In 1999 the Simón Bolívar Youth Orchestra won UNESCO's International Music Award "for being an example to the youth of the world." And increasingly, as the orchestra has toured more and more widely, the reactions of audiences have become as much the subject of media commentary as the performances themselves. Listeners of all ages, from the Kennedy Center to the decorum-steeped venues of Vienna and Lucerne, Milan and Berlin, have responded to the orchestra with a visceral excitement seldom felt in the concert halls of the twenty-first century. The particular gift of these young musicians is their capacity to bring their listeners into their own experience of music as joyful community, so that audiences feel a sense of participation rather than merely passive attendance. At the orchestra's Salzburg Festival debut in 2008, according to one critic, "The audience went wild. It was like a party."

In what proved to be a performance of historic importance, the orchestra made its London debut at the BBC Proms in 2007, with a concert that included a rhapsodic Latin American work, Danzón No. 2 by contemporary Mexican composer Arturo Márquez, as well as Bernstein's "Mambo!" from *West Side Story*, and ended with the colorful Venezuelan jackets and dancing en masse I witnessed at the Kennedy Center concert. The audience was roused to a decidedly un-British frenzy. "I am not sure anything quite like Gustavo Dudamel and his extraordinary group of young musicians has ever hit the Proms before," wrote the music critic of the *Guardian*, Andrew Clements. "There are some great youth orchestras around today, but none of them is as exciting to behold as this."

A video of the Proms performance found its way to YouTube a year or two later, and that link has been orbiting cyberspace ever since, providing millions of viewers across the world with their first introduction to the Simón Bolívar Youth Orchestra of Venezuela. Orchestra members say they sensed at the time that the Proms concert was a watershed. "Six thousand people in the Royal Albert Hall," remembers Dani, the French horn player, "all on their feet, going wild. It was kind of stunning."

The orchestra encountered a similar reception several months later at its New York debut in Carnegie Hall, where the two hundred players nearly spilled off the edge of the historic stage. The famously skeptical New York critical establishment fell hard. *New York Times* critic Anthony Tommasini raved about "the technically astonishing and powerfully communicative playing of these dedicated and accomplished young musicians." "*Qué Fantástico!*" ran the headline in *New York Magazine*. Dudamel shared the Carnegie Hall podium with orchestra supporter and mentor Simon Rattle, the conductor of the Berlin Philharmonic. Wrote Tommasini, "When it ended, Mr. Rattle, with not a trace of British reserve, dived among the players and engaged in a hugfest."

The orchestra embarked upon its first Asian tour the following year, visiting Beijing, Seoul, Tokyo, and Hiroshima. Verónica Balda de Carreño remembers the Hiroshima concert as particularly moving. "We went to the museum before the concert, and to the memorial," she says, "and we all took off our Sistema medallions and left them at the memorial. Everyone was crying. And at the concert—we always play with a very bright, joyful attitude, but this time the emotion was at a whole different level. When the audience applauded, we were clapping for them. We wanted to say to them, 'You are the special people here. You are the survivors.'"

My own first encounter with the Simón Bolívar, when their *Rite of Spring* raised the roof of the Kennedy Center, was part of a U.S. tour in the spring of 2009, which also included an appearance as featured guests of Chicago's first Festival of Youth and Music. Dudamel took the helm of the Los Angeles Philharmonic in the fall of that year, but his touring schedule with the Simón Bolívar did not slow down; the same season found Dudamel and his "*muchachos*," as he calls them, in Toronto, Paris, Boston, Lucerne, Scandinavia, Russia, and Greece. Typical of the acclaim that greeted them everywhere was this notice from a classical music blogger about the Boston concert: "The crown jewel of *El Sistema* rode into Boston this week on more classical music hype than the town has seen in years. And the enormous orchestra managed to justify all the hype. This orchestra doesn't just perform; they make you feel like part of a movement."

During a dinner in Caracas with members of the orchestra and a group of young musicians from the United States, a question is tossed on the table for general discussion: "What is the worst job you ever had?" The visitors from the States take up the question first, recalling horrific summer jobs in fast-food joints and spirit-stifling stints in cubicles. The Venezuelan musicians listen to these tales with something like wonder. "We have only worked in the orchestra," one says finally. "We have never had a bad day of work in our lives."

Here is a crucial element in the story of the Simón Bolívar: the orchestra plays the way it does not only because of exceptional teaching, intense collective discipline, and highly developed musicality, but also because its members receive salaries, which allows them to devote their time to working together in rehearsals and performances. Says Valdemar Rodríguez, "The reason they can tour so extensively and sound so good is that they are really a semiprofessional institution. They get salaries, and they get benefits." For the players, many of whom come from families of very modest circumstances, this is essential; it means they do not have to choose between pursuing their art and finding a job to contribute to the family income.

Nor do they have to choose between playing in the orchestra and pursuing their formal education. Valdemar explains that because the University of the Arts has allowed them great flexibility as to how they move through the degree program, almost half the current members of the orchestra are involved in getting a university degree. "There are many weeks of the year when they cannot study at all, of course, because they are rehearsing, performing, or touring," he says. "So the university allows them to take six or seven years or more, instead of four, to complete their degree. It is understood that the informal education they are getting when they are with the orchestra—playing in the best halls in the world, with the best conductors, with the most difficult repertoire—is an invaluable part of their education. But it is also important that they get their degrees. So the university is very flexible, to accommodate the needs of each one."

In the spring of 2010, the Simón Bolívar Orchestra goes on a tour that ends at the Lucerne Easter Festival, an event founded by Claudio Abbado in 2003, with concerts directed by both Abbado and Dudamel. Reviewers compete to find favorable adjectives strong enough to do justice to the orchestra's performances: the solo playing is "stunning," the sonorities "wonderfully thick," and the overall effect "enthralling."

Several critics, however, remark on the fact that the players have matured past what some would define as "youth." "The truth is that this is no longer a youth orchestra except in name," writes Richard

Morrison of the online edition of the *Times* (London). "Many are now in their late twenties." And Tom Service of the *Guardian* writes, "The Simón Bolívar Youth Orchestra is youthful no longer."

While an ensemble of players in their twenties is undeniably youthful in the context of the great symphonic stages upon which the Simón Bolívar now moves, the critics have a point; the young teenagers whom Abreu brought together in the late 1990s to form the B ensemble of the Simón Bolívar Youth Orchestra are far from teenagers now. No one is more aware of this than Abreu himself, who has decided that the time is once again ripe for new, younger national orchestras. Given the breadth and depth of the Sistema across Venezuela, it's inevitable that remarkable talents are emerging at younger and younger ages, and the number of accomplished young musicians is rising exponentially. Abreu has met this welcome challenge by establishing several new top-tier ensembles.

Most well known of the new national orchestras is the Teresa Carreño Youth Orchestra, a two-hundred-member ensemble made up of high school–age musicians and named after a legendary Venezuelan pianist. According to FESNOJIV director Eduardo Méndez, the Teresa Carreño will eventually become a semiprofessional orchestra in the mold of the Simón Bolívar ensembles. "And our long-term plan is that each state in Venezuela will have its own professional youth orchestra, each with a new building where it can be based," says Eduardo. "So we are creating a new cultural life for each city."

The conductor of the Teresa Carreño Orchestra is Christian Vásquez, a charismatic twenty-six-year-old whose career trajectory has been similar to that of Dudamel's: he grew up within the Sistema, studied conducting with Abreu, and spent formative years conducting a Venezuelan youth symphony before emerging on the international stage to win critical acclaim for his guest appearances with major European orchestras.

Maestro Vásquez, who has been closely mentored by Dudamel, led the Teresa Carreño Orchestra on its first international tour in the fall of 2010, performing at the Beethoven Fest in Bonn and in Vienna, Berlin, Amsterdam, Madrid, and London. Their reception was no less enthusiastic than the raves that have greeted their seniors in the Simón Bolívar Orchestra; a radio commentator in Berlin said of their rendition of Beethoven's Fifth that "these young Venezuelans gave it new life, and opened Germans' ears anew to our own music."

In addition, there is the Caracas Symphony Youth Orchestra, composed of the best high school–age musicians in the city and conducted by Dietrich Paredes, who has chosen not to aim for an international career because he is so strongly committed to working with young teenagers. It is this ensemble I have seen in performance with Jamie Bernstein, and it is striking how thoroughly they have absorbed both the unrestrained fervor and the high musical standards of their slightly older compatriots.

The repertoire of these orchestras includes many of the same pieces that the Simón Bolívar Orchestra frequently plays—the symphonies of Mahler and Shostakovich, Beethoven and Tchaikovsky, the symphonic works of Strauss and Stravinsky and Bernstein. And while youth orchestra leaders in the United States might see this as a mistake, preferring to let a younger ensemble develop its own identity with its own repertoire, the principle of shared repertoire is strong within the tradition of the Sistema.

The power of this tradition is clear to me when I watch a video of the Teresa Carreño playing Márquez's Danzón No. 2, a work that has become a kind of signature piece for the Simón Bolívar, thanks to the ubiquitous YouTube clip from the London Proms. Having seen that clip many times and heard the Simón Bolívar play the work in concert, I'm now used to associating its musical gestures with the expressive young faces of individual players—Luisa playing the bittersweet piccolo solo, for example, or Alejandro brooding over the violin's romantic melody. It is moving to see the younger players of the Teresa Carreño summoning the emotive force and nuance of their older role models as they enact these same musical gestures, making the music at once their own stirring statement and a tribute to the more mature orchestra.

And I imagine it will be even more overwhelming to hear the Sistema's touchstone symphonic masterworks played by Abreu's most recent creation, a new National Children's Orchestra with 358 members, all under the age of sixteen and some as young as eight. With twenty double basses, eighteen bassoons, instrument coaches for every section, and numerous apprentice conductors, the sheer size of this enterprise surpasses any orchestra even Mahler could have envisioned. Abreu himself, now in his early seventies, often works personally with the new orchestra, just as he has done for the last thirty-five years with every national youth or children's orchestra he has created. "He rehearses with these young children until eleven or twelve o'clock at night," says Bolivia Bottome. "He wants to make sure they experience the full musical and social spirit of the Sistema."

Bassoonist Dantes Rameau, one of a group of U.S. musicians who visit Caracas in 2010, writes in his blog about his chance to watch the new National Children's Orchestra at one of its first rehearsals, with Dudamel as surprise guest and Abreu watching from a seat behind the podium. "The kids go nuts when Gustavo walks in," he writes. "They play the fourth movement of Mahler's First Symphony for him, and then they want to play it again with him conducting. Of course he can't say no. The kids play amazingly, like it's their last day on earth."

After the Mahler, an eight-year-old percussionist replaces Dudamel on the podium, and Dudamel and Abreu watch together as the boy conducts his 357 peers in the Venezuelan national anthem. Clearly, the Sistema has not yet encountered limits of possibility for children making music together.

Whether the players are eight or twenty-eight, the true miracle of the youth orchestras of Venezuela is not how young they are but how deeply they communicate through music, with one another and with audiences. In all the ensembles of the Sistema, artistry is inseparable from the spirit of collective endeavor. And that is a connection that will only strengthen as they mature. "I hope to be with the Sistema as long as I live," says Alejandro Carreño. "I love the way we do music. It's that feeling of knowing where your musical partners come from—really understanding them and loving them."

He adds that the experience of empowerment and belonging that comes from a childhood in the Sistema can remain strong even for those who do not become musicians. "Everybody who has been in the Sistema understands that the way you behave in an orchestra is the perfect way to behave in society," he says. "It's a social program, but we use music to get there. It's like the Sistema plants a chip in you, a chip of positivity. And it never leaves you. That chip of positivity stays with you for the rest of your life."

# CHAPTER 5

# An Idea Worth Spreading

I N FEBRUARY 2009, THE DEAN OF THE PREPARATORY AND Continuing Education Schools of the New England Conservatory bought a last-minute plane ticket to Caracas. Mark Churchill had been to Venezuela many times before; as one of the first prominent music educators in the United States to discover and champion El Sistema, he had spent more than a decade working with José Antonio Abreu to develop relationships between the Venezuelan youth orchestra system and the venerable conservatory in Boston. But this plane flight had a greater degree of urgency than usual. Maestro Abreu had recently been offered the highly prestigious prize given annually by the TED organization, a nonprofit dedicated to the support of "ideas worth spreading," to one or more individuals with an original and compelling vision in the field of arts, science, business, or one of the "global issues facing our world." The prize offer involved not only a generous financial award but also the opportunity for Abreu to make a speech, streamed live on the Internet, articulating his vision and making a public wish for help in realizing it. The prize administrators, however, were growing concerned; the date of the awards ceremony was fast approaching, but they had not been able to get the Maestro on the telephone.

"When it came close to the time for Dr. Abreu to receive the award and make the speech, they tried to call him," recalls Mark Churchill. "The folks at FESNOJIV had given them a dozen different phone numbers to try, but their calls weren't getting through. Finally, they called me and said, 'What should we do? We want to give the prize to Maestro Abreu, but we can't reach him!' "

The TED Prize, established in 2005, has gone to a remarkably eclectic array of recipients, ranging from Bill Clinton and Bono to lesser-known visionaries in fields including medical research, photography, film, architecture, and journalism. The two other 2009 winners were oceanographer Sylvia Earle and astronomer Jill Tarter, a specialist in the search for extraterrestrial intelligence. But the prize had never gone to an educator, and never to a Latin American. Mark Churchill had helped guide the TED organization toward honoring the creator of El Sistema. And he had been a witness to the initial communication between TED and Abreu—an occasion when one of those dozen phone numbers had in fact worked, and Abreu had picked up the call from a Spanish-speaking secretary in the TED office. "They asked him if he would accept the prize and make the speech," says Mark, "and he said, 'Of course!' "

Mark knew from experience that personal contact is often more successful than the telephone as a mode of communication with Venezuela. So when the TED people called with their problem, the solution seemed obvious. "I just got on a plane and went to Caracas," he says, "and I went directly from the airport to Abreu's office. And there he was. And I said, 'Maestro! TED needs a speech!' "

Abreu wrote a speech. He was not able to travel to the TED conference in Long Beach, California, on what was, at that point, very short notice, so Mark helped to arrange for the speech to be videotaped in Caracas. Less than a week later, a standing-room-only audience of conferees in Long Beach came together to celebrate the 2009 TED Prize winners, with viewers across the world watching as the event was streamed live on the Internet.

What the California conferencegoers and Internet viewers watched on that February day in 2009 has since become classical music's version of a YouTube phenomenon—a pair of video clips that, for hundreds of thousands of viewers across the globe, have offered a first introduction not only to Abreu but also to Dudamel and the world of the Sistema. One clip captures the latter part of the awards ceremony: a Venezuelan youth orchestra performance, conducted by Dudamel himself, carried live via satellite to the conference in Long Beach. "And now we go live to Caracas," announces TED director Chris Anderson, "to see one of Maestro Abreu's great protégés. He is the new musical director of the Los Angeles Philharmonic, and he is the greatest young conductor in the world!"

The giant screen behind Anderson projects the Teresa Carreño Youth Orchestra onstage in a packed Caracas concert hall, the young musicians dressed informally in jeans and short-sleeved shirts and looking shyer than usual as Gustavo Dudamel walks to the podium in a green sports shirt and gray sweater vest. Dudamel leads them in a stirring performance of the second movement of Shostakovich's Tenth Symphony, and then turns to address his live audience and the cameras linking him to the TED conference.

"Hello to everybody in L.A.," he says, panting a little from the exertions of the Shostakovich. "We are very happy to be with you. And we are very happy to have"—he extends his hands toward the front row of his audience—"this angel in the world." The camera pans on Abreu in his overcoat, with his hand over his heart. "To have him not only in our country, Venezuela—but in our world. He has given us the possibility to have dreams, and to make true the dreams."

Dudamel gestures around the stage at the Teresa Carreño Orchestra. "And here is one of the results of this wonderful project that is the System in Venezuela. We hope, our Maestro, to have such orchestras in all the countries of the Americas." Dudamel bows his head toward Abreu, and the camera shows Abreu clasping his hands together. Then Dudamel turns back to the orchestra and leads them—now in their signature Venezuelan jackets—in the Simón Bolívar favorite, Danzón No. 2 by Márquez.

The second YouTube clip shows Abreu's videotaped speech itself, which was played for the TED audience immediately before the live performance by the youth orchestra a continent away was streamed via satellite. The pairing of oratorical advocacy and orchestral performance was a perfect instance of the Maestro's long-standing habit of showing the results of his system as well as advocating for it, the kind of strategic choice that has served him so well ever since the very first Sistema orchestra played for the Mexican minister of culture in 1975.

The speech itself has none of the celebratory exuberance of the orchestra performance. It was recorded in an empty rehearsal room in Caracas, and is stark in its simplicity: the frail dark-suited figure of the Maestro and the thicket of black chairs and music stands surrounding him are in sharp contrast to the blond wood of the rehearsal room floor and the white pages of an open orchestral score, creating something close to the austere feel of a black-and-white movie.

Abreu speaks to the camera, to his hundreds of listeners at the conference, and to the many more streaming the proceedings online, with his characteristic combination of grave warmth and laser intensity. Speaking in Spanish, with English subtitles on the screen, he relates the story of the very first orchestra rehearsal of eleven musicians in 1975, and he spreads his hands wide to illustrate the moment of decision that confronted him. "I thought to myself, 'Either I close the program right now, or I multiply it for thousands.' I decided to accept the challenge, and on that same night I told those eleven kids I'd turn their orchestra into one of the leading orchestras of the world." Abreu describes his joy in seeing that promise fulfilled over the years, and says he has been particularly moved by the responses of audiences across the United States and Europe to the Simón Bolívar's message of "music, vitality, energy, enthusiasm, and strength."

Abreu's speech is the only TED Prize talk that has been delivered by videotape; the other recipients thus far have spoken in person at the conference. Understandably, TED's videographers took the opportunity to add modest cinematic touches, interspersing audio and video excerpts of Venezuelan youth orchestras playing and children cradling instruments. But the speech would be equally powerful if it had been filmed with a single handheld camera. Abreu's eloquence, at once philosophical and poetic, has the force of great oratory. "In their essence, the orchestra and the choir are much more than artistic structures," he says. "They are examples and schools of social life, because to sing and to play together means to intimately coexist toward perfection and excellence. This is why music is immensely important in the awakening of sensibility and in the forging of values."

Abreu quotes Mother Teresa's belief that the most tragic aspect of poverty is the lack of self-esteem and identity it engenders—"the feeling of being no one, of not being anyone." The opportunity to develop a distinct role and voice in the model society of an orchestra can overcome this feeling, he says. "That's why the child's development in the orchestra and the choir provides him with a noble identity and makes him a role model for his family and his community."

He closes his speech with a reference to the spiritual crisis of the modern world. The promise that music holds for children and adolescents, says Abreu, can serve as "a beacon and a goal for a vast social mission—no longer putting society at the service of art, but instead art at the service of society . . . at the service of the weakest . . . at the service of the children . . . and at the service of all those who cry out for vindication through the spirit of their human condition and the raising up of their dignity."

The sound of a flute solo begins in the background as Abreu concludes. The melody is haunting and inconclusive, and gives his final words a sense of solemnity rather than simple celebration. As applause swells in the TED conference hall, the live satellite feed from Caracas reappears on the screen, showing the Maestro now standing at a lectern.

In slow and deliberate English, he reads his TED Prize wish: "I wish that you would help to create and document a special training program for fifty gifted young musicians, passionate about their art and social justice, and dedicated to bringing El Sistema to the United States and other countries." The image fades out as the TED audience rises to its feet once more to applaud for ten full minutes, long after the screen has gone blank.

In 1977, when José Antonio Abreu was a young conductor and economist struggling to use classical music as a catalyst for change in the lives of Venezuelan children and youth, Mark Churchill was a young cellist and educator doing research in Brazil for his doctoral dissertation at the Hartt School of Music. As he explored the world of Brazilian chamber music, he was impressed by how much he, like most North Americans, had to learn about the vitality of Latin American musical culture. "I got a sense of what music means in Latin America—hope, youthful energy, passion," he says. "And I realized that the feeling of solidarity between Latin American and North American musical cultures that had been so strong in the 1940s and '50s had mostly disappeared, and now there was a rigid wall between the two."

Over a decade later, in the 1990s, Mark had the opportunity to work with the Asian Youth Orchestra as resident conductor. "These kids were from all over Asia," he tells me, "from countries with long histories of animosity toward each other. And they played together, and the animosities and preconceptions disappeared. This reaffirmed my belief in what providing a musical community and in-depth musical training can mean for kids. It was an idea that stayed with me. When I came back to the States, I thought, 'What could be more obvious than a youth orchestra for all the Americas?'"

As dean of Preparatory and Continuing Education at the New England Conservatory, Mark inaugurated a series of Latin American tours for the conservatory's youth orchestra. The dream of a pan-American ensemble persisted, and in the late 1990s he found an ally in Hilda Ochoa-Brillembourg, a prominent Venezuelan businesswoman who was founder and CEO of the major international investment firm Strategic Investment Group. Hilda Ochoa is an ardent advocate of the arts and of international cultural exchange, and she was enthusiastic about the idea of creating a youth orchestra whose membership would span the American continents. "Hilda knows everybody in Washington," says Mark, "and she put together a meeting there of potential supporters for the idea. At that meeting, we realized that we could not create this unilaterally—that it had to be a collaboration between equal partners in North and South America. So we needed a Latin American partner."

There was no doubt among the meeting attendees as to who that partner should be. "We called José Antonio on the spot, while we were meeting in Washington," Mark remembers, "and he was walking on the street in Caracas, and he answered his cell phone. And he said, 'Of course!' He told me later that this overture from us had great significance for him. It was the first time in his lifetime that a North American organization—*any* organization—had approached a South American organization with the intention of equal partnership."

As Mark Churchill began working closely with Abreu and others to create and launch the Youth Orchestra of the Americas, he came to realize that the Venezuelan youth orchestra phenomenon was grounded in a vision equally as far-reaching as the dream of a pan-American youth ensemble. El Sistema not only embraced young people's musical collaboration as the path to cross-cultural understanding; it went further, to imagine musical engagement as a social as well as an artistic phenomenon. "I knew immediately," he tells me, "that we in the United States had everything to learn from them. And so I wanted as much synergy between El Sistema and the New England Conservatory as possible."

Both the newly formed Youth Orchestra of the Americas and the conservatory's youth orchestra toured Venezuela several times, sometimes playing alongside members of the Símon Bolívar Youth Orchestra and other Venezuelan ensembles. Mark particularly relishes the memory of a five-hour concert in Caracas in 2001, when the NEC youth orchestra and the Youth Orchestra of the Americas joined forces and were conducted by Dudamel. "That was thrilling," he says. In 2002, the New England Conservatory gave Abreu an honorary doctorate. And in 2005, a formal friendship agreement between the conservatory and FESNOJIV was signed by Abreu and NEC's then-president Daniel Steiner, pledging to work together toward the common vision of music as a powerful force for change in education and society.

In 2007, NEC made an ambitious plan to host a residency for the entire Símon Bolívar Youth Orchestra of Venezuela, in conjunction with a concert in Boston's Symphony Hall. "We saw what was happening in Europe, the fame and adulation they were getting," says Mark. "And we knew it was just a matter of time before they took the United States by storm. So we wanted the New England Conservatory to host them. But bringing two hundred and fifty people here for a week was an expensive proposition!"

He approached the Boston-headquartered Liberty Mutual Insurance Company with a request for help. "Liberty Mutual is affiliated with a major Venezuelan insurance company, Seguros Caracas," he says. "So the Liberty Mutual people in Boston called Seguros Caracas and said, 'What is this El Sistema?' The CEO of Seguros Caracas didn't know about it at the time, but he made some inquiries. And he got so excited that Seguros Caracas went on to donate several million dollars to El Sistema in Venezuela."

Mark, a tall, lanky man with an errant fringe of white hair, tells me he was delighted that his initiative resulted in an unlooked-for windfall for the Sistema—and equally delighted that Liberty Mutual helped make it possible for the Simón Bolívar Orchestra, with Dudamel as conductor, to play in Boston's Symphony Hall and to have its first U.S. residency at the New England Conservatory. "They were with us for four days, and it was fantastic—not only performances, but master classes, joint rehearsals, all kinds of opportunities to play together. And lots of chamber music—it was a chamber music love-in. We were the first people in the United States to do this for them, and they were very excited.

"For me," adds Mark, "it was a pivotal moment. I knew this was the first big step in the journey to bring El Sistema to the United States."

⁓

During the time that Mark Churchill was launching this journey at the New England Conservatory, the same impulse was spontaneously emerging on the other side of the country. At the Los Angeles Philharmonic Orchestra, a keen interest in Gustavo Dudamel was evolving into a fascination with the Venezuelan system that produced him. L.A. Philharmonic president Deborah Borda says that even before Dudamel was appointed to the position of music director, the process of developing a relationship with him became the catalyst for an in-depth rethinking of the orchestra's community education mission. "In 2006, I had spent quite a bit of time observing Gustavo," she tells me, "traveling around the world to watch him conduct in a number of cities and getting to know him both as a musician and as a person. And it became clear to me very quickly that the two key components of his life are music and home—and for him, home is not only Venezuela, but El Sistema."

In order to understand this fundamental aspect of Dudamel's identity, Borda felt she needed to experience it firsthand, and in November of 2006 she made a trip to Venezuela along with the directors of the orchestra's education department and Ernest

Fleischmann, the famed orchestra impresario who had been general manager of the Philharmonic for many years. A brisk, authoritative executive who has presided over a decade of artistic and financial success at the L.A. Phil, Borda is openly emotional when she speaks of her trip to Venezuela. "It was overwhelming," she says. "As everyone knows who has been there and seen the Sistema, you are so moved—you spend the first few days in tears. I'm a musician and I have been in music management for many years, and I have always said that music is fundamentally about our humanity. But this was the apotheosis of that idea. So I knew that whether or not Gustavo became our music director, I felt a sort of moral imperative to bring this kind of program to Los Angeles."

After her trip to Caracas, Borda won approval from the orchestra's Board of Directors for a substantial investment of resources in creating a program based upon Sistema principles. "Gustavo was the inspiration," she says. "But we decided to do it whether Gustavo became our conductor or not. We were doing it no matter what."

Chad Smith, the orchestra's vice president of artistic planning, adds that he and his colleagues were already pursuing the goal of aligning educational programs with overall artistic mission. "We were doing a great job of giving kids a first exposure to classical music, through children's concerts and school partnerships," he says. "And we were doing a good job of offering education programs to adult ticket-buyers. But as for actual opportunities for young people to make music—we just weren't doing much. And we realized that was just completely counterintuitive. We're an orchestra. We're fundamentally about making music.

"And then we went to Caracas," he adds, "and we were completely blown away. It was a tremendous, synergistic moment."

Jessica Balboni was the L.A. Phil's education director at the time. "When we went to Venezuela," she tells me, "I think I was most overwhelmed by how the Sistema addresses and cares about the whole child. And it was such a dramatic demonstration of how playing in orchestras can give children a strong sense of their own efficacy in the world." Jessica says that when the L.A. Phil group returned home, they were all aware that the orchestra was "poised to become a different kind of leader—an educational as well as artistic leader."

Out of this synergistic moment came a remarkable document created by the Philharmonic's Education and Community Affairs departments and titled "Youth Orchestra Movement: The Opportunity and the Need." The document stated the Philharmonic's intention "to establish a community-wide network of youth orchestras, confident that the lives of young people engaged in music learning are changed through the hard work, self-satisfaction, skill-building, and teamwork of orchestra ensemble playing." Community and civic organizations across Los Angeles, as well as arts and education organizations, were invited and urged to join the "movement."

Major symphony orchestras often support youth orchestras, but rarely do they advocate for movements. And this document had the bold feel of a manifesto. Leni Boorstin, who has headed the Philharmonic's Department of Community Affairs for many years, tells me that the L.A. Phil was, in fact, determined to create something entirely new in the orchestral world. "We wanted to make it clear that we were looking at ways of turning traditional music education on its head," she says, "and asking questions about social justice and social outcomes." Leni adds that the orchestra could never have created such a movement by itself. "We said to ourselves, we need to engage everybody," she says. "This is bigger than just us."

According to Gretchen Nielsen, the orchestra's current education director, the driving motivation for the new initiative came directly from the example of Dudamel and El Sistema, and was guided by the vision of José Antonio Abreu. "This was about reaching kids in our city who had never been reached before, and giving them an orchestral experience they could never have had otherwise," she says. "We've had a commitment to youth orchestras and music education for a long time. And there are many existing youth orchestras already in L.A., and of course we continue to be supportive of them. But they do not represent, and they do not look like, the population of Los ·

Angeles as a whole. And that is where we were inspired by Gustavo and by El Sistema to seek change."

⌣

In November 2007, Gustavo Dudamel took the Simón Bolívar Youth Orchestra of Venezuela on their first tour of the United States, performing in Los Angeles and Boston and culminating in New York with a Carnegie Hall debut. For the El Sistema movement builders in Los Angeles and Boston, the arrival of Dudamel and his flagship youth orchestra served as a potent catalyst. With the virtuosic, ebullient young Venezuelan musicians crowding the stages of venerable concert halls and turning staid season ticket-holders into frenzied fans, the Sistema-inspired momentum that had been simultaneously building on both coasts reached a new peak of energy and excitement. In each city, there was a spontaneous convening of arts educators and social reformers on the day the Venezuelans came to town, focused on how to bring the dream of an El Sistema in the United States closer to reality.

In Los Angeles, the meeting took the form of a symposium attended by representatives from over twenty "stakeholder organizations" who had rallied to the Los Angeles Philharmonic's call for a city-wide youth orchestra movement—people who rarely found themselves in the same room together, much less engaged in alliance-building toward universal music education. "There were academic people from the universities," says Leni Boorstin. "There were people connected to public after-school programs. There were music schools, and there were charter schools. There was the Harmony Project, which was already working to bring music education to underserved kids in L.A. And there were people from the public school system—the Los Angeles Unified School District."

This assemblage of urgent and often competing interests had been able, over the course of meetings throughout the previous year, to achieve unanimity around the common cause of creating a youth orchestra movement in Los Angeles. At the symposium, their new mission was officially announced by the Los Angeles Philharmonic, on the very stage in Walt Disney Concert Hall where the Venezuelan ensemble would perform later that evening.

"It was so exciting!" remembers Gretchen Nielsen. "They all stood on the stage in Walt Disney Concert Hall behind Deborah Borda, kind of in a big rally call. It was such a strong symbolic statement: 'We are all behind this! There's going to be a youth orchestra movement in L.A.!' "

It was especially exciting, both Gretchen and Leni tell me, that along with the orchestra leaders and arts educators onstage, there were representatives from the mayor's office and his office of Gang Reduction and Youth Development. There was no mistaking that this rallying cry for a new movement was social as well as artistic in nature.

To the crowd of artists, educators, and policy-makers that packed the hall, Deborah Borda formally announced the new partnership, called YOLA—Youth Orchestra Los Angeles. "This is possibly the first time," she said, "that an orchestra has taken the initiative to lead a coalition of partners to take on a social issue. El Sistema shows us what is possible: never before has the power of music been concentrated in this way to change the lives of children."

YOLA's goal, she continued, was to build between three and five children's orchestras in underserved communities in Los Angeles, in partnership with community organizations, over the following decade. As a first step forward, the L.A. Phil planned to collaborate with several partners to create a brand-new children's orchestra at the EXPO Center in the mostly Latino and African-American district of South Central Los Angeles. In an Abreu-style move, Deborah Borda promised the audience that the new orchestra—which at that moment did not exist—would perform a public concert within a year at the EXPO Center.

The Los Angeles symposium was guided and moderated by Eric Booth, a renowned leader in the fields of arts education and arts engagement in communities. Eric remembers that the Walt Disney

Concert Hall was filled with excitement that day. "It was really hot," he says. "There was a clear sense that something big was happening."

After Deborah Borda's speech, Dudamel took the stage for an interview with a local radio host. "Gustavo wasn't a superstar yet," Eric says. "He hadn't yet been formally appointed by the L.A. Phil. But hearing him speak was incredible. And it wasn't the thrill of celebrity—it was simply the sense that he was an amazing guy, with a great story."

Gretchen Nielsen agrees that the excitement in the air that day was palpable, and points out that it was deeper than simply fanfare. "It was a day of asking questions," she says, "of asking 'What's possible? Could we actually bring El Sistema here?'"

She adds that when symposium participants gathered that night to hear Dudamel and the Simón Bolívar Orchestra, the young Venezuelans "answered the question of 'What's possible' in a way we could never have dreamed of."

The week after their Los Angeles debut, Dudamel and the Simón Bolívar arrived in Boston for their residency at the New England Conservatory. Here as well, their presence provided the impetus for a daylong gathering of leaders in the diverse fields of music and arts education, professional and youth orchestras, and community arts engagement. As in Los Angeles, the question on the table at the Boston seminar was whether "Venezuela's message of social transformation through music could be a model for education, social reform, and human development in the United States."

Eric Booth, who led this seminar as well as the Los Angeles gathering, challenged seminar participants to be audacious in reimagining the limits of the possible. "We in the arts world are so marinated in scarcity thinking," he told them. "It can seem inconceivable to us to reach for something as grand as El Sistema."

While the movement in Los Angeles had clear roots in the L.A. Phil's professional interest in Gustavo Dudamel, the motivating force for Boston's activism lay in the strong connections between the New England Conservatory and José Antonio Abreu. Maestro Abreu himself was on hand in Boston to deliver the keynote address, in which he expressed his delight at the prospect of joining with the conservatory and other musical institutions in the United States to create a pan-American movement. "The New World," he said, "is nothing less than all three Americas. And so what we are in the process of creating is really an expression of a new, transcontinental social and musical culture."

The seminar ended, as had the Los Angeles meeting the week before, with participants flocking to the concert hall to witness firsthand the phenomenon of Abreu's "new, transcontinental culture." And after Dudamel led the Simón Bolívar in electrifying performances of Bernstein and Beethoven, jackets flew—but not Venezuelan jackets: during the tumultuous ovation, the patrons of Boston's Symphony Hall twirled their double-breasted suit jackets above their heads. It was a potent reminder that the transformational power of music crosses the boundaries not only of continents but of classes, cultures, and generations as well.

⌣

On October 3, 2009, less than two years after the El Sistema sparks first flew in Boston and Los Angeles, Dudamel stood on the podium at the Hollywood Bowl conducting the children of YOLA in Beethoven's Ninth Symphony—and the Sistema was suddenly and squarely on the map of media and public consciousness. Ten days later, the New England Conservatory made its own substantial contribution to the expansion of the movement by launching the first class of the Abreu Fellowship. Eric Booth speaks of this coincidence of timing as proof that El Sistema was, for the United States, an idea whose time had come. "It's unusual enough in this change-resistant field of arts learning to have any synchronous occurrences support the launch of a new movement," he says. "As El Sistema has come to the U.S., there have been a series of synchronicities that speak to a suppressed hunger for this kind of work and for the benefits we believe it can bring."

The successful launch of the Abreu Fellowship in the fall of 2009 was a direct result of the wish Maestro Abreu had made six months earlier, in his speech accepting the TED Prize. That speech, and that wish, were exceptional among TED awards not only because they were delivered on-screen rather than in person, and not only because they have become the object of hundreds of thousands of YouTube hits. His TED Prize wish also had the distinction of combining a large-scale philosophical and spiritual vision with a very concrete goal. The wishes of previous awardees have been always inspirational but often general, calling for "a global conversation about sustainability" or "a global system to detect each new disease or disaster as soon as it emerges." One of the two other 2009 prizewinners, oceanographer Sylvia Earle, made a wish "that you would use all means at your disposal—films! expeditions! the Web! more!—to ignite public support for a global network of marine protected areas." And Jill Tarter, the third of the year's prizewinners, wished "that you would empower Earthlings everywhere to become active participants in the ultimate search for cosmic company." Abreu, by contrast, made a wish informed by philosophical ideals but grounded in a specific number, a clear program, and a clearly realizable goal.

The TED organization responded immediately, mobilizing to help bring Abreu's wish to realization according to his timetable—which was, typically, all about immediate action. In just a few months the application process for the Abreu Fellowship was initiated; funds were raised for stipends, faculty, and administration; and a curriculum was designed to offer two semesters of intensive study of the principles and practices of the Sistema. TED production manager

Anna Verghese says that TED's support for Abreu's wish, as for other projects, has been partly financial but has also taken the form of networking and offering public visibility. "The TED talks get spread online," she tells me, "and they just go like wildfire, and people get inspired to get involved. That's one of the ways we help to make things happen."

Anna explains that TED often works in partnership with communities or organizations to help realize TED Prize wishes. "It was clear that in order for the Abreu Fellowship to grow, it needed to be part of a major institution," she says. "And it was also clear that Abreu believed the New England Conservatory should be that institution."

In 2009 the commencement of the Abreu Fellows Program and the launch of a new Web site marked the official beginnings of El Sistema USA at the New England Conservatory. Says Anna Verghese, the TED administrator, "Maestro Abreu knew that he could really trust the New England Conservatory to create and lead the kind of pedagogical program he has dreamed of."

The launch of a small-scale academic fellowship program is not a media event on the order of a glamorous national conducting debut. Still, there is some modest hoopla when the Abreu Fellows arrive in Boston to begin their studies. Newspaper and television reporters solicit interviews from the Fellows, and in the first week of the program they are shadowed by a camera crew under the direction of Jamie Bernstein, who plans to make a documentary about the fellowship program. My appearance as an inquisitive author in their midst during their first few days is taken in stride.

They are a young group, but self-assured and serious about their mission, and their professional lives have already been guided by "a passion for their art and for social justice," in Abreu's phrase, in a dramatically diverse number of ways. Christine Witkowski is a

French horn player who started a mentoring program for inner-city kids during her college years; Rebecca Levi, a singer and flutist, led a music program in Peru for abused children. Lorrie Heagy has taught elementary school music for years at a school for at-risk kids in Juneau, Alaska. Clarinetist David Malek has taught inner-city children with the Harmony Project in Los Angeles; violist Katie Wyatt was director of education and community affairs for the North Carolina Symphony; trumpet player Stanford Thompson went to Kenya to start that country's first instrumental education program. Dan Berkowitz, who plays trombone and has a dual degree in music and economics, taught master classes to children in China, while Jonathan Govias, a conductor from Canada, worked with a youth orchestra in India. Álvaro Rodas, a percussionist from Guatemala, has worked to bring El Sistema to his native country. Dantes Rameau, a bassoonist born in Canada of Haitian and Cameroonian parents, taught at the Yale School of Music's community outreach program while earning his master's degree there. And managing director Stephanie Scherpf, whose youth, energy, and idealism match those of the Fellows, has founded a community dance program in Mozambique and written a thesis on the pedagogical implications of hip-hop.

It is a rich mix of experience and, clearly, a convergence of passions. On their first day together, the Fellows trade stories about how they first heard of El Sistema. "I was a student at the Curtis Institute of Music," says Stanford, "and Simon Rattle came to work with our orchestra. And he said to us, 'You guys are good, but you play like robots. There are groups of little kids in Venezuela who could bury you.'"

Álvaro tells of being shown a video of those groups of little Venezuelan kids when he was growing up in Guatemala. "They were playing Tchaikovsky's Fourth Symphony at lightning speed," he says. "It was incredible. But what we were all most impressed by was that the kids looked like us! We had never seen a youth orchestra that was not blond and blue-eyed and European-looking."

"I toured Latin America with the Youth Orchestra of the Americas," says Katie. "And the best instrumentalists were always Venezuelan. I would ask them what conservatory they had studied at, and they would tell me, 'Oh, we just learned to play with our friends in the neighborhood.' I was completely mystified."

For a number of the other Fellows, the first exposure came through viewing the now-ubiquitous YouTube clip of the Simón Bolívar Orchestra playing at the London Proms in 2007. Dan, who was living in London when the orchestra played a return concert the following year, says that a scalped ticket for that concert cost 700 pounds—though he lucked into getting a free one. "They played 'Nimrod' from Elgar's *Enigma* Variations, which is like sacred music in Britain," he says, "and not only were people in the audience crying, but orchestra members were crying too—they understood what this music meant to people."

Each Fellow's story ends with almost exactly the same sentence. "I just knew I had to find out more about El Sistema," they say.

Mark Churchill speaks of his personal stake in bringing the Sistema to the United States. "When I first went to Venezuela and saw it in action ten years ago, I said, 'This is it,' " he tells them. "I knew it was the next really important idea in music education—even education in general. What is most striking, to anyone who sees it, is that from the very first time a Sistema child holds an instrument or does a rhythmic exercise, music-making is always about human connection."

He encourages the Fellows to be bold in their ambitions. "We have an elegant triangle in place now," he concludes. "Venezuela, Los Angeles, Boston. And the need now, in order to grow El Sistema in the United States, is informed leadership. So here you are."

"You are musical astronauts," adds NEC president Woodcock. "You are going where we in this country have not gone before." During the Simón Bolívar Orchestra's 2007 residency, he says, "they took us apart with their passion. They reminded us all about the power of music, which we sometimes tend, in our civilized way, to forget."

Because of the long-standing connection between NEC and El Sistema, there are a number of Venezuelans currently studying music in Boston, and these young musicians meet with the Fellows to share firsthand their experiences of growing up within the Sistema. "Here in the States," a flutist says, "the orchestra is the second thing, and the first thing is your playing. In Venezuela, in the Sistema, it's the other way around. Here you are preparing to be a soloist. There, you are working to develop an orchestra."

"When you go to orchestra every day, you're going to your social environment," adds a violinist. "And it is just so much fun to be inside of that. We all grew up not only learning how to play together but also learning how to take care of each other."

A horn player talks about the natural connection, for Venezuelans, of music and emotion. "No one there has to tell an orchestra to 'be passionate,'" he says. "It is something we do naturally. It's part of our culture."

Eric Booth, who has been at the forefront of efforts to identify and articulate guiding principles for the El Sistema movement in the United States and who is the senior advisor for El Sistema USA, urges the Fellows gently and relentlessly to examine their preconceptions about the work they are undertaking. As a mentor and facilitator, he has an uncommon ability—equal parts high energy, verbal brio, and a keen sense of play—to open new and more penetrating ways for artists and teachers to think about the work they do. He asks the Fellows what they are most interested in learning during their fellowship year, and their answers are prompt. How to create a business model! How to fund-raise! Grant writing, managing a budget, marketing and public relations!

Eric acknowledges that these are important issues, but guides them back toward the complex question at the heart of the issue—namely, the ways in which the principles and practices of El Sistema may challenge fundamental assumptions of the arts education community in the United States. "In this country, we tend to think of 'deep' and 'broad' as two mutually exclusive ways to approach arts learning," he tells them. "In El Sistema, they coexist. Music learning there is both deep and broad. We have no model for that here."

Another dichotomy we tend to take for granted, Eric continues, is the relationship between entrepreneurial and artistic energy. "Here in the States, we think we have to choose one or the other," he says. "If you want to be an entrepreneur, you have to sacrifice your artistic goals. But in El Sistema those two kinds of energy seem to be integrated." He describes Venezuelan núcleo directors who are at once "ferocious teaching artists" and avid activists for the expansion of their programs, and he urges the Fellows to be open to using their creativity in every aspect of their work.

Eric asks the Fellows to explore their own individual answers to a question central to their mission. "We are all here," he says, "because we assume that the experience of learning deeply inside complex music is an effective way to support and develop urban youth. Why do we assume this?"

This is, indeed, the inquiry at the center of the enterprise. The leaders of the Venezuelan Sistema have their own answers, based in their culture and their experience. But for the Fellows—as for all music educators in the United States—the question requires a hard look at basic assumptions about music, about learning, about childhood and poverty and possibility.

"The Fellows are on a quest to determine what is the right verb to use when we talk about moving El Sistema from Venezuela to the United States," Eric tells me. "Do we mean to 'adopt' the Sistema? Or 'adapt' it? Transplant it, or re-create it? It's hard to say. The truth is, we're still not sure what this process actually looks like."

As they study and analyze the most effective ways to adapt and transplant El Sistema, the Fellows are constantly challenged to keep abreast of the ways it has already arrived—because the movement to bring the Sistema to the United States is not waiting for them. It is growing, suddenly, like wildfire.

Even before the mainstream media discovered El Sistema, two *60 Minutes* specials featuring Dudamel and some viral YouTube clips of the Simón Bolívar Orchestra have fired the imaginations of social welfare–minded musicians and music-loving social activists in cities across the country. It's too late to ask, "Could it happen here?" Through the spontaneous creation of Sistema-inspired orchestra programs for underprivileged kids in big cities and small towns, in the South and the Midwest and the Rocky Mountains, with resources ranging from substantial to shoestring and faster than anyone can keep track of, it is already happening.

El Sistema USA managing director Stephanie Scherpf tells me that calls and emails come in weekly, and sometimes even daily: "We want to bring El Sistema here! How do we do it? Can you help us?" And the calls don't come only from U.S. locations. Just as suddenly and dramatically as El Sistema has burgeoned in the United States, it has begun to catch the imaginations of musicians elsewhere in the world; in addition to Latin American countries, most of which already have Sistema-like programs in place, El Sistema–inspired programs are now springing up in Canada and Jamaica, in England and across Europe, in Australia and New Zealand and South Korea. Programs such as Big Noise in Raploch, Scotland; the Leading Note Foundation, in Ottawa, Canada; and In Harmony in Lambeth, England—to name just a few—are duplicating El Sistema's mission of bringing orchestral opportunities to children in poor areas with many social and economic problems. Mark Churchill's "elegant triangle" seems to be evolving, rapidly and of necessity, into a geometric entity large and complex enough to encompass the entire world.

The Glenn Gould Prize is one of classical music's most prestigious music awards. Given triennially in memory of the great Canadian pianist, the prize honors individuals who "promote the vital connection between artistic excellence and the transformation of lives." Past honorees have included Yehudi Menuhin, Oscar Peterson, André Previn, and Yo-Yo Ma. In October 2009, two weeks after the Abreu Fellowship begins in Boston, José Antonio Abreu is awarded the prize in Toronto. Instead of the $50,000 cash associated with the award, Abreu has asked for musical instruments, and the Glenn Gould Foundation has collaborated with the Yamaha Corporation to turn the prize into $150,000 worth of instruments for children in the Sistema. The prize also includes an invitation to choose the next recipient of the City of Toronto Protégé Award, for which Abreu, to no one's surprise, has named Gustavo Dudamel.

To honor Abreu and to commemorate the award, the foundation throws a weeklong city-wide "Celebration of Music," convening the first international symposium to focus upon El Sistema as a world model for music education as social change, and—following the precedent of Los Angeles and Boston—hosting a residency in Toronto for Dudamel and the Simón Bolívar Orchestra of Venezuela. Brian Levine, the executive director for the Glenn Gould Prize, tells the Canadian press that hearing the Simón Bolívar musicians is "one of the most moving experiences, and certainly one of the deepest experiences of music, I've had in twenty-five years of professional life in music."

The Toronto festival is proof of Abreu's increasingly iconic status in the classical music world. And in a nicely genre-defying gesture, the Glenn Gould Foundation invites one of North America's reigning pop stars, Linda Ronstadt, to introduce the Maestro to the overflow crowd at Toronto's prestigious Royal Conservatory of Music, where the symposium is held. Ronstadt has recently addressed the United States Congress about the potential of programs like El Sistema to change children's lives for the better, and she pays tribute to Abreu with a reverence not often seen in pop music superstars for classical music education reformers.

By now I am used to the way the diminutive figure of the Maestro can command a stage; but I am newly impressed, at the Royal Conservatory, to see that he can do it with equal aplomb sitting down. With Rodrigo Guerrero translating, he speaks to the audience, mostly school music teachers who have come from across Canada, about the many thousands of Venezuelan children who are "spiritually wealthy through music" and of his desire to create a world where music "becomes an insurmountable barrier" to drugs and violence. "Music is essential for the social development of a community," he says, "and every achievement of an orchestra is also an achievement of the children's families and of their community."

To a question from the audience about how much time children in Sistema núcleos devote to music every day, the Maestro responds animatedly, "They play music whenever they are not in school! They play music on weekends, on holidays! And it is the most joyful experience of their day! It gives them identity and self-worth, and fills them with a sense of hope."

Abreu ends his speech by proposing the establishment of a Venezuelan-Canadian youth orchestra. "I want Venezuela and Toronto to develop a fraternal bond through music!" he says. "In one year, we can premiere this new orchestra in Toronto!"

Rodrigo tells me afterward that this kind of bravura flourish is not unusual. "Everywhere we go, he inspires musicians and policymakers to form connections, to make things happen," he says. "Everywhere, agreements!"

To an afternoon workshop audience of people interested in bringing El Sistema to their own communities, Rodrigo speaks about the dream of an international Sistema. "From the early days, ours has been a global vision," says Rodrigo. "Our musicians are always touring, and we are always hosting foreign visitors." He and his associates, he adds, are constantly sought out for guidance by educators all over the world. "Most of the emails we get are asking us, 'How do you do it? How can we do it?' " he says. "We can't tell you exactly how to do it.

"But we can tell you this: if you do it, your community will support it! Because the results you provide will make it clear that it is worthwhile—in fact, that it is a necessity. Wherever there is a núcleo in Venezuela, its community comes to see it as a necessity. There is no better way to build the life of a community than children playing music together."

# CHAPTER 6

# "Being, Not Yet Being": El Sistema in Action

ESTEBAN IS NINE YEARS OLD. HE LIVES IN ONE OF THE MANY barrios of Caracas, in a dwelling that is little more than a shack, among a welter of similar structures spilling haphazardly down the hillside above the center of the city. Sometimes there is running water in Esteban's home, and sometimes electricity; often, there is neither.

His older brother, Jesús, and his younger sister, Carolina, share his bedroom, which is one of the three rooms in the house—the other two are the kitchen and the living room, where his mother sleeps. Carolina sometimes gets into bed with Esteban; she is scared by the sounds of raucous shouts and gunning car motors that come through the tiny bedroom window at night. They haven't seen their brother for months. At the age of fifteen, Jesús has dropped out of school and is hardly ever at home anymore. "I know he is in a gang," says Esteban. "My mother won't tell me, but I know."

Another thing Esteban knows is that his father is in jail, and he thinks that has something to do with gangs too. He can't remember the last time he saw his father. He says that he used to hate school, and that he used to get in trouble a lot for beating up other kids. He has trouble with schoolwork; when he was seven, his teacher told him he was stupid.

These days, he is beginning to think she was wrong. "I can play the violin," he says.

Every day after school, Esteban plays the violin, and learns that he is not stupid, at the núcleo la Rinconada. It is some distance from his home; his mother walks him to a metro station where he gets on a Sistema-run free bus that takes him, along with many other children from the nearby barrios, to the núcleo. Esteban has only been coming to la Rinconada for a year, but he was given a violin at the very beginning of his time there, and already he is playing pieces by Mozart and Vivaldi in a string orchestra of his peers. He loves his instrument, and he takes it with him in the evening when he gets on the bus for the ride home, so that he can play at night before he goes to bed. "At first my sister didn't like how it sounded," he says. "But now she says she wants to play it too."

Esteban is small and thin, with a crew cut and a wary look in his eyes. His mother, he says, is looking for a second job and is worried about who will care for Carolina while she is gone the extra hours. He has said to his mother that he will just bring Carolina to the núcleo. "You won't have to walk me to the bus stop anymore," he has told her, "because I'll be walking her."

⌒

The centerpiece of the Abreu Fellowship year is a two-month sojourn in Venezuela, for a total-immersion experience of El Sistema. In the winter of 2010 I join the Fellows' group for their first two weeks, and it is then that I meet Esteban, at the núcleo la Rinconada.

Rodrigo tells us that this núcleo is a historic landmark of sorts for the Sistema, as it was the first núcleo in Caracas and has been in continuous operation for more than thirty years.

The "found space" of la Rinconada actually comprises two found spaces, he says; the younger children's program is housed in an elementary school, and the older children gather in the unused facilities of a nearby racetrack. Both spaces are large, and they need to be: there are twelve hundred students at the núcleo. Some of the younger children are students at the school, but many other children come from elsewhere in the neighborhood or from other parts of the city. For these, the Sistema provides free metro buses from several subway stations. The buses arrive at both núcleo locations filled to bursting with children.

Our visitors' van is brimming too; the Fellows have a considerable entourage. "We love visitors," says Rodrigo. "The more visitors, the more chances we have to share our music." He leads us into the younger children's section of la Rinconada and introduces us to Josbel Pulce, the núcleo director. Josbel explains to us that the núcleo is particularly well known for its early childhood programs, and that therefore she has planned for us to observe the children in order of age, beginning with the youngest and progressing to the most advanced youth orchestra. "Here is our youngest group, our Baby Vivaldi orchestra," she says, opening a classroom door.

The Baby Vivaldi orchestra uses no instruments and does not play Vivaldi, but it lives up to at least one part of its name: these are toddlers young enough to be considered bona fide babies. They are in the laps of their mothers, who sit cross-legged on the floor leaning against the bare walls. The room is so small that our large group has to stand in the doorway and peer in. Led by the teacher, a young woman sitting cross-legged and facing them, the mothers and children sing a folk song and tap rhythm sticks; the children follow and imitate every move their mothers make. They are dressed in tiny Rinconada uniforms, dark blue pants and shirts with the núcleo's colorful insignia. "We meet twice a week," the teacher tells us. "We try to teach traditional Venezuelan songs whenever we can, and we work on a sense of rhythm. But mostly, with parents and with kids, we are working toward empathy."

Josbel Pulce explains that the emphasis on traditional children's songs is a deliberate effort to revive an aspect of Venezuelan culture that is threatening to disappear. "Venezuelan mothers have lost the habit of singing to their children," she says. "We have had a rich tradition of 'crib' songs in our culture, but mothers today are mostly listening to pop and reggaeton, and they are not singing at all. So in these 'baby orchestra' groups, we are teaching the mothers as well as the children. We don't want the old songs to be forgotten. And we want to bring back the tradition of children hearing music first through their mothers' songs and lullabies."

She leads us to another small room to observe the Baby Corelli orchestra, a group of three-year-olds who come together every day for an hour. It seems to have been renamed since my visit here the previous summer, when it was called the Baby Mozart orchestra, but the name change is probably more whimsical than significant; there is no Corelli going on here, and no Mozart either. It seems clear that these names are used not to indicate the music being played by the "babies," but to introduce the great composers into children's lives at a very early age, as familiar names and presences, so that when the children grow older and encounter the actual music of these masters, they will seem like old friends. This is a common practice throughout the Sistema—and I have been told that, in the provinces, rural children often lobby to name their favorite farm animals after the composers they've learned about in their núcleos, so that the fields ring with "Here, Mozart! Come, Beethoven!" as cows are herded and chickens fed.

The fourteen children of the Baby Corelli ensemble are not with their parents, but there are three teaching aides in addition to the teacher, so the room is full of adult guidance and positive reinforcement. The children are singing and moving, first walking in a circle and then facing each other in pairs. When the song arrives at the word *abrazo*, the pairs of children hug each other.

Like good preschool teachers everywhere, the head teacher keeps the kids constantly engaged, seldom pausing between activities. After the song they sit down in their circle and the teacher passes out maraca eggs. "The eggs are sleeping," she whispers, and the children hold the eggs with solemn care so they will not wake up, until she announces that "it's morning," and all the maracas become instant roosters. Most of the children in this group were in a two-year-old Baby Vivaldi orchestra last year, and it seems likely that they have already absorbed a great deal not only about music, but about group discipline; these three-year-olds sit startlingly still when they are not singing or shaking maracas. They too wear the dark blue shirt of the núcleo uniform, and since they are not quite so tiny, the insignia can be seen more clearly: a musical staff blooms with bright notes in the Venezuelan national colors of red, yellow, and blue, with the words "National Foundation of Children's Orchestras" arching over the top, and the words "Núcleo la Rinconada" at the bottom. We will see these uniforms and this insignia on all the children, of all ages, for the rest of the afternoon, and will be consistently impressed by its power to convey in simple form the unity of the núcleo, the connection of the núcleo to the entire Sistema, and the musical language that unifies and connects all.

In the Baby Haydn string orchestra (or is it Baby Mahler?), we watch four- and five-year-old children playing actual small-scale stringed instruments. Each string is given the name of an animal: from low to high, the strings are elephants, lions, dogs, and cats. "Let's hear the lion roar," says the teacher, and the children play a rhythmic pattern on their second-to-lowest strings. They sing a song about the animals, with each sung phrase indicating a different animal sound and answered by bowed rhythms. As they play, four assistants circulate constantly to check each child's posture, bowing technique, and fingering; with a teacher-student ratio of about one to four, it's possible to detect and correct most mistakes instantly. Occasionally, a child's attention wanders, and is gently refocused, but in this setting of dynamic communal activity there seem to be few discipline problems. As in the other ensembles, the children are delighted to perform for us, and stage fright is not in evidence. "Performing for people helps them focus," one teacher tells us. "They always pay special attention when visitors are here."

Núcleo director Josbel tells us that she grew up in la Rinconada, beginning her musical life there in 1985 at the age of twelve and then going on to apprentice with Susan Siman at Montalbán and to study early childhood education in Caracas before returning to Rinconada as teacher and then director. She has been responsible for creating and developing the early childhood programs here, and it is obvious that this work is the focus of her life. She explains that the Sistema establishes general guidelines for pedagogy at each level, but within those guidelines she has written much of her musical curriculum herself.

Like Josbel, most of the teachers we see at la Rinconada grew up in this núcleo and received all of their early training here. Some went on to the university to get pedagogy degrees, and the rest, to whom she refers as "teaching musicians," are given frequent professional workshops. Josbel trains all her teachers in an eclectic mixture of musical pedagogies that variously emphasize the use of singing, physical movements, percussive rhythm instruments, and free play. She encourages them to use these techniques flexibly, freely borrowing and adapting what works best in particular circumstances. "We don't have a rigid 'set curriculum,' " says the teacher of a Baby Mozart class. "We always adapt our work to the specific needs of each group."

The overall program at Rinconada, says Josbel, is scaled in very gradual, incremental stages, so that children can continually experience success. And at each level, learning takes place in ensemble, with children constantly playing together. "That's the basis of everything," she says.

And now we are treated to a demonstration of what is perhaps the best-known early childhood innovation of the Sistema, the Paper Orchestra. Josbel leads us into a much larger, gym-sized room where forty children between four and six years old sit waiting for us with their instruments; it is a full-sized, formal string orchestra—except that all the instruments are made of papier-mâché. They are beautiful, elaborate, full-size creations, painted in bright colors and with fanciful designs. Josbel conducts *"La Gran Orquesta de Papel"* in a song she has written about the instruments; as they sing about each string section, the members of that section hold their instruments high (or, in the case of the cellos and basses, twirl them on their carefully crafted pins). "We are the violins, mmm mmm mmm," they sing, and "We are the violas . . . we are the cellos." The children could not be more proud of their instruments if they were actually playing them. For an encore, they offer us a cha-cha version of "Twinkle, Twinkle, Little Star," drawing their papier-mâché bows across their many-hued instruments and singing the sounds the instruments might make.

"In the beginning," says Josbel, "the Paper Orchestra developed partly out of need. There simply were not enough instruments for all the children." As the concept evolved, it became clear that the orchestra served a variety of pedagogical purposes. "When they play in the Paper Orchestra," Josbel goes on, "children develop a sense of what an instrument feels like, even at an age when they might be too young to really play one. They get a sense of how that instrument is supposed to be held, and what the basic positions are, and how it feels to hold it for the duration of a whole rehearsal.

"Just as important, they get a sense of what an orchestra is, and what it is to be a member of an orchestra. They learn about the discipline of the orchestra—to be patient, and not to talk while the teacher is talking. And most important, they learn to love an instrument." In addition, she adds, a rich kind of parent involvement develops as mothers and fathers work with their children to create instruments.

Susan Siman, the Sistema violinist who was a principal figure in founding and shaping its string pedagogy, has explained that the idea for the first Paper Orchestra came in part out of her own experience as a mother, as she was working at the Montalbán núcleo to develop musical learning strategies for very young children. "When my own kids were two and three years old," she said, "I watched how their fine motor skills progressed as they learned to draw and color. They loved to help me make little ornaments for our Christmas tree. And I thought to myself, if we can make little Christmas balls we can make musical instruments!" Susan first experimented with this idea by having her students make mobiles of musical notes, and then by creating model instruments out of wood for them to paint. "They enjoyed decorating the instruments, and then they loved the instruments they made. And that was the concept that eventually became the Paper Orchestra."

Josbel spent several years at Montalbán working with Susan and helping to develop the concept, and she brought it with her when she returned to la Rinconada. "The Paper Orchestra is kids' first real encounter with orchestral activities," she tells us. "Once they've been in it, they feel like serious orchestra members. They want to be in orchestras all the time from then on. "

When children move from the Paper Orchestra to real instruments, they immediately become part of a children's string orchestra, and progress within a year or two to another, more advanced children's ensemble. On the day the Fellows and I visit, these full ensembles are not rehearsing; instead the children are meeting in "sectionals." It's a different kind of window into the pedagogical culture of the Sistema: the students are not in orchestral performance mode, but are learning the kind of disciplined practice that prepares for it. All the sectionals are led by very young teachers—for the second violins, the teacher is a high school student who has been at the núcleo since the age of two—and all are rigorous in relation to multiple goals: intonation, technique, rhythmic accuracy and, above all, ensemble precision.

It is fascinating to see that even in these sessions, which lack the sensuous satisfactions of orchestral sound and beguiling music, the children stay mostly energized and engaged. The incentives, it seems, are both collective and individual; there is clearly fun in the intensity of working together, but it is also apparent that kids are pleased and gratified by individual attention. In the cello and bass sectional, for example, the teacher addresses mistakes by asking kids to play one at a time, and many kids profess to be making mistakes, in order to be given this opportunity—in striking contrast to most youth orchestra players in the United States, who would consider it an embarrassing form of punishment.

As I watch the sectional rehearsal of first violins, my attention is particularly drawn to a small, slight boy in the fifth row. He is sharing a music stand with a somewhat larger boy, and I notice him because even among this group of focused children, his air of acute concentration is striking; his eyes never leave the teacher's face. And he never smiles.

The teacher, on the other hand, smiles a great deal. We watch her lead the group in playing a D scale as she claps out a beat so strong it cannot be resisted. Over and over, they play that D scale . . . over, and over, and over. She sings the solfège syllables of the scale as they play—"Re, mi, fa, sol, la"—and many of them sing along with her. From time to time, she stops for brief breaks, leading them in physical stretches and exercises, and then claps them right back into the scale. "If just one of you plays staccato while the rest of you are playing legato," she tells them, "the whole group sounds off."

Just when it seems impossible that they will submit to another repetition, she divides them in half and has one group start the scale two beats after the other, so that they are playing in thirds—which sound so gorgeous after the twenty minutes of unison scales that the kids lean into the task with renewed fortitude. She flashes them another smile. And then makes them do it one more time in unison—twice as slowly.

"We're going to play a piece of music now," she tells them finally. "You can take a short break while I get my music organized." Three or four assistant teachers roam around the room, applying rosin to bows and retuning instruments. The kids stay in their seats, some talking and giggling with each other. The small boy in the fifth row continues to play scales.

The piece they play is a simple Baroque air by Corelli, and it is rehearsed in the same way the D scale was—phrase by phrase, over and over and over. The teacher is as ruthless as any symphony conductor about their entrances and cutoffs being exactly, precisely together. There is one particularly difficult passage in which some children are playing C natural instead of the C sharp that is called for. The teacher takes the violin of the nearest child and plays the phrase, demonstrating the fingering for the C sharp. "Everyone, let's play a C sharp," she says. They play a C sharp; it's better, but there is still a C natural lurking somewhere. The larger boy at the fifth-row music stand reaches over and very matter-of-factly moves the small boy's finger very slightly up the A string. "Once more, everybody," says the teacher. This time, the C sharp is perfect.

As the rehearsal goes on, we notice other instances of peer teaching—nearly always done unobtrusively, without arrogance or condescension. In the course of our week in Caracas, we will find that this is a primary cornerstone of Sistema pedagogy; rather than trying to inhibit interaction between kids, teachers welcome and encourage it in the direction of mutual support. Every child seems to have absorbed and internalized the idea that if you know A, B and C, you can help others learn A, B and C too.

The assumption that everyone has something to teach, and musical knowledge and skills are meant to be shared, seems to be rooted in the Sistema's very beginnings—in that group of young music students meeting in a garage, who knew that the principle "Whatever you know, teach it" was the only way to build their improbable orchestra. Thirty-five years later, that fervor both for teaching and for learning—the sense that there is something almost sacred about sharing musical skills—still seems to permeate every aspect of life in the Sistema's núcleos and orchestras.

When the sectional ends, the serious little boy in the fifth row spends a very long time putting his violin back in its case. I approach him, and one of the núcleo teachers helps with translation. "*Me llamo Esteban*," he tells me.

Shy at first, he warms up when I tell him I am from New York. "Francisco Cervelli, he plays for the Yankees," he says. "He is from Venezuela." We talk baseball for a while, and then Esteban's story comes spilling out: his worries about his brother, his troubles at school, the pride he feels about his violin. He says that already he has made friends at the núcleo. "Manuel, he is my best friend," he adds, pointing to the chair where the larger boy sat next to him.

I ask Esteban if he can imagine being a violin teacher himself someday. He does not quite smile. "I am already a violin teacher," he tells me. "I teach my sister."

The older students of la Rinconada núcleo may be the only young musicians in the world—even in Venezuela—who spend their formative musical-training years at a racetrack. The bleak stadium-like building at the edge of the track is no longer used for betting or spectators, but horses still race every weekend, and the setting still has the feel of a crowd venue—rock and pop concerts happen here, in fact, on a regular basis. Rodrigo leads the Fellows' group through an open-air lobby and up an escalator to the second floor, where bets used to be placed and music is now heard from behind every doorway. Here he abandons the tour guide format and encourages us to explore on our own, assuring us that we will be welcome wherever we go.

We are, as it turns out, so welcome that for the duration of the afternoon the Fellows become honorary teachers at la Rinconada.

In every room they enter, students and teachers greet them like visiting musical celebrities and are eager for them to teach. Most of the Abreu Fellows are teachers as well as performers by profession and by inclination, and after a semester of studying and theorizing, they jump at this chance. Fellow Stanford Thompson, a trumpet player from Georgia whose charm goes a long way toward making up for his almost complete lack of Spanish, works with a section of eleven- and twelve-year-old trumpet players. "If you play more softly, you have more breath control," he tells them. They stare at him, game but mystified. "You know, breath? Air? *Aire?*"

He picks up his trumpet and begins to play a low note very, very softly. Twenty seconds . . . forty seconds . . . a minute passes. The note goes on and on. The children's eyes are as round as the bell of his trumpet. When he finally stops, they burst into cheers. Then they take turns trying, with Stanford coaching gently in a Spanish-English dialect of his own spontaneous invention.

At the end of the session, I talk to several of the trumpet players. Rafael and Andrés tell me they are both twelve years old and have been playing the trumpet for three years. Jonas, who is fifteen, has only played for one year but is already playing at the level of his peers. "They help me out a lot," he explains. His favorite composer is Richard Wagner.

Without exception, the kids say that what they like most about the orchestra program is the sound of the orchestra when everyone plays together. Their parents, they tell me, are happy they are in the program, because otherwise they might be in the streets and getting into trouble. I ask them what they want to be when they grow up. "A musician," says Andrés, and they all nod. Rafael adds that he will definitely be a musician but might be a scientist too.

Down the hall, Abreu Fellow Christine Witkowski is also working on breath control, with four French horn players, three boys and a girl. One of the boys has an elaborate Elvis haircut. She lets them try her horn, and they are giddy with the sound; they have never heard a horn of such quality. In another room, Dan Berkowitz gives a private lesson to a fourteen-year-old trombonist. The lesson goes on and on . . . and on . . . until finally Dan expresses concern that perhaps he is keeping the boy from being somewhere else he is supposed to be. "I was supposed to be somewhere else a long time ago," the boy responds, "but I didn't want to leave as long as you were able to keep teaching."

Neither Dan nor Christine speaks Spanish fluently, but like Stan, both find themselves able to manage a variety of satisfying musical communications. Katie Wyatt, with more Spanish at her command, plays musical games with a group of violists; the games are hard work, but they are only aware of having fun, and some of the girls are so excited they jump up and hug her. When she takes up her own viola to demonstrate a difficult passage, the kids begin to dance.

I look in on the rehearsal of one of the núcleo choruses, made up of children around twelve or thirteen years of age who have joined the núcleo within the past year and so have missed the stages of early childhood ensemble instruction. The songs include rhythmic clapping and solfège hand motions. The teacher tells me that the choral program at this level is designed to introduce students to the musical concepts and skills they have missed by coming late to the process; they are required to complete a year of chorus before they are given an instrument.

I ask whether this may create a feeling that choral ensembles are less important than, and merely a stepping-stone to, instrumental ensembles, and the teacher agrees that this can be a problem. During the course of the following week, I will find this concern acknowledged by a number of Sistema teachers I speak with. Nevertheless, the children sing with evident enjoyment, and unlike most North American choruses, who seem to have forgotten that singing is a physical activity, they are almost always swaying, clapping, or moving together in some way as they sing.

There are two full-fledged youth orchestras in the racetrack section of la Rinconada, distinguished not so much by age as by level of skill. When I visited this núcleo on my first trip, the orchestras were taking turns rehearsing in a room where they barely fit; cello bows narrowly missed neighboring cellists, and the percussionists' drumsticks and mallets overlapped with one another. The room's bare concrete walls were adorned with whimsical, almost cartoonlike color sketches of Beethoven and Haydn and Brahms.

This year there is a new orchestra room with much more space and better light (although I miss the goofy composers on the wall, and wonder if the kids do too). The advanced orchestra performs in this room for us, and once again a number of the Fellows are pressed into service: Dan plays with the trombone section, Christine with the horns, and Jonathan Govias is drafted without warning into conducting. He begins a little stiffly, but his learning curve is fast, and the kids help him; they want him to succeed. The oldest players are no more than fifteen, but they play with considerable skill and huge sound. Stan says he is "knocked out" by the quality of the trumpet section's sound and technique. The energy in the room is almost overwhelming. And by the end of the rehearsal, Jonathan and "his" orchestra have found their groove together.

During a break, I try out my halting Spanish in a conversation with a thirteen-year-old violinist, Isabel. She speaks as slowly as a teenaged Venezuelan girl can possibly speak—which is still faster than any English-speaking teenager I know—and tells me that she has been playing for many years and cannot imagine a life without the orchestra program. With pride she shows me her music folder; it is black with embossed gold letters, "N.L.R.," for "Núcleo la Rinconada." I look through the music inside: Tchaikovsky's "Marche Slav," the march from Verdi's *Aida*, Rossini's *William Tell* Overture.

These pieces have been showing up with noticeable frequency in the repertoires of the youth orchestras I've heard in Venezuela, and I ask Rodrigo about this. He confirms my understanding that there is a central set of musical works that forms the core of the repertoire for all Sistema orchestras. "This way," he explains, "a child who moves from one núcleo to another or from one city to another will be able to begin work seamlessly where he left off." He adds that the continuity of repertoire stretches not only across núcleos but also across skill levels; children in less advanced orchestras play simpler versions of the same pieces they will play in original form when they are more advanced. "They meet up with the same music again and again," he says, "each time at a higher level of complexity. The music becomes a part of them—something internalized for all of their lives."

Before we leave la Rinconada, I ask núcleo director Josbel Pulce about the home lives of the children here. She tells me that most come from working-class families in Caracas barrios, and that for almost all of the families, the Sistema is their first exposure to orchestral instruments and classical music. "People hear about it through word of mouth," she says, "and they want their kids to be here." As with all núcleos in the Sistema, every child who wants to come is accepted. There are no auditions, and there are no costs; everything is free, including instruments, instruction, uniforms, snacks, and family support services.

Josbel tells me that the Sistema has made a transformative difference in many families' lives. "They are thrilled when they hear what their children have accomplished," she says. "They hear the kids practicing at home, and they hear concerts here, and they feel a kind of pride that gives them hope for the future of the whole family."

Children are streaming past us down the hallway now; it is almost dismissal time. I recognize Esteban, who—though still not smiling—is swinging his violin case back and forth. "Esteban is doing beautifully," says Josbel. "His mother was very worried that he would go to the streets, like his brother. Now she tells me that if her older son had been here, he never would have gotten into trouble.

"It's really very simple," she adds. "In a nutshell, El Sistema keeps kids busy. We socialize them, we immerse them in music and beauty, we love them. And we keep them busy."

"The best and closest friends in my life," says Norma, "are not my friends from high school or my friends from college. They are my friends from my núcleo."

Norma's núcleo is Montalbán, known as the "flagship" núcleo of Caracas because of its impressive facility and its particularly accomplished orchestras. Norma is so excited to show the Fellows' group her musical birthplace that she comes with us on our visit to Montalbán, even though she isn't officially on the job that day. The núcleo is housed in a large concrete building that began life as part of a housing project in the 1980s but was converted into a núcleo in the early 1990s. A highway runs right by the núcleo, but the mountains that rise abruptly on the other side of the highway are thickly forested, lending a slightly pastoral touch to what is otherwise a dense urban environment. "I learned everything here," Norma tells us as we walk through the courtyard. "And for my whole childhood, it was my community, my extended family. Coming back always feels like going home."

The Fellows and I have already become used to being greeted with spirited impromptu performances. At Montalbán the element of spontaneity is altered by something closer to premeditated shock and awe: the large lobby is filled with a concert band of at least a hundred children, who burst into music as soon as we enter. They play a sophisticated medley of U.S. movie themes and pop tunes, and then the fastest and most spirited rendition of the *William Tell* Overture any of us has ever heard.

Zobeya Márquez, the director of Montalbán, is another fiercely dedicated young woman in the mold of Josbel Pulce, and another disciple of Susan Siman, whom she has replaced in this position. As she describes the sequence of musical learning through six different levels, from groups of three-year-olds through children's ensembles to advanced teenage orchestras, it seems fundamentally similar to what we have seen at Rinconada. As at Rinconada, children at Montalbán spend five or six days a week at the núcleo, for hours each day; orchestral rehearsals are the central focus, and are supplemented by individual lessons and classes in recorder, choral singing, and music notation. Like Rinconada, the Montalbán núcleo places a strong emphasis on early childhood education—naturally enough, since it was here that Susan Siman first developed many of the practices we have seen in action at la Rinconada.

And as at Rinconada, the teachers are focused always toward the twin goals of sound musical technique and empathic human community. "This experience has a huge effect not only on the kids themselves, but on the whole community," Zobeya says, echoing what Josbel has told me. "These children become the role models for their families."

The two núcleos are not alike in every way, however; Zobeya explains that while all núcleos share an extensive core set of principles, goals, and practices, there is also considerable room for each núcleo to be shaped by the specific strengths and interests of its staff, and to respond to the specific needs of its own community. Montalbán, for example, has a Cuatro Orchestra, an entire ensemble of children playing the small four-string guitar that is Venezuela's most popular folk instrument.

In addition, Montalbán is well known as a leader in youth orchestras. The highest-level youth orchestra here is a substantial notch in quality above even la Rinconada's most advanced group, because it draws from all across Caracas and is an audition-only ensemble. Called the Children's Orchestra of Caracas, its prestige is such that teenagers in other Caracas núcleos sometimes switch to Montalbán so they can be eligible to try out. "Many of the kids in this orchestra go to the conservatory or to the Center for Social Action for additional private study," says Zobeya. "And some go on to audition for the Teresa Carreño Orchestra."

We do not have the opportunity to hear the Cuatro Orchestra in action during our visit, but we do hear a performance by the Children's Orchestra of Caracas, and it is another shock-and-awe experience. An ensemble of over two hundred kids between ten and sixteen, they regale us with two El Sistema signature pieces, Danzón

No. 2 by Márquez and Bernstein's "Mambo!" Like the young musicians of the Teresa Carreño Orchestra, these children re-create the by-now famous choreographic movements of the Simón Bolívar Orchestra; the violinists sway together, the cellists twirl their instruments, the horn players dance, and the percussion players juggle their sticks. It reminds me of the way kids in the United States commit to memory every move of their favorite hip-hop acts . . . with the difference that these moves accompany the particular splendor of orchestral music-making.

Norma, who played in this orchestra as a young teenager, shakes her head in admiration. "These kids are playing music that we weren't playing until we were two years older than they are," she says. "The quality everywhere in the Sistema is getting better and better, faster and faster. Standards just keep rising."

During our afternoon at Montalbán, we observe and listen to ensembles of all ages, much the way we did at the Rinconada núcleo. For sheer delight, nothing surpasses our experience of watching a class of three-year-olds whose teacher is a young man playing a cuatro. The children sit in a circle, and a pair of egg maracas is given to one child at a time, to play in time with the teacher's strumming. Fellow Christine Witkowski is able to record one child's turn on her Flip camera—an enchanted forty seconds that still resides on YouTube, entitled "Egg Maraca Dance." The concentration of the very small girl with the maracas, the intent focus of the children in the circle, and the uninhibited joy with which some of them get up and dance to the music—the scene captures the essential spirit of the Sistema as fully, in its own way, as does a performance of the Simón Bolívar Orchestra. "*Muy bien, muy bien,*" says the teacher at the end, with a final flourish on his cuatro.

At six o'clock, when the núcleo day is over, the courtyard fills with children waiting for bus or car rides home, playing and chattering and running in the mellow light of the sun setting over the mountains. Zobeya Márquez sits on the steps of the núcleo and talks with us as she keeps an eye on the children. The student population here, she tells us, is a mixture of middle and lower economic classes. But all the kids are wearing uniforms—yellow shirts instead of Rinconada's blue ones—and it's difficult to sense differences among classes. "That is an essential part of what we do here," Zobeya says. "We take away class distinctions. And truly, it's a social education for all classes."

She speaks about her commitment to creating a network of support for each child. "We stay in constant touch with their schoolteachers, to track their academic development," she says. "And if a child is struggling with behavioral issues, we bring in a therapist or social worker." I ask her if this kind of support helps to keep children in the núcleo over many years, and she smiles. "We have a low attrition rate," she tells me. "*Very* low."

Zobeya herself came up through the Sistema playing the cello and went to the university to study music education. "There are a thousand kids coming to this núcleo," she says, gazing at the controlled chaos of the courtyard, "and sometimes it can feel like a lot. But we never forget that we are committed to the holistic development of every single child."

Sunday morning in Caracas, and the núcleos are quiet. But José Antonio Abreu, typically, is not at rest; he is sitting at a large oblong table in a spacious meeting room at the Center for Social Action Through Music, meeting for the first time with the ten Fellows whose training program he has wished into existence. This meeting with the Maestro is a moment the Fellows have been eagerly anticipating for six months, ever since their program began, and now that it has arrived, they are as awestruck as a group of highly self-assured young professionals can possibly be. Abreu begins to talk informally, as though resuming a conversation that has been interrupted. "You know, I've never really liked the term 'Sistema,'" he says to them. "The name arose because here in Venezuela, any

A barrio in Caracas, 2009 (*Jeffrey Stock*)

The núcleo Los Chorros, Caracas, 2009 (*Jeffrey Stock*)

Children's orchestra at the núcleo Los Chorros, Caracas, 2009 (*Jeffrey Stock*)

Jamie Bernstein performing with the
Caracas Symphony Youth Orchestra, 2009 (*Jeffrey Stock*)

Young violinists at the núcleo la Rinconada,
Caracas, 2010 (*Stephanie Scherpf*)

Beginning violinist at la Rinconada, 2010 (*Stephanie Scherpf*)

Violin class at la Rinconada, 2010 (*Stephanie Scherpf*)

White Hands Chorus at Barquisimeto, 2009 (*Frank Di Polo*)

National Children's Orchestra of Venezuela, 2010 (*Frank Di Polo*)

Dudamel with the Simón Bolívar Youth
Orchestra of Venezuela, in Asia, 2008 (*Frank Di Polo*)

Dudamel conducting the Simón Bolívar Youth Orchestra in the Caracas barrio La Vega, 2009 (*FESNOJIV Archives*)

Maestro Abreu congratulating Dudamel at La Vega concert, 2009 (*FESNOJIV Archives*)

Maestro Abreu, 2010 (*FESNOJIV Archives*)

The first class of Abreu Fellows in Caracas with Maestro Abreu, February 2010. From left to right: Mark Churchill, Dantes Rameau, Stanford Thompson, Lorrie Heagy, Rebecca Levi, David Malek, Jonathan Govias, Christine Witkowski, Dan Berkowitz, Katie Wyatt, Álvaro Rodas, Stephanie Scherpf (*Joaquin Avellan*)

Children's orchestra at Harmony Program, New York,
with director Anne Fitzgibbon in white skirt, 2010 (*Arpi Pap*)

Beginning cellist with teacher, Harmony Program, 2010 (*Stephen Pile*)

Violinists at YOSA Music Learning Center, Good Samaritan
Community Services, San Antonio, 2010 (*rickpatrickphotography.com*)

YOSA Music Learning Center String Orchestra, 2010 (*Nicté Hayes*)

Violinist in OrchKids Program, Baltimore, 2010 (*Stephanie Scherpf*)

Baltimore Symphony Orchestra conductor Marin Alsop
working with OrchKids, 2010 (*Nick Skinner, OrchKids site manager*)

Flutists in the YOLA program, Los Angeles, 2010
(*Craig T. Mathew/Mathew Imaging*)

The Paper Orchestra, YOLA at HOLA, Los Angeles, 2010
(*Craig T. Mathew/Mathew Imaging*)

Children's first moments with their violins, at the ICAN Music Project
in Santa Barbara, 2010 (*Clint Weisman*)

Dudamel conducting the Gothenburg Symphony Orchestra
at the BBC Proms, 2008 (*Chris Christodoulou*)

Dudamel conducting the Simón Bolívar Youth Orchestra
at Carnegie Hall, 2007 (*Jennifer Taylor*)

Dudamel with his wife,
Eloisa Maturén,
on tour in Italy, 2007
(*Frank Di Polo*)

Maestro Abreu conducting the first Sistema youth orchestra, 1978
(*Frank Di Polo*)

Doralisa de Medina,
childhood piano teacher of
Maestro Abreu
(*FESNOJIV Archives*)

time an element is replicated in a network, we call it a system. But we are not really a system."

Rodrigo stands behind Abreu, translating with his usual ease and fluidity, sometimes almost seeming to read his mentor's thoughts. Abreu muses about the highly unsystematic way his project came into being and developed through the years, with no viable models to imitate and no overall grand plan to follow. "This is not really a system," he repeats. "This is a . . ." Uncharacteristically, he hesitates. Then, quietly: "It is a '*ser, no ser todavía.*'"

Rodrigo looks surprised. "This is not easy to translate," he tells us. "But it is a 'being, not yet being.'"

"*Permanente,*" adds the Maestro.

"Permanent," repeats Rodrigo.

Abreu leans toward us. "The day we define a system," he says, "it's already dead." He says that instead of a system, the through-line of the Sistema has been an unwavering belief that a youth orchestra is first and foremost a project of social action. "In the beginning, when I insisted on this, the Ministry of Culture considered it a scandal," he says. "But as an artist, I have always insisted that my art be dignified with the mission of creating better human beings."

The Maestro speaks of the ingrained cultural conventions he has devoted his life and work to overcoming: the assumption of the educational system, for example, that the development of intellect is more important than the cultivation of feeling and expression, and the idea that education in the arts is a privilege reserved for the elite. "Culture for the poor must never be poor culture," he says, and while we all know this quote by heart, it is thrilling to hear him say it to us on this Sunday morning in 2010 with fresh conviction. "We must have the best instruments for the poorest children—the best teachers for the poorest children—the best buildings for the poorest children." He describes having recently heard a children's orchestra in an impoverished city play the symphonic poem *Don Juan,* by Richard Strauss. "Even to me," he says, "this was almost mysterious. I can't explain fully to myself how it can happen. But it happens."

He is talking faster and faster now, his phrases overlapping with Rodrigo's and sometimes overtaking them completely in a lively bilingual counterpoint. He speaks of the young generation of Sistema leaders and educators, saying they are the key to the future. "I have learned that we must put our faith in the young teachers!" he exclaims. "Very often the finest teachers are teenagers. Very often the best coaches are the youngest coaches."

He addresses the Fellows openly and in personal terms, expressing his pleasure that these ten young teachers from the United States have come to Venezuela to immerse themselves in the Sistema. "Please don't hesitate to tell us what you see, and what you think," he tells them. "We are all ears to the wealth of experience and insight that you bring. And when you return to the United States, we can really begin to make an international Sistema—to multiply by the millions! This may sound excessively romantic or philosophical. But it is the truth of what I feel."

Even in this informal meeting, there is a kind of symphonic build to Abreu's oratory. And he concludes, as all good symphonists do, with a return to his original theme. "There is no 'system,'" he says. "I have no scruples in saying this. I want you to go all over Venezuela and to create a small chaos that will eventually lead to order."

*Ser, no ser todavía*—permanently being and not yet being. For the rest of our time in Caracas—and the rest of the Fellows' stay in Venezuela—this idea frames much of the way we think and talk about our experiences. I have spent the better part of a year, since my first visit to Venezuela, trying to understand the elements that make El Sistema so unique and so extraordinarily successful. And the Fellows have spent weeks and months in Boston trying to define, categorize, and codify the Sistema's essential characteristics—its core values, its main principles and practices. Abreu's words clarify what has made our efforts so difficult: the "system that is not a system" lives by and thrives on constant evolution.

Certainly, it's possible to identify key and enduring principles of the Sistema. And certainly there are clear consistencies across núcleos, both in assumptions and in practice. But it's also true that these elements are continually being reimagined in an endless variety of ways, to meet the particular needs of particular children in different places, at different times. To observe the Sistema in action is to experience, over and over again, a highly dynamic balance between constancy of purpose and flexibility of means.

It is also a forceful reminder of the primacy of process. In the Sistema, the process of human interaction through music learning is not a means to an end; it is the all-important end in itself. Whether in rehearsal or performance, making music is experienced both as a creative activity and as a profoundly satisfying way of being together.

It's for this reason that a program conceived around the primary idea that an orchestra is an agent of social transformation has been able to produce musicians and orchestras of superior achievement on purely artistic levels. In the Sistema, aspiring to artistic excellence is an inseparable part of building orchestral community. The orchestra is a collective enterprise and a model for social life in which collective goals and high individual ideals are synergistically related.

We have seen this "unity in duality" exemplified in many ways during our núcleo visits. The teacher painstakingly summoning a perfect D scale from her young violinists; the cello sectional leader gently insisting that his students execute an exactly synchronized move together from "ready position" to "playing position"; the teenaged clarinet player in the orchestra helping his friend with the rhythm of a difficult passage—all represent a unity of musical and social purposes. Children are simultaneously learning the discipline they will need to be successful orchestral musicians and the social and emotional skills that will make them successful in family and community life.

Many of our observations about the Sistema seem to be illuminated by Abreu's elegant koan "*Ser, no ser todavía,*" with its
implications of flexibility within unity and primacy of process. The
importance of a common repertoire and a consistent curriculum
across núcleos, for example, has been frequently emphasized by
Abreu and Rodrigo and by many teachers. And we have been shown
a set of documents compiled by a Sistema committee ten years ago,
hundreds of pages long and setting forth curriculum standards and
guidelines in meticulous detail for every developmental level, along
with recommended repertoire. On the other hand, we have seen and
heard teachers spontaneously creating and shaping their methods
and curricula to the particular needs of the children they work with.
At la Rinconada, teachers have told us that they are used to adjusting
to the developmental characteristics of each class; if a group of kids
loves to play percussively and fast, they'll play Tchaikovsky, and if
they need to work on style and phrasing they'll play more Mozart.
And this kind of flexibility extends to individual children as well as
classes. In the words of El Sistema USA senior advisor Eric Booth,
who is traveling with the Fellows' group, "They are willing to mess
with a policy for the benefit of a child."

As the Fellows' group and I share thoughts and impressions about
what we are seeing, it becomes clear that El Sistema constitutes a
challenge to some fundamental aspects of our conventional wisdom
about children, education, and art. Among those fundamentals is
our tendency to equate intensity with work, and fun with play. The
Sistema insists upon intensity—learning several hours a day, five or
six days a week—as an essential principle of its success. And yet a
commitment to fun and joy is equally central; Dudamel is frequently
quoted as saying, "In the Sistema we never forget fun." It requires
a suspension of some long-held mental habits to understand that
within the world of the Sistema, the fun is, precisely, inside the
intensity of the music-making.

The teachers communicate this spirit to their students through
the power of example: the teachers themselves feel genuine delight in

the intensity of the process, and the energy they exude is overwhelmingly positive and generous. Most of them are young products of the Sistema, and they clearly learned from their own teachers that there can be joy, not exhaustion, within intensity. As Frank Di Polo said to me, "We try to give as much as we can, without thinking about what's coming back. This is part of the Venezuelan spirit."

Another element of conventional wisdom we are forced to rethink is our notion that private practice and public performance are two very different kinds of musical experience. In the núcleos we have seen, that dichotomy simply doesn't seem to exist; performance seems a natural extension of rehearsal. From the very beginning of musical training, there is an easy continuum between practicing a D scale with the teacher and performing Mozart for parents or visitors. The habit of frequent performance is so thoroughly integrated into the learning experience that performances are not triggers for anxiety or stage fright, but simply incentives to work hard and occasions for feeling pride in accomplishment. Fellow Álvaro Rodas notes that whenever we visit a class or rehearsal, even if the musicians are only tuning up, we are asked to stand at the front of the room facing the players. "We are not put in the back, to minimize potential distraction," he says. "We are always the guests to play for."

Finally, the Fellows and I are consistently challenged to reconsider our assumption that a primary emphasis on ensemble development necessarily means a lack of individualized musical training. While the balance between individual and group instruction is certainly different from the one we are used to, we observe that the núcleos we visit have worked out a variety of resourceful ways in which individual, one-on-one learning can exist simultaneously with the emphasis on ensemble work. In many instances, private lessons begin soon after children are introduced to their instruments, and tend to increase in frequency and intensity as players become more advanced.

Even within ensemble situations, there is a great deal of individual coaching by assistant teachers. Eduardo Méndez, who as executive director of FESNOJIV is the Sistema's second-in-command, speaks to the Fellows' group about the sense of responsibility felt by every teacher and teacher's aide to help guide students toward excellence. One reason that students progress so fast, he tells us, is that teachers do not allow them to waste time on mistakes. "It is not the child's responsibility to correct a mistake," says Eduardo. "No matter how intelligent or talented a student, he or she is still a child. It is our responsibility. So our teachers see and hear each child every single day. And in that way a mistake that happens on Monday will be corrected on Tuesday and Wednesday, and will be gone by Friday."

Helping to make this possible, he adds, is the high ratio of teachers to students—a ratio hard to imagine from the perspective of standards in the United States. Already, the Fellows and I know how this looks in practice: in every orchestra and sectional rehearsal we've observed, many teaching assistants support the work of the main teacher by circulating among the players, continually correcting mistakes, adjusting positions, clarifying rhythms.

Eduardo is an intense, serious man with black-rimmed glasses; he has been a violinist since childhood, receiving his early training at the Sistema núcleo in the Andean city of Mérida. When he was ten, he came to Caracas to join the Simón Bolívar Orchestra. "At first, I was probably the youngest member of the orchestra," he says. "I was like their pet." During the fourteen years he played with the Simón Bolívar, he completed his university education and entered law school, planning to follow a family tradition and become a lawyer. And then—"Maestro Abreu called," he says, "and told me I should come and work with FESNOJIV. So I did, and I have been here ever since."

Eduardo spent seven years as the national director of núcleos, from 2001 to 2008; during his tenure the number of núcleos in the country more than doubled, expanding from 89 to 184. Now, as executive director, he works directly under Maestro Abreu and supervises the activities of the Sistema on many levels. When he speaks with us, he comes back again and again to the Sistema's insistence on high artistic standards for all children. "The children in the núcleos are constantly exposed to the performances of the national youth orchestras," he says. "They hear the Simón Bolívar. They know Dudamel. So they have a very clear perception about what can be achieved—they can identify with their own ears. That is always our 'north.'"

~~~

While most children in the Sistema don't grow up to become professional musicians, there are many—and their numbers are increasing—who do aspire to play at a professional level. For these young people, the Sistema offers a network of learning opportunities that is many-layered, extensive, and still very much in the process of evolution—very much *"ser, no ser todavía."*

Stewardship of these opportunities is the responsibility of Valdemar Rodríguez, the clarinet virtuoso who is now the Sistema's deputy executive director. Like Eduardo Méndez, Valdemar played for many years with the Simón Bolívar Orchestra; he is still principal clarinetist of the A ensemble of that orchestra. Born in the small provincial town of San Felipe, where his father was a professional saxophone player, Valdemar was the first student to register at the Sistema núcleo that opened in San Felipe in 1979. He was seventeen. Two years later, he joined the Simón Bolívar Youth Orchestra. "I never dreamed I would have an administrative job," he has told me. "I didn't go looking for it. But when that day arrived, I decided to give it everything that was inside me."

In a meeting with Valdemar, the Fellows and I learn about the opportunities the Sistema offers young people for developing and honing professional-level musical skills. The Simón Bolívar Conservatory established by the Sistema during the 1980s has grown steadily, he says, providing private instrumental lessons and classes in solfège, music theory, and many other aspects of music. He tells us that on the very morning of the day we meet with him, FESNOJIV has decided that the conservatory will begin to grant bachelor's degrees. "It's important that our musicians have the chance to get real bachelor's degrees, not just certificates," he says.

In addition, provincial conservatories are being established across the country, following the general curricula for each instrument that have been developed at the conservatory in Caracas. And the music institute created by Abreu in the 1990s is now part of a university combining all the performing arts. "Many of the players in the Simón Bolívar Orchestra are enrolled at the university," Valdemar tells us. "They may take five years or seven years or nine years to get degrees, and that's fine—the university is very flexible in working with us."

Perhaps most important, the Sistema has established national "academies" for every instrument. Although Maestro Abreu has spoken of this concept, the Fellows and I have trouble understanding exactly what an academy is—it doesn't seem to be exactly a building, or a program, or an organization. The harder we try to pin down a definition, the slipperier the concept becomes. Says Rodrigo, "It's more about a unified way of teaching than an actual strict curriculum. It is a kind of semiformal association between the best teachers in the country on a particular instrument, and the students they teach."

"You can't really say, 'Oh, academies work this way,'" adds Valdemar, who is the head of the clarinet academy. "It's very flexible, very creative. My clarinet academy doesn't work the same way as the cello or violin or flute academy. But they all make it possible for students to work with different teachers." He tells us that the master teachers of the Sistema have consciously struggled to minimize the competitiveness about methods, and the possessiveness about highly skilled students, that seem so pervasive in the classical music world. "When we stopped competing and started teaching together, we started to grow as people," he says. "And the students started to play more beautifully. So we really try to live by the belief that everyone has something to teach, and our teaching talents complement one another."

I think of Maestro Abreu's assertion that pedagogical technique for each instrument is one of the few absolutely consistent elements that unify núcleo practices. And yet Valdemar's explanation seems to suggest that there is acknowledged value in exposing students to a wide variety of pedagogical approaches. Another dichotomy the Sistema seems to bridge—*ser, no ser todavía,* I remind myself.

Valdemar tells us that a major role of the academies is to produce festivals and recitals that bring together musicians from across the country; at almost any time of the year, a clarinet festival or a flute festival or a viola festival is taking place somewhere. The festivals are catalysts for intensive teaching and learning, as students play for one another and attend master classes with eminent teachers from not only Venezuela but across the world. "At our most recent clarinet festival, there were forty soloists playing recitals," he says proudly, "and not one of them played the same piece. This is such a huge change from when I came to Caracas in 1981, when the only clarinet repertoire anyone knew was the Mozart clarinet concerto and maybe a few Brahms sonatas. And it's incredible to think that in 1975 there was only one professional oboist in the country who was Venezuelan. Now we have weeklong oboe festivals."

Even if none of us has managed to form a precise mental picture of an academy, an oboe festival that lasts a week is a wondrous thing to contemplate. "Maybe someday," says Valdemar, "we'll sit down and write it all down, the way we do things. But as soon as we write it down, it will change. No matter what we write down, it will be something different."

During our ten days in Caracas, the Fellows' group and I have the opportunity to attend rehearsals and concerts of the major national youth orchestras—both the A and B ensembles of the Simón Bolívar Orchestra, and the Teresa Carreño Orchestra—before they leave to go on international tours. There are some heated discussions among the Fellows about how to characterize and account for the signature sound of Sistema orchestras—the distinctive combination of lushness and vigor that can be traced back to Abreu's first orchestra. Susan Siman has said that this sonic tradition has its origins in the string teaching of José Francisco del Castillo, the Sistema's first and most influential violin master. "Above everything, it's the string sound that is most important," she has told me. "And that flows from him. Whenever you hear any Sistema orchestra, there is José Francisco, there in the sound of the strings."

Some of the Fellows find the Sistema's signature sound too loud, or too rhythmically emphatic. Others defend those qualities, saying that playing loudly may be a by-product of a pedagogical culture that encourages children to be unafraid of making mistakes. As for the strong rhythmic pulse: "They make Saint-Saëns sound like a Venezuelan," says Rebecca Levi, "and maybe that's a good thing, not a bad thing."

A concert by a Sistema chorus, consisting of children and youths from núcleos across the city, surprises us with its solemnity; the chorus sings formal, complex motets and madrigals with dense contrapuntal textures, in Latin and English as well as Spanish. "The choice of this music is quite purposeful," explains Rodrigo. "The Maestro wants to set the bar very high for Sistema choirs." It is likely that for the Sistema, the choice of seventeenth-century European choral works represents a conscious statement that the highest of choral art forms belongs equally to poor Venezuelan children as to Latin American elites and a privileged European tradition.

In the area of instrumental music, by contrast, this statement no longer needs to be so strenuously made; thirty-five years and hundreds of youth orchestras later, it is abundantly clear that symphonic music belongs to all Venezuelan children, regardless of class. The Sistema is therefore embracing and exploring other genres of music, to enrich and amplify the musical palette offered to its students. Jazz is now an important focus; several Fellows pay a visit to the Simón Bolívar Conservatory to hear its first and only official jazz big band, a new initiative. Many of the young conservatory musicians have grown up playing classical music and have only recently begun to play jazz, and not all are comfortable in the new idiom. But the groove is strong and fluent—the rhythmic skill and versatility so typical of Sistema musicians take care of that—and there is a virtuosic female soloist on trumpet, a feature most big bands in the homeland of jazz can't claim. In true Sistema style, the ensemble is huge, with a sound to match; the lineup includes ten saxophonists and at least that many clarinetists, a very large brass section, and a drummer who seems to be channeling Buddy Rich.

We hear more jazz when we are taken one night to a concert at a cultural center in the neighborhood of Chacao, a beautiful little pavilion open to the warm night air and the sounds of crickets and taxi horns. There is a packed house on hand to hear a brass quintet play sparkling Baroque fanfares, tangos accompanied by a percussionist who sits on and slaps a box-shaped instrument called a cajón, and finally a few standards from the American Songbook, including "Misty" and "Sweet Georgia Brown," spiced with conga rhythms. Afterward, I ask the musicians whether they have connections with the Sistema, either as teachers or former students. The trumpet player replies, "Every musician in Venezuela is connected somehow to the Sistema."

While the Sistema's interest in jazz is relatively new, there is a long-standing practice of including Venezuelan folk music and instruments in the curriculum and repertoire of núcleos across the country. Bolivia Bottome tells me that in the early, developing years of the Sistema, there were skeptics who feared that its emphasis on European classical music would accelerate the disappearance of Venezuela's strong folk music tradition. "Exactly the opposite has happened," she says. "Folk music has become stronger than ever. And something really wonderful has happened. As Sistema musicians have worked within the folk idiom, new and more complex versions of the traditional musics have evolved. It's become kind of our own, particularly Venezuelan chamber music."

By far the most popular folk instrument is the cuatro, similar in shape to a ukulele but somewhat different in tuning. The thin, sweet sound of the plucked or strummed cuatro is an essential part of many Venezuelan folk traditions, and the Sistema is passing on those traditions to new generations of children and young people; many núcleos have cuatro ensembles, often using instruments made in Sistema luthier workshops, and a cuatro academy has recently been established.

The Fellows and I are treated to a concert of cuatro music on the rooftop veranda of Seguros Caracas, the Venezuelan company associated with Boston's Liberty Mutual. Seguros Caracas has been a major supporter of the Sistema, and has recently established a nonprofit foundation that makes substantial contributions to three causes: diabetes, highway safety, and El Sistema. "We give FES-NOJIV a grant each year, with which they can do whatever they want," vice president Gerardo Perozo tells me. In honor of the Abreu Fellows' visit to Venezuela, Seguros Caracas has organized a soirée, with black-suited waiters pouring scotch and red wine and passing trays of smoked salmon and stuffed grapes, and entertainment by a group called C4—three cuatro players with an electric bassist.

The music is just as Bolivia has described—complex, but also moving and soulful, with simple, haunting folk melodies punctuated by strumming in intricate, irregular meters. Dusk falls as they play; a breeze stirs the giant ferns that surround the veranda, and the clouds draped across the mountains in the distance turn lavender. During the final tune, the three cuatro players take turns on particularly long, fantasialike solo improvisations, and as the last solo ends, they lean close together, and each puts his left hand on the fingerboard of another. And they finish the tune that way, every player fingering his friend's instrument as he plucks or strums his own. A circle of overlapping arms and hands, in complete musical interdependence—it is a lovely metaphor for the spirit of the Sistema.

Speaking to the players afterward, I find that not all were trained within the Sistema. "I learned in the streets," says one of the cuatro players. But they tell me that the Sistema has made Venezuela an extraordinarily fertile place to be a musician. "It's incredible, what's happening here," says the bass player. "There is an explosion of kids playing music, people playing music, everywhere. And it's because of El Sistema."

⌒

As the Fellows prepare to leave Caracas and visit núcleos in other parts of Venezuela, they are given a stirring sendoff by Eduardo Méndez. "You will see many similarities between núcleos, and also many differences," he tells the Fellows. "There is no written formula—there never has been. But you will see beautiful things. This is a wonderful, incredible country, and each núcleo and orchestra has a personality of its own. You will see fantastic things, and as the Maestro said, you will see some chaos too."

He suggests, as Valdemar has, that the Fellows not try too hard to pin down exactly how everything works. "Because probably, we will change it again in a couple of years," he says. After a pause he adds, "Probably, we will change it in a couple of months."

As he speaks of the hurdles the Fellows will encounter when they return home and begin the work of starting núcleos in the United States, Eduardo adds a bit of advice. "Maestro Abreu will always tell you that everything is possible," he says. "And that is true. But it's my job to tell you how difficult it can actually be. No matter how good your plans are, at some point you will run into difficulties. And you will have to persevere, and you will have to stick together. The more strength you can gather among yourselves, the more power you're going to have."

Eduardo speaks with vehemence, pacing back and forth in front of his small audience and sometimes wiping his brow. But he comes close to smiling when he talks about the enormous rewards to be found in teaching music to children. "Every time you see a student doing something wrong, and you know you can actually help him—that is something you never forget," he says.

"Everything is possible," he concludes. "But you have to start somewhere. Here, we started in a garage. And for a long time it was really difficult. So on the day when you come up against something really difficult, remember that garage. And remember the guy who told you it's not going to be easy."

The industrial city of Barquisimeto sits on a large plateau in the state of Lara in western Venezuela, surrounded by mountains. The city is best known for a centuries-old religious tradition celebrating the Divina Pastora—the Madonna as a divine shepherdess, holding the infant Jesus in one arm and a baby lamb in the other—with a yearly procession bearing her statue from a rural village to the central cathedral; several million people fill the streets for this ceremony every January. But the city also has great significance for music in Venezuela. Barquisimeto is not only the city of José Antonio's childhood, where Doralisa de Medina so memorably gave piano lessons; it is also the birthplace of Gustavo Dudamel and a number of other prominent Sistema musicians, including Diego Matheuz, one of the young conductors whom Dudamel mentored during his first year at the Los Angeles Philharmonic.

Caracas and Barquisimeto are only 160 miles apart, but the highway connections are so poor that the drive by car can take four or five hours. So when Bolivia Bottome and I set out to spend a day at the Barquisimeto núcleo, we go by plane, a ride that has no sooner begun than it is over. Coming with us to tour the núcleo is Isabella Abreu, the twenty-two-year-old niece of the Maestro. Isabella speaks fluent English and is highly engaged in social issues; she talks to us about the struggling Venezuelan economy and the way poor Venezuelans are hard hit by current shortages of water and electricity. "There will probably be a power outage at noon in Barquisimeto," she says while we are on the plane. "There usually is. Almost everywhere in the country, we are having to ration electricity."

A communications major in college, Isabella lived and worked in Mexico after graduating, until her uncle made the call she had always suspected would come. "I'm not a musician," she tells me, "and I wasn't sure what I could do for the Sistema. But when he asked me to come, I knew I had to be here."

The classical music world knows of the Barquisimeto núcleo mostly as the place that produced Gustavo Dudamel. Within El Sistema its renown goes further; the núcleo is regarded as a model for integrating special-needs children into the life of núcleo orchestras and choruses. Jhonny Gómez, the director of the special-needs program, picks us up at the airport in his minivan, and as he drives into town, he begins immediately to talk about the goals of his program. "Our main task," he says, "is to integrate these children into the mainstream ensembles of the núcleos and thus, symbolically, into society."

Of the 3,000 children who come to the núcleo, he tells us, 340 have major special needs, including deafness, blindness, autism, and mental retardation. They come from all over the state of Lara, of which Barquisimeto is the capital city. Jhonny Gómez has directed the program for some years, and he began the process of mainstreaming special-needs children fifteen years ago, as a pilot program. "We have grown very slowly and carefully," he says, "to make sure every single child is truly integrated. It must be done in a careful and sensitive way, taking the needs of each child into account."

Dudamel has told me that for many years the núcleo at Barquisimeto was located in the house where Doralisa de Medina gave piano lessons and a lifelong love of music to many hundreds of children, most memorably José Antonio Abreu. I feel a momentary pang of regret that we will not be visiting that hallowed place. But the new location is spacious and impressive; unlike the núcleos we've seen in Caracas, this facility was built to be a núcleo, with low red brick buildings surrounded by beds of purple bougainvillea and a huge treble clef sign carved into the grass of the front lawn. A boom box playing classical music sits at the entrance to the driveway where children are dropped off and picked up.

The halls are quiet as we enter; it is still morning, and the children have not yet begun to arrive. But there is a violinist—a teacher or teacher's aide, perhaps?—playing in the sun-dappled courtyard at the building's center, and the open hallway that wraps around the courtyard reverberates with the sound. High on a wall in the hallway hangs a tremendous poster featuring the face of the núcleo's most famous alumnus, along with a quote: SOME PEOPLE THINK THAT MATURITY COMES WITH LIVING MANY YEARS. I THINK IT IS ABOUT FEELING AND PLAYING.—GUSTAVO DUDAMEL. Directly underneath the poster is a small shrine, complete with plastic flowers, to the Divine Shepherdess.

Jhonny Gómez escorts us first into a small dark room where six people are seated at computers and technical equipment. They are working, he tells us, to translate musical scores and parts into Braille, a complicated process that involves first transcribing music into a music software program and then using a machine that creates Braille documents. A young woman at one of the machines prints out a Braille part to a simple Allegretto by Suzuki and hands it to me; the symbols are elegant and intricate, but it's hard to see how they could possibly represent musical notation.

A young blind man is introduced to us as Gustavo. "I am another Gustavo of Barquisimeto," he says, smiling. A student of composition, this Gustavo now works full-time for the Sistema supervising the creation of the Braille musical arrangements. He tells us that blind children play side by side with seeing children in the orchestra. "If a blind clarinetist is going to play a Beethoven symphony with his orchestra," he says, "he will get his part in Braille ahead of time, learn it and memorize it, and then play it from memory with the orchestra."

Jhonny tells us that the núcleo teachers and staff also produce

Braille translations of literary works they consider important for students to read, such as biographies, histories, and works about music and culture. "We are concerned with every aspect of our students' lives," he says. "Often, the blind kids here don't have much access to Braille books at all. So if there are books they need in Braille and they can't get them at school, we try to provide them. Our mission is to break the barriers that exist for these kids around the world!"

It is noon, and the winking computer screens go abuptly black; as Isabella Abreu predicted, the power has gone out. There is general agreement that it is lunchtime. Out in the courtyard, the violinist is still playing.

At lunch on a restaurant terrace with views of the mountains in the distance, I ask Jhonny about the evolution of the núcleo. "I grew up here in Barquisimeto, and I was formed musically in this núcleo from an early age," he tells me. "In 1978, when I was sixteen, Maestro Abreu organized a kind of Sistema convention, with young people coming from all over the country. Frank Di Polo was there, and he showed a video of Itzhak Perlman playing the Tchaikovsky Violin Concerto. And when I saw that—Perlman sitting in his chair because he cannot stand, playing so exquisitely and so happily—I was very inspired. I thought to myself, why can't we have handicapped children in our orchestra?"

Jhonny Gómez returned to Barquisimeto determined to pursue this goal. But it was not until 1995, seventeen years later, that the núcleo began to work with special-needs children. "I was very aware that we should not start this until we were ready to do it in the right way," he tells me. "The núcleo itself had to become well established and strong. And teachers had to be prepared with special education—they had to be trained both to teach music and to handle children with special needs. I wanted to be able to accommodate children with every kind of disability. So I had to create an intensive training program to enable teachers to do that."

Jhonny is a stocky man with a crew cut and a blunt manner; he speaks of his mission with conviction and not a trace of sentimentality. "Ever since 1995, we have steadily added more and more special-needs children," he says. "What you see here today—many kinds of handicaps, all integrated with nonhandicapped kids—you will not see in many places in the world." He adds that working with hearing-impaired children has been the most difficult challenge of all. "How is it possible for them to be musicians?" he says. "We didn't know. But we have learned from them that it is possible. We have learned everything from them."

The Barquisimeto núcleo has developed a substantial teacher-training program, preparing special-needs teachers to take their skills to núcleos across the country. Jhonny tells me that there are now eighty such teachers at nineteen núcleos in various provinces, working with a total of 1,800 children with special needs. "We want to double that this year," he says, with the matter-of-factness about wildly ambitious goals that so many Sistema leaders seem to have absorbed from Maestro Abreu.

In 2009, Jhonny received Italy's prestigious Nonino Prize, which honors international contributions to culture in the fields of the arts and sciences, for his pioneering work in transforming the lives of special-needs children. The Italian conductor and longtime Sistema advocate Claudio Abbado had received the prize in 1999 and had recommended that Gómez's program be considered. "I went to Italy, and we set up a chorus of Italian children with special needs," Jhonny tells me. "And when the parents saw what their children were able to do, they said, 'This is a miracle.' But for us, this miracle is normal."

The power is back on when we return from lunch, and the núcleo is in full swing, swarming with hundreds of kids. Standing in the central courtyard, we can hear the sounds of instruments tuning and warming up coming from all directions. Jhonny tells us that the students of the núcleo are excited that we are here, and that we will see and hear performances this afternoon by a number of groups, some made up entirely of children and young people with special needs, and others where special-needs children are combined with children without special needs. We will begin, he says, with Lara

Somos, a vocal quintet of young men who are blind, autistic, or both. He leads us into a small room and seats us in folding chairs, and the young men enter and stand directly facing us. "Professor Jhonny," as they call him, introduces each one to us, and explains that they have all been in the núcleo for many years and are proficient instrumentalists, arrangers, and composers as well as singers.

The youth on the right, who is blind, takes a step forward. *"Buenas tardes,"* he says. With Bolivia translating, he thanks us for being there, and explains that the name of the group means "We are Lara," referring to the province of Lara. "We have arranged for you a sample of the music of our dear Venezuela," he says. "As Professor Jhonny has said, we sing our own arrangements of these traditional folkloric songs. Several of us do the arrangements, and that makes the ensemble grow stylistically.

"Our first song is a tonada, a traditional song that is sung in the *llanos*—the Venezuelan plains—by cowherds when they are milking their cows." He indicates the young man on the far side of their line. "José has arranged it for five voices." He hums the starting pitches. José taps his foot twice to signal the tempo, and they begin to sing.

I have come to Barquisimeto thinking I was prepared for this moment. For several months I have been reading and hearing about the work of the núcleo here, and I have imagined how affecting it must be to experience these young musicians. But I have not come close to imagining this. I am overwhelmed—by the strength and purity of their voices; by the sharp poignancy of the music, its melody arcing upward across a minor arpeggio and then breaking apart into a major chord; and most of all by the almost ecstatic sweetness in their faces as they sing. The tune is simple but the harmonies are dark and intricate, and the series of ending chords, with one of the blind youths singing high notes in a pure falsetto, has the majesty and tenderness of a hymn.

They sing two more songs for us, another tonada arranged by one of the other singers, Gregorio ("We have a little competition going on as to which of us can arrange the best tonada," says José), and then a merengue with a complex five-eight rhythm. They are wonderful musicians, with a purity of vocal blend and a rhythmic finesse that many a college a cappella group in the United States could only envy. But what makes their performance unforgettable is the innocent, unselfconscious quality of their joy—and the contrast between who they have become through this music and what their lives would have been without it.

After hearing Lara Somos, I have a strong inkling that I am not remotely prepared for anything I will experience this afternoon. And of course this turns out to be true. There is a chorus of small children with various kinds of special needs, all holding hands as they sing. There is a bell choir that mixes special-needs and non-special-needs children, making a splendid and precisely coordinated clangor with an array of colored bells; most of the children have two bells, but there are children with only one bell, because they have only one hand.

There is, incredibly, a percussion band of teenagers and young adults whose special needs include deafness and cerebral palsy as well as blindness and autism; the youths in wheelchairs are playing maracas, and the conga player is both blind and deaf. The band plays a Latin piece with extremely complex rhythms, executed flawlessly and completely together. Of all the Sistema ensembles I have seen, these young musicians are the least connected to us as an audience— and the most intensely connected to one another. The blind players are acutely listening, the deaf players acutely watching; the degree to which they are locked into their mutual connection is almost frightening in its intensity. They are gratified when we applaud, but it's clear that the social and emotional world of their ensemble is what matters.

There are four young men without special needs, part of a twelve-trombone ensemble, who welcome us into a small rehearsal room to hear them sight-read a beautiful and difficult new piece of Latin American music. And there is an older children's chorus with special-needs and non-special-needs children singing side by side, accompanied by a small boy who switches expertly between piano and cuatro. The chorus sings some lively songs and some melancholy ones, rendering three- and four-part harmonies easily and fluently. It is clear that for these children, the chorus is not a social experiment in mainstreaming but a close community of friends where song is the language of connection and affection.

This particular choir has gone to considerable lengths to celebrate our visit; a special program has been created and printed for the occasion, announcing the presentation of a *"Muestra Musical a invitados especiales internacionales"*—a "musical sampling for specially invited international guests." The program is decorated with musical motifs and credits the conductor, Imelda Fréitez, with arrangements of two of their three songs. After the presentation, Bolivia and Isabella and I speak with Imelda, who explains that the núcleo's choral program has many levels, beginning with an infant choir who sing in unison "whenever we can get them to stay in one place." At the age of five or six, children graduate to the preschool choir, learning to sing both folk songs and simplified arrangements of symphonic choral works in two-part harmony; the next level is the children's choir, ages nine through fourteen, which we have just heard. There are two advanced choirs, the youth choir for teenagers and the Camerata Larense, for young people aged fifteen to thirty. And finally there is the Cantoría Jhonny Gómez, made up of parents of núcleo students.

I say to Imelda that the carefully structured progression of choral levels from beginner to advanced seems to be as sophisticated as the structure of instrumental and orchestral levels in most núcleos. She agrees, saying that this complex curriculum for choral work has been created and developed by Jhonny Gómez's daughter Libia Gómez, who is the director of the Foundation for Children's Choirs in the núcleo system of the state of Lara. "As a result of this system, our youth choirs sing at a very professional level," Imelda tells me. "They have made recordings and won many international prizes. In 2005 they won second place in sacred music at a choral festival in Rome.

And recently we won three medals at a festival in Graz!" Imelda has been at the núcleo for many years, and adds proudly that the conductors of the younger choral ensembles are her former students.

In the courtyard of the núcleo, I speak with a parent, Sonia, who has two children here. The older one has Down syndrome; the younger is visually impaired. Both of them, she tells me, have been in orchestras and choruses here for years. "Music has saved them," she says. "It has filled their lives."

Our afternoon at Barquisimeto ends with a performance by its most famous ensemble. The White Hands Chorus, a double choral ensemble with a section of deaf children and a section of hearing children, was invented here by Jhonny Gómez and his wife Naybeth García, and has rapidly become one of the indelible international faces of the Sistema, making appearances in documentaries, television features, and YouTube clips. Often they perform symphonic works with the Barquisimeto núcleo orchestra or other Venezuelan orchestras, but they also sing just as a chorus accompanied by piano, which is how we hear them today.

As they file into the large room where we have been seated to hear them, slowly filling up six levels of wide risers, I'm surprised by the sheer size of the ensemble; there must be several hundred children here. They are wearing bright-colored shirts of yellow, aqua, and red; the deaf children, who are grouped on the right, wear white gloves; and all the children are chattering—the children on the left side noisily, the children on the right silently, with their hands. Several young men in wheelchairs position themselves on the side of the hearing children. Bolivia tells me she has seen these young men before, and has been informed that they were abandoned as children and taken in by the núcleo. A deaf girl of about fifteen, Jessica, is brought over to us and introduced. Jhonny Gómez tells us that last year Jessica set herself the goal of conducting the núcleo youth orchestra in Beethoven's Fourth Symphony, and that she achieved her goal this year. She smiles shyly as she receives our congratulations.

Two conductors stand before the ensemble, one in front of the hearing children's section and the other—Naybeth García, Jhonny's wife—in front of the deaf children. In tandem, the two conductors give the downbeat. The hearing children begin to sing a soulful ballad, *"Somos mucho más que dos"*—We are much more than two—while the white-gloved hands of the deaf children begin to dance, tracing graceful shapes and patterns in the air in rhythmic accord with the music. Once again, I realize there is no way I could have been truly prepared for the experience of hearing and seeing this chorus. It is not simply that the hearing children sing tunefully and expressively, and that the deaf children move with poise and freedom, their gestures evoking the meaning of the words in a way that literal translation never could. It is the strong sense of spiritual unity that is most moving—the sense that this is not a chorus of singing children with movements added, but an inseparable whole, in which each half of the ensemble completes the other.

They sing—and the white hands dance—several more songs, traditional folk songs of the province. At the end of the presentation, as Naybeth thanks us for coming, two little girls step out of the chorus and walk over to me. The girl from the hearing section hands me a large color poster of the White Hands Chorus, with the title *Somos Venezuela*. And the girl who is deaf hands me a small box made of clear plastic, bound with decorative ribbons, containing a pair of white gloves.

Both girls put their arms around me. Then they lead me into the chorus and many pictures are taken with me surrounded by deaf children, hearing children, and groups of both.

Jhonny Gómez tells me: "When Itzhak Perlman visited us last year and experienced the White Hands Chorus, he felt transported—he felt that something was reborn in him. He took a pair of white gloves with him when he left, and he said he would never forget what he had seen and heard here." I am sure, I tell him, that no one who has seen this chorus will ever forget it. He nods. "In Bonn," he says with pride, "in Beethoven's birthplace, there is a pair of white gloves."

As Jhonny drives us in his van to the airport for the flight back to Caracas, I reflect on the interesting coincidence that the Venezuelan núcleo most focused upon special-needs children is also the núcleo that has produced several young conducting virtuosi who have already achieved international stature. Or perhaps this is not a coincidence. Perhaps, in fact, there is a depth of musical and spiritual understanding to be gained from the experience of learning to play music with young people who accomplish their artistry against every conceivable odd.

Jhonny Gómez is certain of this. He is certain, too, that the núcleo's work with special-needs children cannot be regarded as music therapy. "For a long time," he says, "people with special needs were taken care of from a therapy point of view. But a handicap is irreversible. There is no 'therapy' to be done." What happens at the Barquisimeto núcleo, he says, is better described as the formation of children. "We try to identify what each child *can* do, and develop that," he says. "The handicap is put aside, and the rest of the child is worked on. Every human being has talent and potential. Every human being has capacities that can grow. And the soul doesn't have special needs. The soul is whole."

As I leave Venezuela on the first of March and return home to my piano studio, the Fellows leave Caracas to spend six weeks traveling, in subgroups of three and four, through the states of Venezuela. They travel through eight of Venezuela's twenty-three states, visiting núcleos in small villages and middle-sized cities, in the mountains and the plains and on the seacoast. They see a núcleo housed in a church on weekdays and at a university on weekends, and a núcleo at an abandoned beach volleyball college. They see núcleos in old houses and bus terminals and warehouses. Wherever they venture, they are welcomed as honored guests and as "maestros," and they are besieged with requests for lessons. Their missives from the field, in the form of emails, data reports, Google Docs, and blogs, provide glimpses of their adventures and a wealth of information that complements, expands, and illuminates what I have seen and learned in Caracas and Barquisimeto.

One of the most common themes in their reporting echoes Abreu's exhortation to have faith in young people. Almost everywhere they go, they find responsibility entrusted to youth—young teachers, young núcleo directors, young regional administrators. At a núcleo in the central plains city of Calabozo, they are told that the conductor of the advanced orchestra will be made núcleo director as soon as he turns eighteen. In many núcleos, teachers are as young as sixteen. Several of the Fellows observe that this is a natural consequence of the Sistema precept that everyone has something to teach; children practice teaching as well as learning throughout their formative years. "Teaching starts very young," writes Rebecca Levi, "and grows out of peer mentoring practices." Álvaro Rodas notes that often the teachers' assistants are the núcleo's most advanced students, working on a volunteer basis.

The Fellows are consistently impressed by the high percentage of Sistema graduates who return to work in their núcleos. Very frequently, a núcleo's entire teaching staff is made up of former students, who have firsthand knowledge and experience of the núcleo's pedagogical practices and who identify strongly with their students. "We are part of them," a twenty-four-year-old núcleo director in Guatire tells Rebecca. "There isn't a feeling of division between teachers and students."

"Those who go to conservatory and become musicians are expected to come back and teach what they have learned," a teacher in Calabozo tells Christine Witkowski. A regional coordinator in the state of Guárico says that Sistema teachers consider themselves servants of the children and young people.

Stanford Thompson says that he was told by a teacher in the province of Mérida, "I can never walk away from this. Because no one here ever walked away from me."

These observations remind me of an observation by Anne Fitzgibbon, the founder of several núcleos in New York City, that spending a year in Venezuela has given her an understanding of how deeply the ethic of giving back to one's childhood núcleo pervades and renews the momentum of the Sistema. "They really know," she has told me, "that from those to whom much is given, much is expected."

Similarly, Mark Churchill has told me of watching Maestro Abreu address a group of six núcleo orchestras at a provincial concert. "Who here would like to be a teacher?" the Maestro asked. In the group of six hundred young people, every hand went up.

A particularly clear expression of this ethic comes from Valdemar Rodríguez. "I have lived incredible experiences," he has said. "Fabulous trips to play music in the best venues around the world. The immense experience of playing under the direction of the greatest orchestra conductors. But the most beautiful of all has been the experience of teaching. To have had excellent students who have taught me, and continue to do so, in my modest knowledge and teachings of music and the clarinet—there is nothing as satisfying as this."

The impulse to return and to give back is strong even among the vast majority of núcleo graduates who do not become musicians; many come back as administrators or volunteer teachers. Dantes Rameau writes in his blog about "the dedication to the núcleo that many former students demonstrate, and not just through lip service. Many have jobs as engineers or accountants, for example, but continue to teach at the núcleo on a regular basis."

During the course of their travels, some of the Fellows develop the acronym CATS to refer to the way they understand the El Sistema teaching model: núcleo teachers take on the multiple roles of "citizen, artist, teacher, and scholar." By assuming responsibility not only for teaching music, but also for modeling good citizenship, high artistry and continuing study, the teachers of El Sistema encourage these qualities in their students. There seems to be a common understanding of these multiple roles, even among the very youngest teachers.

In virtually every núcleo the Fellows visit, there is a very high ratio of teachers per student. And certain teaching practices seem universal. The philosophy that children learn by doing, and by teaching one another, prevails to a degree that would confound most traditional music teachers. At a núcleo in the port city of Puerto La Cruz, children tell the Fellows of joining the orchestra before they knew how to play their instruments. "For me," says a young cellist, "the best part of the children's orchestra was just playing for the pleasure of playing, before I really knew how to play."

Dan Berkowitz recalls watching as a young girl was handed a violin for the first time and shown to a seat in the back of the violin section of her núcleo orchestra. "The kid next to her turned and showed her where to put her hand," says Dan. "Like 'Oh, here's how you play this note. And here's how you play that note.' Pedagogically, it probably wasn't perfect. But within an hour that girl felt like she was part of an orchestra."

Christine Witkowski recalls a similar scene with a boy who was given a viola. "His stand partner spent the rehearsal helping him understand the fingerings and bowings," she writes in a blog. "No one told her to do this." Christine also relates hearing a teacher tell students who have been playing for two years that they need to be helpers to children who have just gotten their instruments. "She told them, 'You are not their teacher, but you are their helper, and we need you to do that well.'"

The peer-teaching phenomenon is particularly touching at several núcleos where, as in Barquisimeto, there is a special emphasis on including and integrating children with special needs. Núcleos at Maracay and at Calabozo, among others, have established White Hands choirs and a number of other special-needs ensembles, often with the help of specialists trained at Barquisimeto. At Calabozo, in the province of Guarico, the Fellows are told that all the students at the núcleo, whether hearing-impaired or not, know how to say their names and simple phrases in sign language, and that all understand how to applaud the White Hands Chorus by waving hands in the air. The older deaf students frequently act as guides for the blind students, and older children without special needs volunteer to help teach their special-needs peers.

Christine Witkowski reports watching a sixteen-year-old horn player help the deaf percussion ensemble stay together by lightly tapping rhythms on their backs when they lose track of the beat. And when there is a concert for núcleo ensembles from across the province of Guárico, all the children respond to a duet by two very nervous young snare drummers, who are blind, with the same enthusiastic applause they give to the most advanced youth orchestras.

Also universal is the primacy of the orchestral ensemble—as pedagogical context, as artistic goal, as social world. While one-on-one lessons and small-group training go on regularly, it is the orchestras that are the heart and soul of every núcleo the Fellows visit. "The words 'núcleo' and 'orchestra' are often used interchange-ably," observes Katie Wyatt. "The orchestra is where the núcleo lives, where everyone comes together."

Lorrie Heagy appreciates the fact that every núcleo has orches-tras at different levels of musical skill, so that children can move from one skill level to the next without disrupting their experience of ensemble. "It's become commonplace for us," she adds, "to enter a room of a núcleo and be deeply affected by music played in ensemble by hundreds of kids."

Just as they did in Caracas, the Fellows spend considerable time, in conversations and at their word processors, trying to identify exactly what makes these orchestras so vibrant and appealing. "The orchestras of El Sistema have a way of really drawing in the lis-tener—especially the string sections, who always seem to be playing for their lives," writes Dantes Rameau. "It's not always perfect—no orchestra is perfect all the time, anyway—but it's intoxicating and mesmerizing."

And after observing a children's orchestra in the city of Cagua, Rebecca Levi writes, "How have they achieved such a remarkably

high level after only one and a half years of playing! We are all trying
to figure this out."

There is no doubt that one part of the answer to this question
lies in the seemingly limitless positive energy of the orchestra conductors. Andrés, a conductor at a núcleo in the city of Guarenas,
near Caracas, says that his orchestra's remarkable playing is rooted
in having fun. And at the núcleo in Puerto La Cruz, the Fellows
watch as a conductor named Yuri explains to his orchestra that the
best composers are able to capture the meaning of the universe in
music. "Like the feeling of holding your newborn baby," he says,
"that's the feeling these composers create through music." Most of
the children in the orchestra are closer to the time when they were
newborn babies themselves than to a time they will hold one of their
own; but they are fascinated by his explanation and respond with
highly emotive playing. An eleven-year-old violist tells the Fellows
afterward that she likes playing in the orchestra "because of the
passion."

While all the children's and youth orchestras play with evident
passion, and many play with considerable skill, the Fellows observe
that the most advanced orchestras, which are often referred to as
"professional" orchestras, are clearly more advanced at some núcleos
than at others. These orchestras tend to be made up of núcleo teachers, former students, and advanced current students. Christine Witkowski notes that they have sometimes lost their best players to the
national youth orchestras centered in Caracas, the Simón Bolívar
Orchestra and the Teresa Carreño Orchestra. The Sistema is aware
of this problem, she says, and is making an effort to combat it "by
trying to create great regional orchestras that offer opportunities for
local musicians—so they can flourish economically and artistically
without going to the national level."

There are many times during their travels that the Fellows are
forcefully reminded of Abreu's aphorism *"Ser, no ser todavía,"* and of
his admonitions about flexibility and variety among núcleos. "We
are discovering," writes Lorrie Heagy, "that each site is unique and

flexibly adapts its planning to meet the needs of its children and community." There are few Paper Orchestras outside of Caracas, they find, and there are many differences among núcleos in early childhood training, solfège curriculum, the use of folk music, and other areas. Álvaro Rodas notes that while most núcleos have three levels of orchestral and choral ensemble—young children, older children, and youth—the lines are often blurred, and there are times when children move back and forth between ensembles.

"The more we travel and see," says Dan Berkowitz, "the more we are understanding that everything we see has been born out of necessity. At every núcleo, they take the variables they have and do the best they can with them."

Even in the context of perpetual flexibility, however, the Fellows find a consistency not only of pedagogical principles but also of individual and collective spirit. Students everywhere are driven by a voracious desire to play and to learn music; Katie Wyatt writes of being "floored by the kids who travel hours through Venezuelan traffic on crowded and sometimes dangerous buses, or walk on dirt roads to núcleos with dirt floors and no electricity or air-conditioning, to play Shostakovich, Beethoven, and Brahms for *hours*." Rehearsals and lessons do go on for hours, everywhere, and as a matter of course. "These kids spend so much time in orchestra," says David Malek, "that they memorize symphonies the way we memorize scales." Rebecca Levi reports being told by the núcleo director at Guatire that his more advanced students are often frustrated that they can only come six days a week, and ask whether they can come on Sundays too.

The intensity of this hunger to play and to learn prevails even in the face of conditions that we in the States would be likely to consider prohibitively difficult: the absence of air-conditioning in places where the temperature routinely tops 100 degrees Fahrenheit; rehearsal settings with no running water, and sometimes no walls; frequent power outages. David Malek tells of being at a núcleo one evening when the electricity went out. "Everything was pitch black;

you could not see your hand in front of your face," he says. "But I heard music coming from somewhere upstairs, so I followed the sound, thinking the electricity must still be on in that part of the building. I opened the door to the rehearsal room, and still—pitch black. But with little points of light: some kids were holding open cell phones up to light the music while other kids played. I grabbed my flip camera and started filming, thinking, 'No one's going to believe me when I tell them about this.'"

One group of Fellows visits a núcleo in San Vicente, in the state of Aragua, situated on the edge of a huge garbage dump. The area is impoverished in the extreme, and many dwellings are constructed with remnants from the dump; the neighborhood is so dangerous that the núcleo does not stay open after dark. Rebecca Levi writes of talking to an eleven-year-old girl at this núcleo who has played the violin for two years. "I asked her what had changed for her since joining the orchestra. And she said, 'Before, I used to get in a lot of fights. But now, when I get really angry, I grab my arm as if it were my violin, and start practicing my fingerings.'"

The Fellows tell of young musicians who travel for many hours to attend a kind of floating "conservatory" in the state of Guárico, a mountainous region south of Caracas. The conservatory sponsors master classes by top Caracas teachers every few weeks, and núcleo teachers come from across the province to attend these sessions—as do many of their advanced students, who are considered responsible for helping to coach the less advanced players of their instruments. "Guárico is a big state, so this can be a seven-hour drive, sometimes more," says Dan Berkowitz. "We even heard of an instance where kids came from a bordering state; they had to leave at six P.M. and drive all night, and they arrived at eight the next morning. And they took one or two hours of private lessons and one hour of solfège and music theory class, and then they drove back home. Two days of driving, just to get these few hours of master teaching and bring what they learned back to their núcleo."

To a musician from the United States, such a "conservatory"

would be unrecognizable. "Every lesson is open for casual observation," the Fellows write. "Students wander in and out at will to listen to each other. Doors and windows are wide open, and often lessons take place outside." When they're not actively engaged in lessons, students simply hang out and teach each other informally; younger students often approach older ones for help and advice.

Frequently, lessons go past their assigned times. One master horn teacher explains that the essence of Sistema teaching involves extensive practicing during every lesson. "We don't end the lessons until the mistakes are corrected," he says. "We don't want the students to go home and practice their mistakes."

Just as powerful as the drive to teach, learn, and play within the núcleos, the Fellows find, is the drive to reach out to include and build community. And the spirit of inclusion takes as many forms as there are núcleos. Frequently, it means the active participation of parents and other adults in the life of a núcleo; in the city of Maracay, for example, at a núcleo with a particularly strong early childhood program, Lorrie Heagy observes "a toddler program packed with moms and dads tapping sticks together with their children to the beat of Mozart, and a beginning orchestra for parents learning alongside their children." For núcleos in the city of Calabozo, community outreach is focused on establishing an El Sistema presence within public schools, which in Venezuela do not typically include music in the curriculum. Teachers and advanced students from the núcleos lead music programs they call *módulos* in eight local schools, reaching over a thousand children.

Everywhere, community involvement means performances. Children's and youth orchestras and ensembles not only perform constantly within their núcleos, but also give concerts in public squares, in hospitals, in neighborhoods—wherever there are people to listen. In the coastal city of Puerto La Cruz, Fellows attend a youth orchestra concert one night in a barrio, another night in an elegant hotel. At the barrio concert, audience members dance, and the conductor allows children from the crowd to conduct one piece. "People in the barrios are very proud that the orchestra comes to them," writes Christine Witkowski. "The conductor told us that the people of Puerto La Cruz really feel this is 'their' orchestra." The hotel concert is more sedate, but the venue itself creates a new kind of multiclass community, as the audience combines núcleo parents and family members with well-to-do hotel guests.

One young member of the Puerto La Cruz núcleo orchestra talks to the Fellows about community-building in terms Maestro Abreu might have used. "The orchestra is not about a small group of people," she tells them. "It's about the whole country. It's for everyone. The more we are a cultured people, the more the country will develop."

∼

In the course of their travels through Venezuela, the Fellows begin to get a sense that underlying El Sistema's skein of compelling voices and faces is an extensive and effective, even if sometimes seemingly informal, organizational structure. In every state, núcleos are part of a regional network, and each region has a director who reports to the central office of FESNOJIV in Caracas, which seems to function as the "solar center." While salaries throughout the country are paid by FESNOJIV, fund-raising for all other purposes—facilities, instruments, supplies, and outreach—goes on at the level of individual núcleos and regional networks.

One group of Fellows happens to be traveling in the state of Guárico when word comes that its regional El Sistema network has been awarded a grant of $800,000 from a state foundation. "The grant came through on a Friday," says Dan Berkowitz. "And on Monday the directors and teachers from all the núcleos of the state got together and talked about how the money should be divided up to best meet everyone's needs. They allocated the money in a day." He adds, "They had to, because if they didn't move quickly, there was a good chance the money would disappear."

In the city of Cagua, a few hours west of Caracas, several Fellows have the chance to see the birth of a new núcleo. This núcleo began, just as most El Sistema institutions do—and as the Sistema itself began so many years ago—with an impromptu gathering of determined teachers and enthusiastic young people who found their way to instruments and began to rehearse. After a year and a half of working together, they have formed partnerships with the local government and have received the blessing of FESNOJIV, and there is an inaugural concert for the townspeople and local officials . . . and for Maestro Abreu, who attends núcleo openings as often as he can. "The players were between eight and seventeen," writes David Malek, "and they were all complete beginners who had never read a note of music before being handed an instrument a year and a half ago. And their playing was mind-blowing."

In their memorable meeting with Maestro Abreu in Caracas, the Fellows had been charged with becoming involved in the lives of the núcleos they visit. Throughout their travels, they find it easy to follow this advice—and often, in fact, impossible not to. Brass players Dan Berkowitz, Christine Witkowski, and Stanford Thompson are constantly asked to give individual lessons that can last for hours— as are violist Katie Wyatt, percussionist Álvaro Rodas, and wind players David Malek and Dantes Rameau. Lorrie Heagy, who specializes in early childhood education, and Rebecca Levi, who speaks fluent Spanish, give teacher-training workshops almost everywhere they go, and are always amazed to find that teachers have traveled long distances from other núcleos to hear them. "Where did all these people come from?" asks Rebecca at one workshop. "Are they students or teachers?"

She is told, "They are students becoming teachers."

For three Fellows who travel to the northwestern town of Acarigua, there is an opportunity to enter the life of a núcleo in a particularly exciting way. The director of the núcleo, Roberto Zambrano, has been a Sistema stalwart for many years, beginning as a cellist in the Simón Bolívar Orchestra during the 1980s and then devoting his career to developing núcleos in the Venezuelan provinces. During a telephone interview with me, Roberto has spoken of his conviction that the Sistema's break with traditional concepts of musical training represents the future of music. "The Sistema," he said, "is a sphere of freedom."

When the Fellows arrive in Acarigua, Roberto greets them with a gift of freedom—combined with responsibility. "I would like you to prepare the orchestra for a concert in the town square," he tells them. "The concert will take place in two weeks."

It is a small núcleo with just one orchestra, so the range of age and skill levels among the young players is very wide. "The repertoire was already picked—the main piece was Tchaikovsky's *1812 Overture*—and the date was set," relates Stanford Thompson, "and we went into our very first rehearsal and realized how much work we needed to do."

Acarigua sits on the open plains and is customarily very hot—especially when the electricity fails, as it does during the first week of rehearsals. "The AC goes off, and there is exactly one window, which does not open," says Stanford. "There's sweat everywhere—on the kids' faces, on their instruments, on the ground. And I'm thinking—this is crazy! But that is the moment when everything we have been experiencing makes sense to me. Because it's clear that these kids are completely immersed in the process."

At the beginning of the rehearsal period, Roberto Zambrano introduces Fellow Dantes Rameau to an eleven-year-old boy. "This is Carlos," he says. "Carlos is going to be a bassoonist. And you're going to teach him his first lesson." That morning, Dantes shows Carlos how to put the instrument together and how to blow into a double reed. "I teach him four or five notes, give him some exercises, and tell him to come back in a few days," says Dantes. "And that afternoon, while I'm conducting a sectional rehearsal of the woodwinds, practicing their part for the *1812 Overture*, I see little Carlos with his bassoon case walking toward the back of my section. And during some difficult sixteenth-note patterns, I can hear him making a screeching sound: 'Ehhh! Ehhh!' "

After the rehearsal, Dantes asks Roberto Zambrano whether he actually expects Carlos to be playing in the upcoming concert. "And Roberto says, 'Yes, of course!' "

Dantes spends hours every day with Carlos, moving him gently from "Ehhh" to the bassoon lines of the 1812 Overture. And when the day of the performance comes, Carlos is ready. "No one ever told him he couldn't do it," says Dantes. "None of the other bassoonists looked at him oddly when he sat down in the back of the section on the first day. And that experience will teach him how to get through anything in life—not just music."

Says Fellow Jonathan Govias, a conductor who is charged with leading the concert, "We all know how the 1812 Overture goes . . . but we tend to forget that it's difficult. It's really very difficult. So the bar is set very high. And we have kids like Carlos, with an hour's experience on his instrument, mixed in with kids like the concertmaster, who two weeks later will be in Caracas performing with the National Children's Orchestra. So it's a complicated task to bring them all somehow into the performance. We simplify some parts for some children, and then we start rehearsing, note by note, measure by measure, phrase by phrase."

The concert takes place in Simón Bolívar Plaza, in the center of the town. The temperature is still close to 100 degrees; the evening light is fading fast, and the wind is blowing the music off the stands. As the orchestra begins to play, a drunken bystander wanders up and begins to conduct along with Jonathan, then offers a salute.

Later, Jonathan writes in his blog about what the experience has meant to him. "There were many wrong notes. We were not always together. But it was meaningful. And for me, it was beautiful." He refers to the motto *Tocar y luchar*—To play and to struggle— engraved on the medallion that every child of the *Sistema* is given to wear at performances. "This was really *Tocar y luchar*," he writes.

"Because we had gone through a struggle together. And that is what gave meaning to our playing."

The Abreu Fellows and I came to Venezuela, as do all visitors to El Sistema, with great excitement about this extraordinary program, and tremendous curiosity about how it works. We also came—and so, probably, do most visitors—with a trace of skepticism: is it really as extraordinary as it seems?

As the Fellows near the end of their travels, their answer to this question seems similar to my own. Like any human endeavor, the Sistema struggles with problems and imperfections. Some núcleo orchestras are less successful than others; some teachers do not meet the high standards of skill and dedication set by the majority. There are children who are somehow not reachable by the Sistema's vision of music as community.

The choral curricula and pedagogy in some núcleos are not as developed as the instrumental programs. Still less developed, in many núcleos, are compositional skills. And the high growth rate currently pursued by FESNOJIV means that the demand at new núcleos for good instruments and good teachers sometimes exceeds the supply. The leaders and teachers of the Sistema are the first to admit these problems, and discuss them candidly.

And yet it's difficult for even the most cynical visitor to experience the youth and children's orchestras of Venezuela without concluding that the Sistema is, in fact, as extraordinary as it seems. It's impossible not to be impressed, in every núcleo, by the primacy of empathic connection between and among students and teachers. In every núcleo, it's impossible not to sense a clear and potent common purpose toward the inseparable goals of social harmony and artistic excellence. And the scope of this dual goal, which has touched millions and is growing exponentially to reach millions more, is simply without precedent in our modern world.

Perhaps most inspiring of all is that the Sistema's power derives from a vision of art, and of human nature, that is profoundly and insistently hopeful. Abreu's grounding assumption is that children of poverty—children anywhere—will, if given the chance, choose the self-affirmation and pride that comes with communal belonging and artistic accomplishment over destructive and self-destructive alternatives. To see this assumption borne out in action on so vast a scale, and in the context of such entrenched social and economic distress, is almost necessarily to reconsider the balance, so long and carefully calibrated by U.S. musicians, educators, and activists, between skepticism and hope.

As they come close to the end of their time in Venezuela, there is a clear shift in the tone of the Fellows' observations; they become less preoccupied with defining pedagogical principles and analyzing núcleo practices, and more drawn to exploring the essence of underlying principles. "We keep looking for the key to the system," writes David Malek. "And we always tend to think in terms of speed and efficiency. But they take their time in a life of making music. They 'waste' time together, making music in relationship, for four to six hours every day."

Rebecca Levi agrees: "When a child has a trumpet in his hand for six hours, there is the assumption that there is no hurry."

And Katie Wyatt proposes that the defining quality of the núcleo orchestra is that it is "an environment of contribution. Everyone in the orchestra is responsible for everything in the orchestra."

Others find that Abreu's attitude of limitless possibility is the through-line of everything they have seen. "A violin teacher named Israel, in Caracas, told me, 'Never place limits on what a child can do. Every child is a musician from the very start,' " says Lorrie Heagy. "And wherever I went in Venezuela, I heard teachers say, 'Más! Más!' "

By the end of their stay, most of the Fellows find themselves in agreement with Anne Fitzgibbon, the founder of New York's Harmony Program, who has told them: "Everyone who goes to

Venezuela is searching for models and prescriptions. It's natural—that's the way we think. But the thing that can't be remotely analyzed is the Venezuelan spirit of joy. And that is what allowed the Sistema to grow and flourish in the first place."

～

The Fellows return to Boston in April, to begin planning the creation of brand-new "núcleos" across the United States. The programs they bring into being will be influenced by, and reflective of, the multitude of discoveries and revelations they have experienced in Venezuela. Says Jonathan Govias of the Fellows' trip: "We didn't just see the work—we lived it. We lived El Sistema. We lived all these wonderful ideas: access, integration, community, connection, intensity."

But they will also be able to learn from the experience of a first wave of energetic pioneers from the United States who heard about El Sistema several years ago and were stirred to action, launching Sistema-inspired programs that have been up and running for a year or two. These programs, and a host of emerging ones, are already well into the process of imagining how to combine music learning and social engagement in the lives of children in the United States.

When I spoke with Esteban in Caracas at the outset of our visit, he was thrilled to learn that the Venezuelan baseball players he reveres are heroes in the United States as well. And then he asked whether children in our country play music in orchestras. "Kids there have everything," he said. "They must have orchestras too!"

There are many youth orchestras, I responded. But they are not like his; they are mostly groups of children who take private lessons and come together for rehearsals now and then. Now, though, some people are starting to create orchestras more like his, where poor kids will have the chance to learn together and play together every day. I told Esteban that I have visited some of these new programs and plan to visit more. Is there a message he would like me to take to the children there?

Esteban didn't have to think about it. "Yes," he said. "Tell them to come here and play with us. Tell them we're playing Corelli's 'Air.'" He pronounced it nimbly, in Spanish: "*Aah-eer.*" "Tell them that if they don't know it, we'll teach it to them."

CHAPTER 7

# Faces of El Sistema USA

WEST SAN ANTONIO, TEXAS, DOES NOT, AT FIRST glance, look like a New Yorker's idea of a ghetto. There are no high-rise projects, no grim alleyways; the sun usually shines on the blocks of modest adobe houses painted Easter-egg shades of pink and green and blue. It's not immediately obvious that the predominantly Mexican-American neighborhood is home to many households characterized by poverty and chronic unemployment, or that this is the turf of perennial gang activity and conflict.

Similarly, the Good Samaritan Community Services Center in the middle of the neighborhood doesn't fit the institutional image often associated with the words "social services." Its modern one- and two-story buildings, sunlit and freshly painted, flank a courtyard, basketball courts, a bright-colored playground. But "Good Sam," as everyone calls it, fills an urgent and growing community need. Its social, medical, and educational programs serve over a thousand families a year, providing everything from nutrition counseling to case management, from after-school activities to senior-citizen care; for the most part, the recipients of these services have no other access to such resources. There is a computer lab for kids, a crafts program for seniors; staff members measure and graph children's behavioral and academic progress.

Music education doesn't tend to show up in the charter of a social services agency. For the past two years, however, the hallways and courtyards of Good Sam have come alive every afternoon with the scrape of violin bows, the twang of plucked cello strings. Thanks to a partnership with the Youth Orchestras of San Antonio, Good Samaritan Community Services is the setting for the Music Learning Center, a program modeled after Venezuela's El Sistema.

In San Antonio, one of the most Hispanic of southwestern cities, the "Sistema" story happens to begin with a Brit. Steven Payne, a tall, lanky native of Bournemouth, England, is the executive director of the Youth Orchestras of San Antonio (YOSA for short), a vibrant and ambitious enterprise with 450 students in five orchestras. Before coming to YOSA in 2007, Steve had heard about Venezuela's Sistema through friends at the League of American Orchestras, and had also seen the first 60 Minutes program featuring the Sistema and Gustavo Dudamel.

"YOSA had already been doing a weekend outreach music program on San Antonio's West Side," Steve tells me, "and its board was sympathetic to the idea that music could be used for social good. So when I interviewed for the job of director, I talked about wanting to transform this into a real Sistema-type program. And they were all completely enthusiastic." A committee was born, and the idea of partnering with the Good Sam center evolved. Combining YOSA's musical and pedagogical expertise with Good Sam's social services experience seemed a good way to bring the Sistema's musical and social goals into alignment.

YOSA found immediate allies in the leaders of Good Sam, CEO Jill Oettinger and board president Neel Lane. "We are a good fit for an El Sistema program," says Jill, "because it's about the whole child—which is what Good Sam is all about."

Neel Lane, a prominent San Antonio lawyer, has had a long-standing interest in the damaging effects of poverty on the developing brain of a child. "The research shows that the damage is reversible through skill development," he says, "especially the skills that are brought into play through music."

The question of funding for an El Sistema program loomed large at the outset; neither YOSA nor Good Sam had the financial resources to launch and support the Music Learning Center they envisioned. Enter a Texas-sized personality named Al Silva, a son of Mexican immigrants, who grew up in the West San Antonio barrio and learned to speak English as a child at Good Sam. A basketball scholarship took him to college, and he is now a successful business-man and long-standing member of both the YOSA and Good Sam boards.

The ideals of El Sistema resonated strongly with Silva's child-hood experiences. "I remember being that age, and thinking I had no options," he says, "and then my high school coach took me to a basketball game, to inspire me. I was inspired, but I was terrified too. Those players were so tall! Mexicans don't"—he pauses for dramatic effect—"grow."

Al Silva grew. A handsome—and tall—man with the charm of a born politician and the fervor of a born-again preacher, he approached local foundations and the business community of San Antonio for help in launching the Music Learning Center. "This is not only for music lovers," he told them, "this is about social reform. A kid grows up better when he has an instrument in his hands." No one, Al tells me, said no. He had some formidable fund-raising allies in board members like Barbara Labatt, a philanthropist and music teacher who chairs YOSA's music programs. Within five months they had raised over $250,000.

Maggie Raveneau, a young cellist and music teacher who is the principal instructor for the Music Learning Center, seems at first to be the mirror opposite of Al Silva; she is a soft-spoken woman with a sweet, shy smile. But she is a force in her own understated way. She and her husband, Jon Raveneau, a pianist and bass player from New Orleans, recruited children for the new program by giving musical presentations at two elementary schools in the Good Sam neighborhood. "We played a Bach cello suite, and we played the Sponge Bob tune," says Maggie, "and we played '*Eine Kleine Nachtmusik*' and the Mario Brothers theme. And then we took requests—Jon can play anything. And we got kids just swarming to sign up."

On the hot September day when I visit the Music Learning Center, it is beginning its second year of operation, with approximately eighty children learning to play stringed instruments. I sit in a small chair at the back of an open, sun-filled room and watch a class of beginning violinists. These are very small children—mostly first- and second-graders—with very small violins, and they are both intrigued and intimidated by their instruments. Maggie takes them through a series of slow, graceful movements to arrive at the correct way to hold a violin; the clear message is that there's no hurry about this delightful ritual. She introduces them to the shoulder rest: "See the nice beautiful curve? It fits with the curve of your body," she tells them. After five or six steps, violins have arrived at last under chins. The children stand very still, almost holding their breaths. "See the purple string?" she says, "That's your G string." She is using a method and lesson book she has designed herself, using color codes for strings and for fingers. "We're all going to pluck our G strings now," she tells them. "Ready—set—pluck!"

They pluck. "Now look at your book and find the picture of the red string. . . . Now find the red string on your violin. . . . Are you ready? Pluck!" It's possible that the soaring arc of a Brahms melody never thrilled an orchestral violinist more than plucking the red string excites these children.

She tells them to open their music books. "Our first song!" she exclaims as though she's announcing a birthday party.

"Can we use our bows now?" they ask her.

"Not yet," she says. So they pluck their way through their first song, which lasts all of ten notes. Several assistant teachers move among the kids, adjusting hand positions, correcting faulty plucks. When no help is needed, they sit among the kids with their own violins, modeling how to follow Maggie's instructions. Jon Raveneau is there too, "floating and fixing," in his wife's words. "We call him 'the cool factor,' " she adds.

Watching with me is Troy Peters, YOSA's new music director. He is impressed with Raveneau's ability to foster both high spirits and focused work. "I'd love to see our youth orchestra rehearsals have the spirit of fun I see here," he says. Troy tells me that the children in the Music Learning Center will soon begin to meet together once a week, as a string orchestra, and that he will conduct them.

When the beginners' class ends, we walk around the Good Sam complex and stop in a room filled with boisterous children enjoying snack time. "Who wants to sign up for the music classes?" Troy says.

A chorus of voices responds: "I do! I do!"

"Do it!" he answers, equally boisterous. "Do it!" He rushes off to find the application forms.

Back in the music classroom, the beginners' class has ended and the second-year children have arrived. Now there are bows on strings, playing actual melodies. Maggie takes them back and forth between the "Ode to Joy" and the Queen anthem "We Will Rock You." "Joyful, joyful, we adore thee" . . . Note, note, stomp! Note, note, stomp! Feeling alternately like classical cognoscenti and rock stars, they are actually learning about rhythms and rests.

Maggie has told me that the boy playing cello, Juan, was known at Good Sam for several years as a difficult child. After he began to participate in the Music Learning Center, he carried his cello with him everywhere. "People would do a double take," she says. "They would say 'Is that Juan?!' They barely recognized him."

I watch Juan raise his hand as the ensemble hurtles to the close of "We Will Rock You." "So two eighth notes are equal to a quarter note, right?" he says to Maggie. I'm guessing that he knows the answer and just wants recognition for the question.

"That's exactly right," she says, and he beams. She tells the class it is time to put their instruments away.

"No-o-o!" they yell in unison.

After the kids have gone, Maggie talks with me about the program's mission. "The main point is not how to play music," she says in her soft voice, "so much as how to live. When they come to class, I want them to feel a sense of coming home. And I want them to feel the pride of belonging to something, like belonging to a sports team, but even more powerful."

She tells me that her kids often show her the bad grades they're getting in school, convinced they can't do better. "They actually tell me they're 'bad kids,' " she says. "It breaks my heart. I tell them, 'If you can struggle and succeed at learning this beautiful instrument, then you can definitely get A's in school.' And they believe me, because they know I believe in them."

I ask her about the pros and cons of having the program in a social services organization rather than a school. She tells me that she values the way Good Sam can provide caseworkers to address the emotional needs of individual children and families. "And meals," she adds, "Good Sam gives the kids nutritious meals. That's key." But she acknowledges that it's sometimes not easy to get parents to actively support the program. "One problem is that parents don't want their kids to stay late here," she says, "because they're afraid about them leaving the center after dark. It's a dangerous area. But in these kids' lives, everywhere is dangerous."

Steve Payne and Troy Peters have made efforts to enlist the musicians of the San Antonio Symphony in the work of the Music Learning Center, inviting them to become involved as teachers and mentors. It has been an uphill battle, they tell me; most members of the symphony lead busy freelance lives as well, to make ends meet, and have little time to spare for community volunteer work. This may be just one instance of a larger problem; many symphony orchestras in the United States, where constant financial pressures are felt at both individual and organizational levels, may be slow to see El Sistema as a movement that has meaning and relevance for their own mission.

A luncheon later that day for the advisory board of Good Sam is a different story: the board members are eager to be rallied to their new cause. They consume taco salads and vast quantities of iced tea as they listen to a speech by Eric Booth, who is in San Antonio to help energize and guide the evolution of the Music Learning Center program. "El Sistema in Venezuela is not only producing the best youth orchestras in the world," he tells the board, "but lives are being transformed beyond anything we have thought possible. We are discovering that art is way more powerful than we have allowed for."

Eric adds that among the El Sistema–inspired programs springing up across the United States, the model they are in the midst of inventing is unique. "What's happening in San Antonio is distinctive from what's happening in other cities," he says, "because the partner organization is you folks—a community organization that is really good at working with the very kids we're trying to reach. So this is a particularly important national experiment."

Al Silva delivers the rousing finale for the meeting. "Everyone is frustrated with our national failure to educate poor children," he says. "This gives us a chance to try a really nontraditional approach." He adds, "Everybody likes to talk about 'exposure to the arts,' but exposure doesn't lead to changing a child's life. El Sistema does this. It's not about exposure. It's about life change."

When the luncheon ends, Al stands in the sun-baked courtyard of Good Sam and watches kids play basketball. He points out the graffiti on a metal column. "That's a gang tag," he tells me, "it goes up every night. We paint over it every day."

He recognizes the tag; the gang's name is Ghost Town, and they were around when he was growing up here. "My cousin was the head of it," he says. "My mother, bless her, called my cousin's mother and said, 'Keep your kid away from my kid.'" I can understand why Silva is such a successful fund-raiser: he would not be easy to say no to. When he speaks of giving children hope and skills to lift them out of poverty, his words have the resonance of lived experience.

And Good Sam clearly still feels like home to him. He knows many of the families who come here now, and takes a personal interest in the progress of the kids in the Music Learning Center program. "How about that kid Reggie," he asks Maggie, "that kid who was doing so well on the violin?"

She tells him that Reggie stopped coming, and they haven't been able to contact his family. Silva immediately calls across the courtyard to Jill Oettinger, Good Sam's CEO. "Jill, Maggie tells me that Reggie's missing," he says. "We have to find Reggie. Do you know where he is?" His question is as urgent in tone as his rallying cry to the board about arts education policy had been. He repeats: "We have to find Reggie."

In the weeks and months after my visit to San Antonio, Maggie Raveneau stays in touch with me about the progress of the program. "We are up to 89 kids," she writes at the end of September. In October she writes, "We now have 110 students enrolled!" And in November: "We have closed enrollment at 160 kids, but more keep wanting to join. I say, Why not???"

Steve Payne has explained to me that the space limitations at Good Sam require YOSA to limit the program to 180 children, with a full- and part-time staff of five. "We would love to expand eventually," he says, "but right now we are just concentrating on serving these kids as well as we can."

In December, Maggie sends me a photo of a brother and sister, César and Ytzel, who come from a particularly dangerous area but are devoted to the program. She includes a scanned picture of a handwritten essay by Ytzel about how it has changed her life. "*Toda mi vida,*" the third-grader has written, "*nada ha sentido como amando un violin.*" "All my life, nothing has felt like loving a violin."

Maggie signs all her messages "Hope-full." It's persuasive, the combination of optimism and tenacity I have seen in San Antonio, and I find myself thinking it's possible—I'm even hope-full—that Reggie has been found.

~

The rain is relentless during the bleak November days when I visit Lockerman Bundy Elementary School in West Baltimore. The neighborhood would be bleak even without the rain; across the street from the school, the once-elegant little row houses are run-down and dilapidated, their stoops crumbling and many of their windows boarded up. Lockerman Bundy makes a valiant effort to counter its environment, with brightly painted interior walls and lively murals. At dismissal time, the principal stands at the door to give each child a goodbye hug. And for the past year, the school has been filled with music, both during the school day and afterward, thanks to "Orch-Kids," an El Sistema–inspired program involving 180 Lockerman Bundy students and sponsored by no less eminent an organization than the Baltimore Symphony Orchestra.

I am visiting the OrchKids program in the company of the ten Abreu Fellows, who have come to Baltimore for their first glimpse of an El Sistema–modeled program in the United States. Our day begins with a morning prekindergarten class; OrchKids provides the school's youngest children with twice-weekly music classes during the school day. The Fellows and I take our seats as quietly as possible in the back of the classroom, eleven grown-ups pretending to be inconspicuous in a room full of very tiny children.

The teacher, Eric Rasmussen, is a bespectacled, slightly rumpled man who would be pegged anywhere as a college professor—which, on most days, he is; at the moment, however, he is waving a colored scarf and singing "Hold That Tiger" along with a tinny 1940s big-band recording. The children are waving scarves too, crouching as they move in a slow circle: they are the scary tigers. "Mr. Eric" out-lines a musical phrase with scarf movements, as though drawing the melody in the air, and the children imitate him. On precise cues, they jump, growl, crouch, and leap in time to the music. When the song ends, the children are still jumping and leaping; it's hard to stop being a tiger. But they calm down instantly to a soul version of "Here Comes the Sun" with light, fluttery scarf movements. At the end the scarves flutter beautifully to the ground.

Eric Rasmussen moves them without a pause into the next activity, an improvised song about their favorite Thanksgiving food. "Pie!" they shout, and "Cake!" and cake and pie go immediately into the song. He has devised complex, syncopated rhythms and an odd meter for the song, and these very young children sing fluently, as though it's a nursery rhyme.

"They're totally capable of doing complicated music, and they could do even more if I had more time with them," he tells the Fellows and me afterward. "I have them two days a week. I wish I had them five." Eric is the chair of the Early Childhood Music Department at Johns Hopkins's Peabody Institute. "I love the babies," he adds. "They can't be too young for me. These four-year-olds are already a little old. And by the time they're seven or eight, it's almost too late. The younger they are, the more I can teach them."

The effort to bring intensive music education to very young children is a distinctive feature of the OrchKids program, one of the many ways it emulates the Venezuelan Sistema. The program for the older OrchKids—first- and second-graders—also hews to the basic Sistema model, with children playing every day after school in lessons and ensembles. "Life is not easy for these kids," says Orch-Kids director Dan Trahey. "For me, the most important thing about this program is that we give them a daily sense of a community that really cares about them."

Dan knows firsthand how music education can shape a child's formative experiences. Raised in a working-class city in Michigan, he discovered at an early age that playing the tuba really well was his "ticket out," since good tuba players were always in demand. The tuba took him all the way to the Peabody Institute and then to the Yale School of Music. From the outset, he tells me, he was focused less on a conventional orchestral career than on forging links between music and communities. "I always wanted to use performance for education and outreach purposes," he says. "In high school, in college—I always had a performing group that would go out and play in community venues."

Dan Trahey first heard about the Sistema the same way Steven Payne did: he happened to see the *60 Minutes* feature. He got on a plane to Caracas, making up in curiosity and determination what he lacked in connections. "I've been to Venezuela four times now," he tells me, "and what always impresses me the most is the sheer excitement about playing music. From the tiny little kids to the professionals, they're all just so excited about it. I wasn't always completely impressed with the level of the orchestras I heard; but the community feeling, the energy, the amount of work they were putting in—all of those things were constantly impressive.

"I felt like the Venezuelans were confident poets," he adds. "In this country, educators are always asking the question about music education, 'Is this important?' Not only were they saying it was important, but they were saying it in such an eloquent way."

Confident poets: it is a striking turn of phrase from this straightforward young man. But it's clear as Trahey talks about his program that he has an urgent sense of mission about bringing both confidence and artistry into the lives of the children at OrchKids. "The social impact of the program is enormous," he says. "They learn conflict resolution, leadership skills, empathy, and compassion."

He adds, "Would this work if it were an intensive Ping-Pong program? In some ways, I think it would. But the beauty of the music would be missing. We're talking about people who hardly have money to eat or pay phone bills; you give them something beautiful, and it has a huge impact. And those instruments in their hands: this is something that can last forever."

In the OrchKids classes we visit, there is a perceptible sense of confidence among the kids, and often more than a whiff of poetry.

In one large room a group of kindergarteners make a wide semicircle around their teacher for Bucket Band, an ensemble of overturned buckets played with drumsticks, and they copy the series of rhythms she plays. "OrchKids ready position!" she calls out as they begin, and "OrchKids rest position!" when they end. "OrchKids rest position!" they carol back to her. Even in the context of a simple classroom command, their special identity as OrchKids seems to be just as exciting as making a loud and joyful noise on the bottom of a bucket. We watch classes of very young violinists, flutists, trumpet players; the music they play is simple—sometimes just downbeats and repeated notes in rhythm—but they are absorbed and animated.

Dan Trahey moves among the classrooms, concentrating on the kids. He is handsome in an offhand, dressed-down way: dark hair, dark eyes, jeans, and well-worn cowboy boots. I watch him approach a small posse of second-grade boys who enter a musicianship classroom and sit in a boisterous cluster. He squats beside them, eye-level. "Are you sure you guys want to sit together? Or would you like to spread your leadership skills throughout the whole classroom?" Wide-eyed, feeling the tremendousness of their leadership skills, they spread out.

Later, I overhear Dan talking with DeeShay, a second-grader who plays the cello. "I want you to be the leader of the cello section," he says. She nods, but she's clearly uncertain. "Are you bossy at home sometimes?" he asks. She nods again: no uncertainty about that. "Well then, you can be section leader. What's bossy at home can turn into leadership here."

As the bell rings for the end of the school day, I stop into the cafeteria where the OrchKids students congregate for snacks before they begin their music classes. Presiding over snack time is Dan's assistant, Nick Skinner, who assures me that snack time is no less important a part of the program than is music-making. He moves among the tables issuing quiet guidelines. "No cookies in your pockets," he says. "No eating standing up. Make sure everyone has some before you start."

Taking his cue from El Sistema in Venezuela, Nick sees every interaction, not only musical but social, as a teachable and potentially character-building moment. "We're on it all the time," he tells me. "Everything matters—even hiding a cookie in your pocket. They learn that being an OrchKid means behaving in a certain way."

When the program began, says Dan, he was unhappy about the quality of the food served at snack time. "It was the only low-quality thing we did, and that bothered me. Every single thing about the program should give the message of high quality." He persuaded the public school system to dedicate a portion of its funds from the federal stimulus package to providing healthy meals for OrchKids children, and now the young musicians eat turkey sandwiches and bananas (as well as cookies) instead of Fritos.

Dan and Nick have created an administrative office for OrchKids in a small room at the very heart of the school, a former storage room they cleaned up and painted themselves. The office seems to function as a kind of sanctuary; kids feel welcome to drop in, and safe when they come. I happen to be there when a resource teacher brings in a crying OrchKids child; she has been upset by an aggressive incident in her second-grade classroom and is seeking comfort. "You need to stop crying and smile," says Dan. "How am I going to get through my day if I don't see you smile?"

She manages to sob for a few more seconds before the smile breaks out. "Mr. Dan, can I stay here?" she asks.

"Nope," says Dan. "You have to go back to your classroom and learn lots of stuff, so you can come to OrchKids after school."

Sometimes it is an OrchKids child who acts out in the classroom, and in those cases, Nick tells me, OrchKids teachers "can sometimes discipline them more effectively than their classroom teachers can, because their desire to stay in the program is a huge positive incentive."

Lockerman Bundy principal Cynthia Cunningham confirms this. "The kids in the program—they really want to come to school every day," she says. "And often they don't want to go home." She tells me she loves the program's emphasis on classical music, which most of the students would never otherwise hear. And she is thrilled with the program's general effect on the kids' lives. "It's like a bright new sun is shining on them," she says.

Parent liaison Shirley Dessesow, an ardent advocate for the program since its inception, sees the effect reaching beyond the children to their parents and communities. Shirley asserts that the kids' love of music is changing family conversations, which are changing neighborhood conversations. "Kids ask for instruments for Christmas now," she says.

How did the sun happen to shine so brightly on two hundred children in West Baltimore? There is a fairy godmother aspect to this story, involving the lucky convergence of Dan Trahey with the conductor Marin Alsop, one of the most prominent visionaries in the contemporary classical music world. Alsop was hired as music director and principal conductor of the Baltimore Symphony Orchestra in 2007—the first appointment of a woman to such a position by any major symphony orchestra in the United States. Educated at Yale and Juilliard and mentored by Leonard Bernstein, Maestra Alsop has brought fresh musical energy and a strong reformist impulse to her job. Her concept of starting an outreach program to connect the orchestra with the vast underserved and impoverished segment of Baltimore's population first evolved, she says, as a way to reenergize her musicians, some of whom seemed to have lost their original spark of excitement about music-making. She met with Dan Trahey, who was then working at Peabody as a "music teacher mentor" forging connections with the public school system in Baltimore, and told him of her desire for the orchestra to start a community engagement program. "How would you do it?" she asked him.

"I'd start something like El Sistema in Venezuela," he told her.

Marin knew almost nothing about El Sistema, but Dan's description intrigued her, and she was immediately convinced. "Enrolling the orchestra musicians was a gradual process," she says. "It involved a year of sometimes difficult meetings and conversations. But ultimately it has been very successful."

The Baltimore Symphony hired Dan to head the new initiative, and sent him back to Venezuela to learn the administrative and managerial side of the Sistema. Marin Alsop underscored her commitment to the program by donating a substantial portion of the MacArthur Fellowship she had recently received, to help cover start-up costs. Further substantial support came from Robert Meyerhoff, the Baltimore philanthropist whose family name graces the symphony's concert hall. And partnerships were forged with Peabody, whose president, Jeff Sharkey, was an enthusiastic advocate, and with the public school system. Larry Friend, head of Fine Arts for the Baltimore public school system, has said that when Marin and Dan came to him with the OrchKids idea, he "didn't even know what El Sistema was. But I said 'Let's go with it.' We have nothing to lose and everything to gain."

Dan Trahey speaks of the intensity of the planning process. "We talked for hours and hours and days and weeks about how to structure a Sistema program that would work for Baltimore kids. We wanted more planning time, but Marin said, 'This needs to happen *now.*'"

OrchKids began at the Harriet Tubman Elementary School in the fall of 2008, moving to Lockerman Bundy the following year upon the closing of the Tubman school. "Ms. Marin" has been a visible presence from the outset, visiting often and working with the children. "They're so sweet—they're always hugging me," she tells me with the delight of a high-profile orchestral titan whose typical day does not involve a lot of hugs.

During the after-school OrchKids program on this rainy November afternoon, I watch Ms. Marin rehearse the first- and second-grade instrumentalists for a concert the next day. It's an eccentric ensemble: lots of violins, two cellos, one bass, a few flutes and clarinets, an assortment of trumpets and euphoniums, a single trombone.

The Fellows sit with their instruments among the children and play along, and the kids are elated; they have never heard themselves sound so good. Marin beams and bounces as she conducts, seeking eye contact and dispersing lavish compliments. "You all look so beautiful and professional with your instruments!" she tells them. "We're getting good now, that means we gotta keep practicing. That's how you get to be perfect—always play it one more time!"

They play it one more time—many times. The cello section, consisting of a small girl with a ponytail on top of her head and a tiny intense boy with his tongue between his teeth, sways back and forth with the music, in Venezuelan fashion. Abreu Fellow Rebecca Levi sits between two little boys with flutes; two girls with clarinets flank David Malek, another Fellow. The children are mostly attentive, absorbed in the music; when one flagging violinist puts down her instrument and wanders off, Dan Trahey grabs her instantly, hugs her, and sends her back to her chair.

As we sit watching the rehearsal, Dan points out a very small child standing motionless in front of the orchestra. "Tamir is four," he says. "He has fetal alcohol syndrome, and he lives in foster homes. And he loves music more than anything." A few moments later Tamir approaches and puts a tiny hand on Dan's knee. "Tamir, this is Ms. Tricia," says Trahey.

In one motion, Tamir shakes my hand and climbs into my lap. I ask him if he's going to play in the orchestra when he's older, and he nods.

"I'm gonna play clarinet," he says. "It sounds peaceful."

After more than two hours of rehearsal, these six-, seven-, and eight-year-olds, who have already put in a full school day, are still strikingly focused. And Ms. Marin, who will be conducting the Baltimore Symphony in *Rhapsody in Blue* this evening, shows no sign of flagging. It is after five-thirty when she asks the children if they want to play it one more time. "Yeah!" they shout in unison. They play it one more time, and it's the best they've sounded.

She gives them a thumbs-up. The rehearsal is over, and they are instantly noisy, clustering around the Fellows and me. Tyrone is the only double bass player. "I was playing violin for a while, but I grew up," he says, standing as tall as his eight-year-old frame will allow. "And now I can play double bass. I've been playing it for six weeks."

His arm is draped around his instrument. How long, I ask, does he think he'll continue to play it? He looks surprised at the question. "Forever," he says, and adds, "Playing music fills your mind up with expression."

Second-grader Arkeen tells me he plays the flute. "I can play A, B, C, D, and E flat. And high E." He holds his flute case tightly against his chest, as if no more needs to be said.

The next day, talking with me before the noontime OrchKids concert, Marin Alsop speaks of her fascination with the children's relationships with their instruments. "Very often, there really is a right instrument for every child," she says. "When they find their instrument, sometimes it's an immediate physical reaction—almost a reverence." She tells me of her own childhood discovery of conducting, after becoming accomplished on piano and violin at a very early age. "I saw Leonard Bernstein conduct a Young People's Concert when I was about nine," she says, "and that was it. I said, 'Oh, that's what I'm going to do.' And I never wavered. And my parents, who are both musicians, were completely supportive—even though a woman conductor was almost unheard of in those days.

"In fact, when I finally got to Juilliard and wanted to study with Otto-Werner Mueller, he told me, 'You'll never be a conductor.' " I said to him, 'I don't think you understand who I am and how I feel. If you take me on as your student, I promise I will be the best student you've ever had.' And when I finished my master's degree at Juilliard, I started my own orchestra, Concordia."

From the very outset, Marin says, Concordia had a social as well as a musical mission. "We partnered with a school in Bedford-Stuyvesant for eight years, and worked with an entire generation of kids there."

I ask her if learning about El Sistema has changed the way she thinks about music education's social possibilities. "It's not exactly that my ideas have changed," she responds, "it's that I feel inspired. People are always so quick to say you can't do this or that. Can't, can't, can't . . . And then here is Maestro Abreu, who never, ever says 'can't.' Just one small man, plugging away, relentlessly positive, and doing unbelievable things.

"I would also say that I felt validated," she adds. "The Sistema is not about measuring the level of a child's musical achievement, it's not about judgment—it's about the child's integrated experience. I've always felt that is what is important."

Marin is keenly aware of what such experience has already meant to the children of OrchKids. "They now have a sense of possibility—a sense that they can go on to higher education. That's huge. It becomes a cycle of generating possibility and value and self-esteem."

On the day of the concert, the young musicians enter the auditorium spectacularly well scrubbed in their white shirts and dark pants or skirts, wearing "OrchKids" medallions on blue-and-white ribbons around their necks and looking proud as decorated generals. Their audience—the entire student body, sitting cross-legged on the gym floor—catches the excitement and breaks into prolonged clapping before the music has even begun. And when Ms. Marin, festive in a multicolored scarf, begins to conduct the orchestra in the "Russian Sailors' Dance," their listeners can't restrain themselves from clapping along in time to the music.

At the end, Dan Trahey addresses the cheering audience. "Every single one of you in this room," he tells them, "could do what you heard these kids do today. Every single one of you!"

For Dan, the idea that every child is capable of making music with others is an article of faith, one that needs no translation in the move from the Venezuelan barrios to the inner city of Baltimore. The five-year plan for OrchKids is ambitious, involving the addition of a new grade and fifty or more children each year. And an OrchKids choir will begin soon, in partnership with Lyric Opera Baltimore. "When you think about the dangerous idleness that confronts these kids," he says, "it feels like you just have to expand."

I ask him about OrchKids' ultimate goal. "Well," he says, "there are 83,000 kids in the Baltimore public school system. . . . "

When I mention this comment to Marin Alsop, she concurs without hesitation. "Why not? I'm a firm believer in possibility," she says. "Every kid should have the chance to play an instrument in an ensemble. It develops really critical twenty-first-century skills."

Marin seems incapable of thinking small—and OrchKids is not her only dream for connecting symphony with community. She tells me about a new program she has initiated, Rusty Musicians, that aims to link amateur instrumentalists in Baltimore with orchestral mentors. "Four hundred people signed up in twenty-four hours," she says. And she describes another idea, still in the dreaming stages, to create a space near Symphony Hall for community creativity, "a beautiful new building where mothers can bring their kids to be together, to create, maybe with a listening library—a kind of hub of creativity." Referring back to OrchKids, she says, "Right now, though, my goal is to serve these hundred eighty kids as well as we can."

Dan tells me that he often hears OrchKids children say to people, "I'm with the Baltimore Symphony." They have good reason to think so; they have already had several opportunities to sit on the stage of Meyerhoff Symphony Hall, interspersed with the symphony musicians, during rehearsals. And there are plans to include OrchKids performances as part of regular BSO concerts.

Even in its early stages, OrchKids has some concrete indicators of success. The kids who began the program in the fall of 2008 were surveyed about their futures; only 15 percent could imagine themselves going further than elementary school. At the end of that school year, 55 percent saw themselves going all the way to college. "Most of these kids, when they started, couldn't answer the question of what they wanted to be when they grew up," says Marin. "Now a lot of them say they want to be musicians, or teachers, or doctors."

Dan Trahey tells me that the community has already begun to

provide validation for the work of OrchKids. "I recently drove two kids home," he says, "and was stopped by a cop—he just assumed that, as a white guy, my business in the neighborhood was suspect. I told him I lead the Baltimore Symphony children's program here. And he said, 'You do incredible work. You are going to make our work easier someday.'

"I would like OrchKids to be a place where other people in the country can come and be inspired to go home and create their own programs," he adds. "Twenty years from now, I want Baltimore and our work here to be talked about in the coffee shops as well as in the dissertations."

P.S. 152 is a sand-colored brick building in a working-class area of Flatbush, Brooklyn, a neighborhood of modest frame houses surrounding a vast bustling intersection known as "the Junction" where you can catch the subway train to Manhattan, an hour and a world away. An Irish and Italian enclave once upon a time, Flatbush is now home to Brooklyn College and to a multitude of first- and second-generation immigrants from Africa and the Caribbean; the children of P.S. 152 trace their roots to Haiti, Trinidad, Jamaica, Grenada, Guyana, Barbados, and Belize, as well as Ghana, Zimbabwe, and Nigeria. On a freezing afternoon in December, I stand outside the school with a small group of visitors as the afternoon bell rings and the children pour down the steps into the already darkening streets of Flatbush, talking and laughing, pulling on hats, dropping mittens. We go up the steps as they come down: we are there to observe the fifty children of P.S. 152 who do not leave when the closing bell rings, but stay on until evening in the company of trombones and trumpets, clarinets and flutes, violins and cellos, and some very animated young music teachers. These are the children of the Harmony Program, another of the first programs in the United States to be modeled closely upon Venezuela's El Sistema.

"I chose this school to launch the program," says Harmony Program founder Anne Fitzgibbon, "because it's in an area where children have very little access to music education. And it's near Brooklyn College, which supplies us with our teachers." Walking with her, we can hear music up and down every hallway and around every corner. In one classroom, five second-graders play "O Come, O Come, Emmanuel" on their small cellos, with their teacher accompanying them at a keyboard. "More bow!" she calls out, and five bows move more bravely, with lengthier sweeps across the strings. A percussion ensemble rehearses in another classroom; we watch as the teacher gives a lesson in eighth-note rhythms. She stomps, claps, and sways, and they imitate her, feeling the rhythms as physical movements. In a corner of the school gym, two nine-year-old trombonists play "Jolly Old Saint Nicholas" in harmony, their arms straining to extend the slides of their instruments, their eyes round with effort and probably with the sheer thrill of the gymnasium's clangorous acoustics.

In a classroom upstairs, three even younger boys are producing a startlingly robust sound on their trumpets. Their teacher, Christian Alonzo, is a young Filipino man; he talks to them as they play. "Feel it! Feel it!" he says. "Be confident!"

Feeling it, they play an excerpt from "O Holy Night." We applaud, and confidence blooms. "Can we play the whole thing for them?" they ask. The boy playing the melody line has a particularly beautiful tone. As they approach the climax, where the melody soars to its highest note just before the end, Christian says quietly, "Go for the stars, Jedediah." Jedediah plays the note perfectly. "I'm proud of you, buddy," says Christian, still quietly, as he conducts the final phrase.

The fifty children of the Harmony Program stay after school several hours a day, five days a week, learning instrumental technique and music fundamentals in mostly group settings. We visit a group of six flute players rehearsing in a small library, who have christened themselves "The Flute-ka-teers." The sound of six beginning flutists can border on shrill, but they seem elated, and particularly eager for us to notice their best player, a boy named Supreme who has figured out on his own how to add vibrato to his pure tones.

"What I find most encouraging is the improvement in their attention span," says Anne Fitzgibbon. "When we started the program last year, it was pretty chaotic, and the kids were wild. Now they are so much more orderly and disciplined. It is a testament to what music can do."

Anne is tall, blond, and ebullient, a dedicated advocate for music education El Sistema–style. Trained as a clarinetist, she studied public policy in graduate school and began her career in the deputy mayor's office at City Hall. "I couldn't help but notice all the reports coming through that office about the lack of instrumental music programs in public schools," she has told me. "And I got tired of reading and talking about the problem year after year. I decided I had to try to *do* something."

She began by initiating a privately funded program for kids from public housing developments in all five boroughs of the city, bringing them for music classes on Saturday mornings with young musicians studying at the New School for Jazz and Contemporary Music in Manhattan. "I realized how much demand there was, on both sides of the equation," she says. "The college students were so hungry for teaching experience. And the kids were so hungry to learn to play music. I kept thinking, How do I ramp this thing up?"

The answer came when a friend told her about the *60 Minutes* program introducing a revolutionary music education program in Venezuela—the same program that caught the attention of Steven Payne in San Antonio and Dan Trahey in Baltimore. Like Dan Trahey, she decided almost instantaneously that she had to go to Venezuela. "I knew right away that it was the answer to everything I was questioning," she said. "I wanted to immerse myself in the Sistema, travel the country, teach, and learn how to bring it back and do it here in the States."

Anne decided to apply for a Fulbright scholarship, and submitted her application in May of 2006. The Venezuelan Sistema still had no Web site at the time, and little contact information in English; her requests for support via emails and phone messages went largely unanswered. By the time the October deadline came, she had virtually given up on getting the support letter she needed from FESNO-JIV. "The night before the application was due, I fired off a desperate email: 'If you're there, please help me!' And they came through."

She won a scholarship to spend a year in Venezuela studying El Sistema. "And then I emailed everyone I knew," she says, "asking if they knew anyone in Venezuela. And mostly I got a bunch of discouraging answers back: 'Don't do this! You won't know anyone! It might not be safe!' "

But among all the warnings came a response from a friend of a friend, who wrote, "Come! Life is beautiful here." Anne decided to believe that one. "So I put my New York program on hold, packed my bags, and got on a plane to Caracas."

The friend of the friend came through too; he met her at the airport and brought her back to his gated hacienda in the hills above Caracas. In the weeks that followed, by dint of perseverance, fluent Spanish, and a healthy dose of blond, blue-eyed charisma, she found her way to the offices of FESNOJIV and began to meet people who could show her the Sistema in action.

"I saw things I had never imagined were possible," she says. "I saw a núcleo with twenty-four hundred kids, with an orchestra in every room, on every floor! I saw twelve-year-olds leading some of those orchestras with an astounding degree of maturity. I saw children, tiny children, performing in concerts like pros, as though it was second nature."

Anne began to teach clarinet at the hillside núcleo Los Chorros, and fell immediately in love with her young students. "I remember one little girl—her name sounded to me something like 'Quises.' What an unusual name, I thought. I asked her how to spell it, and she said, 'You know, *como "besos" in inglés!*' Her name was 'Kisses'! A round little girl with a cherubic face, a devilish grin, and this odd name—she was always at my door, even when I was working with other kids. She loved to take my hair down and smooth it. 'Now you don't look like you're seventy years old,' she'd say.

"One day Kisses was doing this crazy little dance. 'I have a secret! I have a secret!' she chanted. I said, 'I know: it's a boy.' Because to me it was clearly an 'I have a boyfriend' kind of dance.

"But it wasn't a boy. The Sistema had provided her with a brand-new clarinet to replace the old, battered one she had had. Kisses was doing an 'I have a new clarinet' dance.'"

After a year of observing and teaching in Sistema núcleos, and total immersion in Venezuelan life, Anne Fitzgibbon came back to New York fired with ambition to re-create her music program in the image of El Sistema. She began the Harmony Program at P.S. 152 in the fall of 2008, and extended it to P.S. 129 in Harlem the following year. Like the OrchKids students in Baltimore, children in the Harmony Program come after school five days a week, and the program's classes and rehearsals are oriented toward group learning, playing instruments, and participating in ensembles. It's no accident that both programs follow the Venezuelan model so closely: like Dan Trahey, Anne has worked to establish both the intensity and the quality of the learning environment she herself experienced while working within the Sistema.

"People told me it would never work in this country," says Fitzgibbon. "They said I would never get kids to come every day. But I said, 'They'll come if it's fun.' And our attendance rate is 96 percent.

"The hook," she adds, "is the instant ability to be part of an ensemble. It's a great feeling, and every kid wants it. I remember how key that was in Venezuela; my students at Los Chorros would often bring me the clarinet parts to the *West Side Story* suite. They knew their orchestra was rehearsing that, and they knew that if they could play it they could be part of the orchestra."

Another strong hook for her program, says Anne, is its concert-going component; each year the children and their families attend a number of musical events at the Brooklyn Philharmonic and at Carnegie Hall and Lincoln Center—for many of the children, their first trip to the never-never land of Manhattan on the other side of the East River.

The Harmony Program works closely with the music teacher at P.S. 152, Jeff Lederer. "I have limited resources, and so little time with each kid during the school day," Jeff tells me. "I only wish every one of my students could have the depth of musical experience Anne's program offers." He adds that Harmony Program participants are often skilled enough—and they are always eager—to act as informal mentors to their classmates during school music classes.

Funding for the program comes from an arduously cultivated combination of sources: colleges, local governments, and private foundations and donors. A particular and key element of the program is its affiliation with several universities; it is housed within the City University's Office of Academic Affairs, and its sixteen part-time teachers are drawn from the graduate music student populations of Brooklyn College and the City University of New York. For Anne Fitzgibbon, the development of a team of socially conscious music teachers is as important a goal as the musical and social education of children. The young teachers are paid salaries and trained through a series of workshops—several with the Sistema's master pedagogue Susan Siman and with El Sistema USA senior advisor Eric Booth—in the principles and values of El Sistema.

Anne rejoices in the teachers' progress just as she does in the musical and social blossoming of the children. "I remember a teacher at the Los Chorros núcleo saying to me, 'I am teacher, I am psychologist, I am parent,'" she says. "And I think our teachers are getting that. They bring a tremendous amount of dedication and enthusiasm to their work."

One of the Harmony Program teachers is Sam Marchan, the Venezuelan violinist who grew up within the Sistema in the Andean state of Mérida, and whose older brother Francisco had been part of the original youth orchestra in 1975 before returning home to start the núcleo where Sam began his musical education. Sam came to New York to study at Juilliard and NYU, and stayed to pursue a freelance career. "I met Anne, and she had a dream of bringing El Sistema here," he says, "and I wanted to help her realize that dream."

Sam says with admiration that the Harmony Program is "very El Sistema, and also very New York." The sense of camaraderie between teachers is very similar to the atmosphere in Venezuelan núcleos, he tells me. "And the energy level of the kids—that's the same too," he adds. "They are rambunctious, they love to fool around. But they love to play. And we harness that."

He believes that New York City, with its wealth of artistic and musical opportunities, could be "a great base for a developing El Sistema." But he is concerned about sustainability in a context where there is no governmental commitment. "Grants, local funding sources . . . they're all finite, and they all run out," he says. "That is the hardest task here."

Anne Fitzgibbon is constantly looking for funding and worrying about sustainability. But so far the Harmony Program seems as feisty and robust as its founder. Its advisory board includes José Antonio Abreu; Yo-Yo Ma; the composer John Corigliano; and Alexander Bernstein, the son of Leonard Bernstein and founding chairman of the Leonard Bernstein Center for Learning. The Facebook page for the Harmony Program is brimming with photos of beaming cellists and violinists and flutists, and lively with commentary from fans. The most powerful testimonies to the program's success, of course, are the images we take with us on our subway ride back to Manhattan that December night: schoolrooms filled with children who have discovered individual self-respect and communal joy in making music.

During the process of researching and writing about El Sistema in Venezuela and in the United States, I have constantly had the sense that my story was running ahead of me faster than I could possibly keep up with it. At the beginning of 2009, there were perhaps five or six programs in the United States based on the El Sistema model. By mid-2011, there were at least fifty such programs—and the list is increasing by the week, and sometimes by the day. Spurred by several recent documentaries and television features about the Sistema, and inspired by the message of José Antonio Abreu and the musical and personal charisma of Gustavo Dudamel, people in cities and towns across the country are bringing El Sistema's example to life in the distinctively "do it yourself" tradition that tends to drive both artistic advance and social change in the United States.

In Newport News, Virginia, French horn player Rey Ramirez and architect Anne Henry have started Soundscapes with a group of first-graders, an initiative modeled on the Baltimore OrchKids program and housed in a trailer donated by the owner of a local storage unit company. In Pasadena, California, the Verdugo Young Musicians Association, headed by Louise Gandhi and Samvel Chilingarian, has partnered with the Pasadena public school system to create a children's chorus and a children's string orchestra. The San Diego Youth Symphony is working with both the public school system and a social service agency to establish a children's orchestra program in Chula Vista, five miles from the Mexican border. And in Chicago, the YOURS children's orchestra at the People's Music School began with 35 children and grew within a year to 150. Bob Fiedler, the school's director, and Deborah Wanderley dos Santos, the conductor, plan to "expand one orchestra at a time, creating an integrated web of youth orchestras throughout Chicago." El Sistema–inspired children's orchestra programs in Vail Valley, Colorado (First Notes), Cleveland (CityMusic), Fort Wayne, Indiana (Club O) and many other cities have already given their first concerts.

Virtually every one of these emerging programs has originated with an individual or a team of people whose imaginations are seized by the vision of El Sistema and who feel impelled to act upon that vision. In Allentown, Pennsylvania, a musician who toured with Slide Hampton has partnered with a Latino social worker to begin creating a program loosely modeled upon the Baltimore Symphony's

OrchKids project. A Des Moines public school administrator has similarly relied on the example of OrchKids in building her "Kid-Ovation" program.

The First Notes program in Colorado's Vail Valley has had an extra infusion of Venezuelan energy through its founder, Dani Bedoni, a Venezuelan-American who began studying clarinet with Valdemar Rodríguez when she was sixteen and became an immediate Sistema enthusiast. "What I saw in the Sistema was something I had never seen before," she tells me. "It was a portal into another dimension. I had never seen so much passion for music, or such commitment and dedication." With a background in languages and business as well as music, Dani began working with the Sistema in 2007 as a translator, international liaison, and tireless enthusiast; in 2009 she teamed with the Vail Valley Foundation to start a Sistema-modeled program at an elementary school. "I hired teachers for the program and took them to Venezuela with me," she says. "And they were totally excited. And Yo-Yo Ma came to our first concert this spring!"

The panorama of El Sistema–inspired programs in the United States has widened considerably as the Abreu Fellows have graduated and set out to pursue the mission, stated in Maestro Abreu's TED Prize speech, of "bringing El Sistema to the United States." They have already spent part of their Fellowship year working to build the El Sistema USA network in a number of ways—developing the Web site, creating interconnections, building a directory of U.S. programs. One of the Fellows, conductor Jonathan Govias, has written a series of articles about El Sistema for various music publications. "They have a passionate sense of themselves as building a movement," says Mark Churchill. Now they spread out across the country to immerse themselves in that movement.

Trombonist Dan Berkowitz, hired halfway through his fellowship year to be the manager of Youth Orchestra Los Angeles, is already in the process of expanding and developing YOLA. He tells me that he can see in Los Angeles the potential for a kind of mini-Caracas, with a multitude of youth orchestras across the city. "Our inspiration is always Maestro Abreu," he says. "Whenever he starts out to solve a problem, and several different avenues appear, he takes all of them. And then more avenues appear. And he takes all of them."

Working closely with Dan is horn player Christine Witkowski, who has been hired to direct YOLA's new children's orchestra initiative at HOLA, the Heart of Los Angeles community after-school program. Beginning with eighty first-graders on stringed instruments and forty fourth-graders playing winds, Christine plans to have an orchestra up and running within a year—which will soon, no doubt, take the stage of the Walt Disney Concert Hall under Gustavo's baton.

Violist Katie Wyatt is returning to North Carolina, where she was previously the education director for the state symphony orchestra, to head a program called KidZNotes, based on the El Sistema model. The program will begin in three public schools, all of which have suffered cuts in the school-day music curriculum. "Our ultimate goal is to extend across North Carolina," says Katie, who like many of the Abreu Fellows has absorbed her mentor's capacity for thinking large.

Two of the Fellows will remain in Boston: Rebecca Levi and David Malek have been hired by the Conservatory Lab Charter School, a public school in the Brighton neighborhood, to create and head an El Sistema–based program. The school is already music-intensive and has adopted an ambitious extended-day schedule: classes, rehearsals, and lessons on stringed, wind, and brass instruments will happen every afternoon, from 2:30 to 5:30, and music will also be integrated within academic subject teaching during the school day. All of the school's 150 children will be involved, and David and Rebecca have hired a staff of fourteen part-time teaching artists; for the youngest children, they plan to start a Venezuelan-style Paper Orchestra. "We will start with the youngest kids learning by ear," Rebecca tells me, "and then build skills in composition and improvisation as well as reading and playing. The idea is total immersion in music as a kind of language."

Bassoonist Dantes Rameau heads for Atlanta to start the Atlanta Music Project, which will bring orchestral music, El Sistema–style, to an after-school program in the city's lowest-income neighborhoods. "We want to target the kids who really need it—kids who wouldn't have access to it otherwise," he says. Lorrie Heagy goes home to Juneau, Alaska, to start a new El Sistema–based music program at Glacier Valley Elementary School: Juneau Alaska Music Matters (JAMM for short) will offer triweekly free violin instruction to kindergarteners after school. In New York City, percussionist Álvaro Rodas has started Núcleo Corona, or the Corona Youth Music Project, in a mostly Hispanic neighborhood of Queens; he divides his time between this venture and helping to create an El Sistema program in his native Guatemala. In Philadelphia, trumpet player Stanford Thompson is launching Tune Up Philly, a new Sistema-based program that involves eighty elementary schoolchildren who come five days a week after school, learning to play stringed, wind, and brass instruments. And by September of 2011, the second class of ten Abreu Fellows will be in the process of launching their own new sites, or working with others to expand existing ones.

All the emerging El Sistema–based initiatives in the United States, whether or not they are led by Abreu Fellows, are beginning as initially modest programs, but most are dedicated to ambitious long-term goals. And they are developing in a wide variety of ways, depending upon the professional orientations of their founders and the particular circumstances of the locations where they take root. Some are affiliated with community organizations: Kidzymphony, in Charleston, South Carolina, is sponsored by the Charleston Academy of Music; the Imagine Syracuse Children's Orchestra operates in a "family center" context; a new Sistema initiative in the Watts-Willowbrook neighborhood of Los Angeles takes place at a local Boys and Girls Club.

In Las Vegas and Miami, El Sistema–inspired programs are

associated with or sponsored by major symphony orchestras—as is Imagine Syracuse, which is run by the Syracuse Symphony's education director. Orchestra affiliations also support emerging initiatives in Portland, Maine; Jackson, Mississippi; and Waterbury, Connecticut. Programs in San Antonio and San Diego are sponsored by the youth orchestras of those cities, and involve collaborations with social service organizations and the public school system. Says Dalouge Smith, head of the San Diego Youth Symphony, "We are evolving a kind of hybrid model, where the public schools are the first núcleo sites and feed into community youth orchestras. We are inspired by El Sistema but not precisely duplicating it."

In Santa Barbara, California, a philanthropic foundation supports an El Sistema—inspired music program as part of its ICAN (Incredible Children's Art Network) initiative. A private foundation in Fort Worth, Texas, has also founded a Sistema-inspired elementary music program. In Ashville, North Carolina, two home-schooling families have sponsored a similar project. And my Google Alerts continue to bring breaking news of yet more El Sistema initiatives: in Birmingham and Aspen, in Indianapolis and St. Louis and Milwaukee.

Each new initiative has its own particular profile and trajectory. And as they grow and develop, many are finding that they need to modify aspects of El Sistema's practice in order to meet the specific needs of their own cultural contexts. For some U.S. programs, having children attend the program every day is not feasible. Others seek a balance between individual and group playing that is slightly different from the norm in Venezuela. And a number of U.S. núcleos are developing strong partnerships with local school systems—a kind of partnership not typical in Venezuela, where there is little or no music in the public schools.

More important than these differences, however, is that all the new programs share the central inspiration of El Sistema in Venezuela. And nearly every new program Web site or Facebook page is anchored by a quotation from José Antonio Abreu. The immense resonance, for so many in the United States, of Abreu's words and vision, and of Dudamel's example, seem to be testimony to a hunger in our culture for authentic and socially progressive arts education.

Long before El Sistema became well known in the United States, there were many noteworthy organizations devoted to filling this void. These organizations continue to be vibrant and powerful presences in their communities. Community MusicWorks in Providence, Rhode Island, where classical musicians live and teach music in a low-income neighborhood; Renaissance Arts Academy in Los Angeles, a charter school with the arts at the center of the curriculum; community music schools in New Haven, San Diego, and other cities, where outreach to underserved children is a primary goal—these programs and many like them have been dedicated for years to the idea of changing children's lives through music.

But the sudden mushrooming of new programs explicitly grounded in the example of El Sistema in Venezuela is something remarkable and unprecedented. These programs have a depth of shared ideals, an ambitiousness of purpose, and a kind of synergistic momentum that could not have developed without the example of El Sistema to expand their collective understanding of what is possible.

In 2011, the New England Conservatory made the decision to discontinue sponsorship of El Sistema USA, while continuing to support and invest in the Abreu Fellowship program. Leadership roles in the El Sistema movement are in the process of realignment; the L.A. Phil will partner with others to focus on teacher training and field-wide learning.

And on their own initiative, the directors of the forty or so U.S. núcleos that are already up and running have begun to deepen their interconnections. At a spur-of-the-moment "Sudden Summit" meeting, they agreed on the need to consolidate their strengths as a network by creating a set of mission and vision statements and establishing a regular schedule for convening. It's rare for a group of local organizations voluntarily to coordinate their efforts on a nationwide scale, and the summit meeting is testimony to the gathering strength of the El Sistema movement.

"We need to define together our vision for what this movement can be," says Dalouge Smith, who runs San Diego's El Sistema–inspired program. "And we need to take a very long view. We should take a lesson from Maestro Abreu, who even now, thirty-five years later, is no doubt thinking thirty-five years ahead." The very first joint action of the núcleo directors was to petition the Nobel Peace Prize Committee to award the prize to José Antonio Abreu.

Lacking the governmental support that sustains the Venezuelan Sistema, U.S. initiatives are scrambling to find resources in various and imaginative ways, and are sometimes launching classes and ensembles from positions of less-than-complete certainty about their long-term financial resources. "I don't know if it was the smartest thing in the world," says Rey Ramirez, who founded Soundscapes in southern Virginia, "but we just jumped in. My mantra has been, 'There is no better time to help children than right now.'"

It may be that for artists and educators in the United States, who have for so long been conditioned to the necessity for caution and prudence, the spirit of "just jumping in" is the most exciting thing of all about the example of El Sistema. Dan Trahey recalls being visited in Baltimore by Roberto Zambrano, the director of the núcleo in Acarigua, Venezuela. "We were sitting on a stoop in West Baltimore, and I was asking Roberto for advice about starting our program," Dan says. "And he said, 'Look, it's really not so hard. You just have to open up your arms.'"

And then, he adds, Roberto stood up, spread his arms wide and approached a group of kids passing by on the street. "Hey," he said, "how would you like to be in an orchestra?"

# CHAPTER 8

# Gracias Gustavo:
# Healing Communities in
# Los Angeles

O F THE MANY FACES OF EL SISTEMA IN THE UNITED STATES, none is more vivid than the face of a fourteen-year-old flute player in Los Angeles named Martin Luther King Aubry, Jr. I first see Martin sitting on a curb playing his flute in front of the EXPO Center in South Los Angeles. His melancholy tune rises clear and pure above the city traffic; it reminds me of the famous dirge that begins the Adagio of Mahler's First Symphony. I approach and ask what he is playing. "Mahler," he says. "Symphony Number One."

He wants to be a musician when he grows up, or maybe a professional golfer. His face is open, eager, and very serious. Mahler is his favorite composer. "And that's my father," he adds, pointing to a stocky man standing nearby.

The father introduces himself as Martin Luther King Aubry, Sr., and he chats with me while Martin, Jr., walks around the courtyard in front of the center, still playing his flute. He tells me that he is a carpenter looking for work and that four of his six children are in the

YOLA program at the EXPO Center; his sons Moses, eleven, and Amajesty, ten, play double bass and violin, and his seven-year-old daughter plays cello. I ask him about the name "Amajesty." "That's what he is," he says. "He's a majesty. Names are important in our family." They have moved out of the neighborhood since the children began in the program, he adds, but he continues to drive them back here every day. "They love it," he tells me. "It's the center of their lives." He adds that the cop in the neighborhood has told him, "Kids like yours are going to put me out of business."

It is May 2010, and YOLA is already three years into pursuing its goal of putting cops out of business through creating orchestral community for children. One of the most ambitious El Sistema–inspired programs in the United States, it is also one of the most visible, thanks to the substantial commitment of the Los Angeles Philharmonic and the dedication of its high-profile conductor, who has been actively involved with the children of YOLA from the outset.

Like most Sistema-inspired programs, YOLA's beginning was modest. "The first time I met José Antonio Abreu," says L.A. Phil president Deborah Borda, "I asked him for advice about how to bring El Sistema to Los Angeles. And he gave me two words: 'Start small.'" YOLA's first initiative, which began in the fall of 2007 at the EXPO Community Center in South Central Los Angeles, served eighty children three times a week.

Helping to jump-start the program was the L.A. Phil's partnership with a strong community organization, the Harmony Project (not related to the Harmony Program in New York), which had years of experience and expertise in bringing music education to impoverished children. The first children in the YOLA program were the Harmony Project students at the EXPO Center, and many of the teachers were, and still are, Harmony Project teachers. YOLA directors speak candidly about the "'growing pains" that accompanied this partnership, and the difficulty of reconciling the Harmony Project teachers' more lesson-oriented teaching style with YOLA's focus on the centrality of the orchestral ensemble. "We learned from one another," says Leni Boorstin, the orchestra's director of community affairs. "There have been bumps on the road, but we always knew we were committed to the same road."

Within a year, word of mouth about YOLA had spread so effectively that the program had a hundred kids and a waiting list. "And we needed to grow," Leni recalls, "because by that time we knew Gustavo was coming, and we needed to have an orchestra for him to work with!"

Says Deborah Borda, "I asked Maestro Abreu, 'Now what?' And he answered—again, he didn't miss a beat—'Grow without fear.'"

YOLA has grown without fear. The EXPO Center program now serves three hundred children in its neighborhood—most of them Latino, but some, like the Aubry family, African-American—who come as often as five days a week for group lessons, private lessons, and orchestra rehearsals. The program has added an early childhood component, serving children as young as two and three. A mentoring partnership with the Colburn School of Performing Arts in downtown L.A. offers YOLA children the chance to study privately with young musicians who are students at Colburn's Conservatory of Music. And a second program has been launched in partnership with a community center in the impoverished Rampart district, Heart of Los Angeles (HOLA for short, so this program is tagged "YOLA at HOLA").

Gretchen Nielsen, education director for the L.A. Phil, explains that YOLA's expansion has been driven not only by Maestro Abreu's advice and counsel, but also by the impact of Dudamel's presence and leadership. "With Gustavo here," she says, "we have to think big. We have to think in terms of thousands of children. We are really impelled by the vision of our leader."

Dudamel first worked with the children of YOLA in December 2008, almost a full year before his tenure as the Philharmonic's music director officially began. "I rehearsed with them at the EXPO Center," he says, "and it was amazing—they were just beginners, of course, but already there was that spark in them, of loving to play music together."

He tells me that he was excited and touched by the L.A. Phil's eagerness to align its social vision with his own. "You know, they asked themselves, 'From where is Gustavo coming? What can we do together?' " he says. "And then they spread their arms, and they created YOLA. This is something very, very important to me."

Of Dudamel's first rehearsal with the children of YOLA, Gretchen says simply, "It was magical. They loved Gustavo instantly, and he loved them. His English was still not too good at that point, so sometimes he would speak to them in Spanish, and the Latino kids would translate for the others. That in itself was empowering! Instantaneously, we had peer teaching going on."

"And he promised them that the next year they would have a rehearsal on the stage of the Walt Disney Concert Hall," adds Leni. "And they believed him."

⌣

Dudamel keeps that promise on an afternoon in May 2010, in front of an enthusiastic gathering of El Sistema activists and advocates who have come to Los Angeles from cities and towns across the United States for the first national symposium on the subject of El Sistema. While it's not quite the audience of 18,000 that attended Dudamel's first public performance with YOLA some months before at the Hollywood Bowl, the hall feels crowded; many families and friends of the YOLA players are also in attendance at this rehearsal, which is free and open to the public. The children are arrayed on the stage of the Walt Disney Concert Hall; they fill every inch of the stage, just as the Philharmonic does, even though they are visibly more nervous, and the feet of more than a few players barely reach the floor when they sit down.

Dudamel walks onstage in his black YOLA tee shirt and greets the children like old friends, then launches them into the Adagio from Mahler's First Symphony—the piece Martin Luther King Aubry, Jr., has been practicing on his flute, curbside in South Central Los Angeles. The tune has the quality of a nursery rhyme darkened by despondency, even despair. Dudamel stops them after a few phrases.

"You know the notes very well," he says, "but now we have to create the atmosphere. Mahler was feeling very sad, you know? Maybe there is a little bit of hope at the beginning"—he sings the first two ascending notes, using solfège syllables—"Re, mi . . . but then . . . fa." He sings the minor third of the scale. "No hope now," he says, shaking his head. "Let me hear that when you play."

They look bewildered. Is it possible to communicate hope with a D and E, despair with an F? He asks the cello section to try it first. "Let's do something musical here," he says. "The sound should swell and grow louder with the first notes, and then fall away as you come back down to re."

They try again. "Good! Better!" he says. "Now we have to breathe, and play with more personality." Once more they play, and this time he closes his eyes and bows his head as he conducts.

Watching him, they get it. "Ahh," he says, and the children grin even as they successfully wring melancholy from their small cellos.

Dudamel has the whole orchestra try it. The sound is subdued at first, and he takes the violin and bow of one of the children. "Look," he says, "you have this whole bow to use, but you are using only"—he indicates a few inches with his thumb and forefinger—"this much." He plays the tune that way, singing along in a squeaky voice: "Re, mi, fa mi re."

The children can't help laughing. They try it again, and he is pleased. "I'm very proud of that," he says. "Okay, so we have the sound. Now we need to play the eighth notes without rushing them. The sound *and* the eighth notes—it's a lot to think about." They play again, and the eighth notes are still rushed. "Look, I know there's a big audience out there," says Dudamel. "But they are all your friends."

He looks over his shoulder at us. "Am I right?" Hearty applause from the audience, and he smiles at the children. "They don't lie, you know!" he tells them.

He continues to lead the orchestra through the Mahler Adagio, patiently, painstakingly, and with clear enjoyment. The children begin to lose their nervousness and play with increasing confidence; every time he asks them for "Sound! Sound!" they respond with more intensity. When the music arrives at the second theme, a warm, lyrical phrase in a major key, Dudamel stops them again. "This tune, it's like a beautiful secret. It's like . . ." He smiles, searching for words. "Let's put down the instruments and sing it," he suggests. Shy but willing, they sing. He folds his hands and puts his cheek against them, closing his eyes, imitating blissful slumber. And when they play the tune again, it has the feel of a song. They have understood the secret.

After the Mahler, Dudamel asks them to get out their music for the Latin piece *Chamambo*. "This piece has beautiful memories for me," he tells them. "I first conducted it when I was twelve." He pauses. "No, I was older." Another pause. "Thirteen," he says, with a comic timing to rival his symphonic finesse. The children are giggling as they tear into *Chamambo*, relaxed now and swaying to the music like Venezuelans.

At the end the parents in the audience wave at their children as Dudamel walks among them, touching or hugging each one. He tells them they will be here again. "The greatest orchestras in the world play here in this hall," he says. "And you are now a part of the community of musicians who play here. That is a big honor. And a big responsibility."

⌒

The EXPO Center of Los Angeles, where the children of the YOLA orchestra have learned to play Mahler's First Symphony and *Chamambo* and many other things, is a vast city-run complex that includes a senior center, a preschool, an outdoor amphitheater, and a recreation building with sports facilities and an Olympic-sized pool. It serves 60,000 people yearly, and 5,000 to 6,000 every day. Belinda Jackson, the executive director of the EXPO Center, sees it as an ideal setting for an El Sistema–like movement. "We are in a very dense community," she explains, "very cluttered, with no open spaces. This is the only place families can congregate."

A tall, elegant woman whose previous experience includes a modeling career and a long involvement with the Boys and Girls Club, Belinda has a strong intuitive grasp of what the Sistema is about and is committed to building the program at EXPO. "I am very moved by El Sistema's idea of a community learning to empower itself," she says, "and of transforming music education into a social reform movement. It is a different model—it brings people together in a totally different way."

Belinda tells me that often the children and young people in the YOLA program arrive at the Center several hours early. "It's beautiful to see them arriving with their instruments," she says. "Sometimes they practice—in the courtyard, on the lawn, everywhere. They would rather hang out here than anywhere else."

She adds that many of the kids in the YOLA program have gang members in their families. "And I am going to bring those gang members to concerts! They will come—I am going to make sure of it. And who knows what kind of impact that could have? It's a very rough community. But I am convinced that the El Sistema model is what will heal this community."

It seems a utopian idea. But on a Saturday morning, filled with the music of YOLA lessons and rehearsals, the EXPO Center has an undeniable feel of intertwined musical and social energies—the feel, in fact, of a núcleo in Venezuela. There is a violin lesson in one hallway and a clarinet lesson in another; a children's orchestra rehearses in an assembly room; a percussion ensemble bangs out energetic rhythms on overturned buckets. Many of the children's parents have stayed to watch and listen, and an intrepid few are participating in a beginning recorder lesson.

"I'm going to teach you the first few notes of *Chamambo*," says Ken Fisher, one of the YOLA teachers. "You've heard your sons and daughters playing it, and now you will learn to play it yourselves!" Slowly, laboriously, four moms and a dad produce a collective squeak that could be construed as an A. "Fantastic!" says Fisher. "*Fantastico! Now we will learn to play a B!*"

Down the hall from the recorder lesson, the children's orchestra is led by YOLA conductor Bruce Kiesling in a rollicking if rough-edged rehearsal of the overture to *William Tell*, which the children have instantly dubbed "Dear Motel" in honor of its Spanish name, *Guillermo Tell*. A parent named Rhonda, whose twelve-year-old son Evan is a cellist, stands on the sidelines and claps softly in time to the music. "Sometimes I'm tired and don't feel like bringing my son to the program," she tells me, "but he won't hear of it. He makes me bring him every time. He loves the music, and the discipline, and the social scene. And he loves being good at it." Another mother tells me that her eleven-year-old daughter Cassandra, also a cellist, is "always playing the cello or just holding it, polishing it. When her grades started to go down, I told her that if she didn't do better in school she would have to stop the orchestra. And her grades got better right away."

Isaac Green, a tall boy with an Afro, tells me after the rehearsal that he's thirteen and has played the double bass for two years. "I like a lot of kinds of music, but my favorite music is Haydn," he says. "Well, actually, I guess I'd have to say Haydn and old-school rap."

I ask him what he would be doing on afternoons and weekends if he weren't playing the double bass in the YOLA program. He gives me a blank look. "If I weren't doing this?" he repeats. "I can't even imagine."

Matthew and Steven, a violinist and a cellist, are ten-year-old twins. I ask them what they like best about playing with the YOLA orchestra. "The sound," says Steven, "the sound is—I don't know how to say it. It feels like a party."

"I hate to sing," volunteers Matthew, "and with my violin I don't have to sing, it sings for me."

Paloma Udovic Ramos, who is the Harmony Project's director for the EXPO Center YOLA program, tells me that she thinks one of the most important things about the program is that it brings classical music to children who would never hear it otherwise. "It's beautiful, and it's different from what they usually hear," she says. "And because it is complex music, it requires a substantial level of commitment from the children and their families."

The most important thing of all, she adds, is the connection between the teachers and the children of YOLA. "There have been such big changes in some of these children since they started the program," she says. "It can seem like magic. But it's really very simple. It's easy for parents and kids in this community to feel overwhelmed. And they need to feel that someone's listening. So it's simple. It's just communication, and love."

One of the most interesting elements of the YOLA story is the process of "stakeholder" networking that began several years before the program opened its doors and has continued ever since. "This is bigger than the L.A. Phil," says Community Affairs director Leni Boorstin, who has guided much of the process, "and we can't do it all by ourselves. We can be a catalyst. But this is not just a program we're talking about—it's a movement. We've known from the very beginning that the movement will come from the synergy of all the stakeholders working together."

In meetings and interviews with YOLA teachers and administrators and with many members of the "stakeholders' network," I have the sense that the animating power of the El Sistema vision has reached both wide and deep into the city's musical and social consciousness. "To be working with an arts organization, and to have a general population who is aware of what you're doing," says L.A. Phil vice president Chad Smith, "even though this is a town that's all about movies—that's pretty fantastic."

One of the major stakeholders in the YOLA network is the L.A. Unified School District's after-school program Beyond the Bell. Says District Supervisor Tony White, "We are talking about social justice programs here, not just arts education. And many people in Los Angeles are working for this cause through music. If we are going to be effective in challenging gangs, we have to offer kids community. That is what music does."

He adds that he himself grew up in South Central Los Angeles; he is a clarinet player, and taught music and led school bands in the city for many years. "I want to see youth orchestras all over Los Angeles," he says. "It's a no-brainer. If we make it relevant and powerful and exciting, this can save kids. And if Third World countries like Venezuela can do it, we can sure do it here."

Like YOLA, Beyond the Bell has established a partnership with the Harmony Project because of its long experience in bringing music education to impoverished Los Angeles communities. The Harmony Project's founder, Margaret Martin, articulates her perspective in terms that evoke Abreu's language. "When you put a violin in the hands of a seven-year-old," she says to me, "and you teach her to make it sing—week by week, she's learning to create something of beauty. It changes everything for her."

Margaret, who earned a doctorate in community health sciences, has a flair for the theatrical and a parallel career as a playwright. When I ask her how she came to start the Harmony Project, she responds with a dramatic personal story. "My third child was a prodigious violinist at a very young age," she tells me. "When he was five or six, he asked me if he could play in public at the Farmers Market, to earn money. And one day when we were there, and he was playing, a posse of hard-core gang members came through. They stopped right in front of my little boy. I was terrified. And they just stood there, and listened. And after a while they all reached into their pockets and took out some money, and very gently laid it in his open violin case."

It was a turning point in her life, she says. "It was the most unforgettable lesson I ever had about the importance of the arts. I understood that these men would rather be doing what my little kid was doing than what they were doing. In that moment, I knew that making quality arts education accessible to every child had to become a major part of my public health work."

Margaret started the Harmony Project in 2001, with a $9,000 grant from the local Rotary Club—enough to give violin lessons to thirty-six kids in a Seventh-Day Adventist Church after school. "I recruited kids by going into school classrooms with my son," she said. "He would play for them, and I would say, 'You can do this too!'"

Nine years later, the program serves eight hundred young people, including the children in the YOLA program at the EXPO Center. "We commit to staying with our students through their entire child-hoods, from the time we get them to the time they graduate from high school," Margaret says. "For many kids, we are the only stable, positive element in their lives."

She adds that the program's success is partly attributable to a rig-orous reliance upon a wealth of clinical research that proves the ben-eficial effects of arts learning for underserved children. "Everything we do is research-based," she declares. "And the research results are clear. What happens is that kids defy their own negative expec-tations. They discover the truth about their own potential, which everything in their lives has conspired to tell them was not there."

Margaret's description of how she has won support for her pro-gram is strikingly similar to the strategic vision of Maestro Abreu and the Sistema. "This must be seen not just as an arts program but as a youth development program," she says. "You have to be able to show city officials and school superintendents that you can help them solve their problems. They need to see you as the cavalry. And then they will support you.

"I was a teenage mom myself," she adds. "I lived homeless in Los Angeles with two kids for a year. So I come to this work with a fire in my belly."

I hear an equally moving personal story from Tony Brown, the director of the community organization HOLA, where YOLA has established its second children's orchestra initiative. Like the Harmony Project, HOLA started as a modest after-school program in a neighborhood church; it offered kids a safe haven with basketball courts and academic tutors. Tony Brown worked as a volunteer for the program at its beginning twenty years ago, and when it expanded into larger quarters, he was asked to come back and lead the organization. "I had gone on to a business career," Tony tells me. "But it took me no time at all to decide to say yes to HOLA. My older brother had died of drug abuse and HIV/AIDS when he was eighteen. So I was really driven to try to make a difference in young people's lives."

HOLA, which offers a broad spectrum of after-school classes in academics, athletics, and the arts, brims with young energy, from the "soda shop" lounge complete with pool table to the children's artwork, bursting with life and color, covering every inch of the walls. Tony tells me that it was the L.A. Phil's Leni Boorstin who suggested the idea of the partnership with YOLA. "Our chorus was giving a concert a few years ago," he says, "and Leni was there. Our kids sang an African thing, and they sang a Latin thing."

He erupts into song to show me how the African thing and the Latin thing sounded. "And Leni said, 'Wow, that was fantastic!' That was our first connection. And last year she called me to say that YOLA wanted its next children's orchestra to be at HOLA."

Tony says that he immediately started reading and learning about El Sistema and Maestro Abreu. "It's such an incredible model for how you energize neighborhoods and give kids tools to lift themselves up. And that is what we are all about here."

It is not a matter of coincidence that the first national El Sistema symposium happens during the week of Dudamel's rehearsal with the YOLA orchestra in Walt Disney Concert Hall. "The L.A. Phil had made a commitment to support Gustavo in his promise to conduct the YOLA kids at the concert hall," says Gretchen Nielsen. "And when we were in the planning stages, we realized that *everyone* wants to watch Gustavo work with children. So we decided to make the event the centerpiece of a national El Sistema symposium."

"It was exciting," adds Leni Boorstin. "We said to each other, 'We've got Dudamel! We've got Disney Hall! Let's put on a show!'"

The "show" is a three-day gathering called "Composing Change: YOLA and the El Sistema Movement," and it turns out to be bigger than anyone has expected. Sponsored jointly by the Los Angeles Philharmonic, El Sistema USA, and the League of American Orchestras, it attracts several hundred people from across the country: musicians, educators, and policy-makers; people who have already started El Sistema–inspired programs in their communities; people who are thinking about starting them. The inquiry that began three years before, with synchronous conferences in Boston and Los Angeles, has flowered into what is unmistakably a nationwide movement, and the sense of collective excitement has, in Gretchen's words, an "almost physical force."

Eric Booth, who moderates the symposium, articulates the general excitement when he says that "while music has been around forever—and while many of us have worked in music education for years—with El Sistema we are relearning the fundamental power of music."

Jesse Rosen, president of the League of American Orchestras, tells the story in his opening remarks of a children's concert given at a public school by the Seattle Symphony Orchestra. "All the kids wrote a thank-you letter to the orchestra members," he says. "And the gist of the letters was, 'I'm sorry you guys are feeling so sad.'" In the area of communicating joyful involvement with music and with audiences, he says, "orchestras in the U.S. have much to learn from the Sistema."

The presence of the League as cohost of the symposium highlights the question of what role professional orchestras should play in the development of an El Sistema movement. Rosen tells me that El Sistema in Venezuela represents "orchestral performance of a totally different nature—there is a total, human, complete connection between the players, the music, and the audience. The first time I saw it in Venezuela, it felt like a different art form."

Polly Kahn, the League's vice president for learning and leadership development, says that "no matter what role you play in the orchestra world, El Sistema is important to pay attention to." She adds, "Even though this is a very new way of thinking about art and education, many in our field are highly intrigued by it. And some are enraptured."

Adds Jessica Balboni, the director of the League's Orchestra Leadership Academy, "Youth orchestras in the United States tend to be about excellence, not about access and equity. The Sistema is all about access to orchestral playing for young people who have never had it. That is very different from our youth orchestra mission statements."

The feeling among symposium attendees that they are participating in something of historic importance is underscored by the presence of leaders from El Sistema in Venezuela: Bolivia Bottome, Rodrigo Guerrero, Norma Núñez, and Susan Siman are all in attendance. Susan leads a demonstration rehearsal of the YOLA orchestra, in no-holds-barred Sistema style. "*Más! Más!*" she urges the children. "We need more sound! More energy!" She asks them to stand up while they play, and to hold their violins high. "Apply more pressure!" says Susan. "Try to break the bow!"

No bows break, but there is definitely more sound. "I was Gustavo's violin teacher," she tells them. "I knew him when he was smaller than you are. So I get to say this: when he conducts you at the concert hall, see if you can blow him off the stage!"

After the rehearsal, Susan discusses some of the Sistema's key pedagogical principles. "From the very earliest years," she says, "our pedagogy was simply this: we put someone who played beautifully next to someone who didn't. Always, one lifted the other up."

She adds that it's important for kids not to fear making mistakes. "Achieving excellence has many aspects," she says, "but it can only happen through rehearsal, and mistakes."

Again and again, Susan and her compatriots remind symposium participants that what they are working so strenuously to understand is often best expressed in the simplest terms. In a panel discussion devoted to issues of pedagogy, Norma says, "You know, I was never conscious of getting a 'music education.' I was just with my friends in the orchestra. Music was all about friendship and communication." She adds that she doesn't remember group discipline as being a problem. "If we started acting up, the worst thing they could say to us was, 'You have to leave! No orchestra for you today!' "

To a group discussing educational research, Bolivia observes that while she understands our interest in hard data, the Venezuelan tendency is more toward qualitative research and empirical evidence. "If a kid who's doing badly in school enters a music program and starts doing better in school," she says dryly, "it's a pretty good guess that it's because of the music program."

The visiting Venezuelans are generous in expressing their admiration for the spirit of the symposium and the zeal of the participants. "I came here with high expectations," says Norma, "and all of them were exceeded."

"We are extremely proud," says Rodrigo, "and at the same time extremely humble, at seeing so much inspiration flowing both ways." He adds that from his point of view, the El Sistema movement in the United States will succeed as long as there is a spirit of support and interdependence among its elements. "Take a look at the people on each side of you," he says. "These are the people you are going to need. These are the people you are going to work with to achieve your goals. You can't work alone."

Adds Bolivia, "I feel very moved by what I have seen and heard here. Sometimes it's been difficult to keep back the tears. There is an atmosphere of reflection, and an open-mindedness, a willingness to receive. I feel that our family has grown now." She pauses and looks around the crowded hall, much as Dudamel had contemplated his inaugural Hollywood Bowl audience half a year earlier. And just as he did, she adds: "*A lot!*"

At the end of the symposium, Eric Booth observes that less than two years ago, "the YOLA orchestra set itself an unreasonable expectation: that these kids, who had just begun to play their instruments, would perform under Dudamel in Disney Concert Hall. That was an act of courage. And they rose to it." He relates a Frank O'Hara story in which some travelers in the Irish countryside come upon an apple orchard with walls too high to climb. "Instead of giving up," he says, "they all throw their hats over the wall. So then they have to figure out a way to get over it."

The work of re-creating and nurturing El Sistema ideals here in the United States, Eric says, is likely to pose formidable difficulties. "Whenever an obstacle seems insurmountable, or a wall seems too high," he says, "I hope you will throw your hats over the wall."

When Gustavo Dudamel celebrates the presence of the YOLA children, in May 2010, as "part of the community of musicians who play here" at Walt Disney Concert Hall, he is welcoming them to a venue, and to an orchestra, where he is already deeply engaged. Dudamel's first season in Los Angeles has included a series of ambitious and successful concerts, featuring nine premieres of new works, an acclaimed performance of Verdi's Requiem, a festival celebrating the music of all the Americas, and a U.S. tour of eight major cities across the country.

At the same time, Dudamel's international star has continued to be in the ascendant. Guest-conducting appearances in Europe have included a headline-making concert in Paris in which the Orchestre Philharmonique de Radio France joined with the two-hundred-member Simón Bolívar Youth Orchestra to play Berlioz's *Symphonie Fantastique*. The logistical improbability of such a feat, as well as the splendor of the music, managed to astonish even the French, who immediately inducted Dudamel and Abreu into France's prestigious Ordre des Arts et des Lettres.

Dudamel has continued to honor long-term commitments to other orchestras as well. Several winter months have been spent conducting Sweden's Gothenburg Symphony Orchestra on a tour that includes the Canary Islands. And the conclusion of the L.A. Phil's spring season is followed by a tour of Scandinavia, Europe, and Russia with the Simón Bolívar Orchestra.

The high-profile intensity of Dudamel's first season brings with it an equally high level of attention on the part of the media. For much of the year, the hoopla skews sharply toward the adulatory; Dudamel's reviews are mostly rapturous, and he is showered with media attention and accolades. *Time* magazine names him one of 2009's "Top 100 Influential People," citing Metropolitan Opera general manager Peter Gelb's declaration that "with what appears to be unlimited talent and charisma, Dudamel has invigorated the sometimes staid world of classical music, and his performances are ecstatic affairs."

The eminent author and *New Yorker* critic Alex Ross writes that "under Esa-Pekka Salonen, the Los Angeles Philharmonic became the most interesting orchestra in America; under Dudamel it shows no sign of relinquishing the title." The Deutsche Grammophon recording of his inaugural concert with the L.A. Philharmonic hits the top of the *Billboard* and iTunes classical charts almost as soon as it is released. And the blogosphere continues to reverberate with fervent tributes to what Anne Midgette of the *Washington Post* calls the conductor's "ineffable star power." Even nonmusical bloggers get into the act, with posts touting Dudamel as a perfect leadership model for entrepreneurs and executives.

In April 2010, the Massachusetts Institute of Technology presents him with its Eugene McDermott Award in the Arts, one of the nation's most prestigious and generous arts honors. The residency associated with the award includes an open rehearsal with the MIT Symphony Orchestra, a visit to its Media Lab, and a panel discussion with the prominent composers John Harbison and Tod Machover.

In the parallel universe of celebrity stardom, Dudamel has been pursued by paparazzi, interviewed about his favorite restaurants and movies, and featured on the cover of *Esquire*. In the satire-defying manner of the contemporary pop culture machine, his hair itself has become a celebrity. The rap artist and composer Daniel Bernard Roumain briefly shares headlines with Dudamel when he sues the conductor for imitating his "trademark" head of crazy hair. "I play with Lady Gaga," says Roumain. "He just conducts some orchestra in L.A."

And a Facebook fan page for Dudamel, established shortly after his arrival in L.A., was followed in short order by a fan page specifically for his hair. "You love Dudamel," says the fan page, "but you also love his hair."

⌒

Such a combination of critical acclaim and celebrity adulation tends almost inevitably to generate a backlash, and this part of the cycle begins even before the end of Dudamel's first season with the Los Angeles Philharmonic. The week after Dudamel conducts the YOLA children's orchestra in Disney Hall, the L.A. Phil begins a national tour of eight cities across the United States. While they are greeted everywhere by sold-out houses, the critical response to Dudamel is decidedly mixed. Some reviewers are disappointed by what they deem "willful interpretations" or a "lack of musical depth." Others complain of "ostentatious mannerisms" and imprecise playing. "Dudamel Falls Short of His Hype," declares a headline in the *Philadelphia Inquirer*.

The negative commentary can be partly attributed, perhaps, to the media's—and the public's—penchant for puncturing the balloon of any highly acclaimed newcomer to the arts world who garners initially hyperenthusiastic raves. As one blogger put it, "It's part of the choreography of criticism." It's also possible that there is an element of envy at work in cities whose orchestra conductors are less currently newsworthy than the leader of the Los Angeles Philharmonic.

There is, too, the simple fact that the initial "hype" about Dudamel has been so great that no one could possibly have lived up to it. As *Washington Post* critic Anne Midgette wrote, "Dudamel is being billed as the future of classical music. . . . It's going to take more than even Dudamel at his best to keep classical music vital in the 21st century."

It is likely, of course, that there are elements of truth in the criticisms, as well as in the tributes, that have greeted Dudamel. He is a young artist still in the process of formation, still growing and developing his strengths. And he is highly spontaneous and adventurous on the podium, so he is bound now and then to try things that don't work.

But it may also be true that the lens of classical music's critical tradition is not quite wide enough to take in what is most valuable about Dudamel. A love for the infinite expressiveness of music; a passion for communicating that expressiveness; a fervor about bringing music into the lives of needy children—he combines these qualities at such a deep level that they are impossible to parse or separate.

To consider Dudamel solely according to the strict criteria of classical music criticism is perhaps to miss the crucial multidimensional quality of his gift. Whether or not his orchestral ensemble is polished to perfection, or all of his interpretive ideas are fully formed, he is a kind of musician—to borrow the word I heard from so many El Sistema núcleo directors, one might say a "citizen-musician"—that we have not been accustomed to seeing.

As a citizen-musician, Dudamel doesn't separate his professional work from its social context. Conducting Mahler with the

Los Angeles Philharmonic seems, for him, to be integrally connected with conducting Mahler with the children of YOLA—and not only on the great stages of Los Angeles but also in the unglamorous rehearsal spaces of community centers, where the real work of educating children in music and social life takes place.

A similar impulse has led him to help create a fellowship program, the Dudamel Fellows, so that he can offer promising young conductors the kind of mentoring that has nurtured his career. Two of the four first-season Dudamel Fellows, Christian Vásquez and Diego Matheuz, and one second-season Fellow, twenty-six-year-old Manuel López, are younger compatriots from Venezuela. "It's the dream of each of us," Matheuz has said, "to follow Gustavo's example not only as a conductor but as a kind person."

Dudamel's sensitivity to the social and communal aspects of his music-making extends to the Los Angeles Philarmonic organization at large; he has insisted that every employee receive opportunities to attend orchestra rehearsals free of charge. "The people who clean the lobby, the people who take the parking tickets, all these people make our music possible," he has told me. "They should have the chance to hear it."

One of the deepest aspects of Dudamel's "citizen-musician" identity is his sense of urgency about breaking perceived boundaries between the music of the different American continents. This strong pan-American vision is reflected in many of his musical choices. The "Americas and Americans" festival of his first season with the L.A. Phil has made a powerful case for the dissolution of musical borders, intermingling Bernstein and Copland with Ginastera, and showcasing the music of Latin American composers such as Mexico's Carlos Chávez, Venezuela's Antonio Estévez, and Argentina's Osvaldo Golijov, whose music blends Brazilian and Afro-Caribbean influences.

"Gustavo is forming a new space for Latin American composers," Alberto Arvelo, the director of two documentary films about El Sistema, has been quoted as saying. And Plácido Domingo, who heads the Los Angeles Opera, has declared that the "fantastic corner" of Grand Avenue and 1st Street, where the Opera's Dorothy Chandler Pavilion faces the L.A. Phil's Walt Disney Concert Hall, "has become a great cultural force in our Latin world."

Dudamel's "citizen-musician" choices—his insistence on and involvement with community children's orchestras; his mentorship of younger conductors and his sensitivity to the community of support staff; his emphasis on transcultural musical connections—are not ideas unique to him; certainly, there are other conductors who have displayed interest in one or another of these avenues toward connection and community. What may be unique is the extent to which, for Dudamel, connection and community are intextricably linked to the process of exceptional music-making. Inevitably, these priorities are evident in the way he conducts—in his understanding of music as a kind of cathartic emotional connection that links conductor, musicians, and audiences.

Particularly revealing in this regard is a comment made by a Philadelphia reviewer, Peter Dobrin, in his critical review of the L.A. Phil's concert in that city. The orchestra, wrote Dobrin, was guilty of "recalculating aspects of the job once considered ancillary," among which were "community relations and education," and has decided those aspects are "primary now."

Perhaps the last orchestra to have merited that accusation was the New York Philharmonic, who managed to make "community relations and education" and splendid musicianship coalesce into one grand goal, under the leadership of Leonard Bernstein.

Dudamel's second season with the Los Angeles Philharmonic does not begin with the kind of euphoric inauguration that characterized his first. Still, the media fanfare continues throughout the season. The conductor is featured in a Tavis Smiley television special and appears as a guest on the Jay Leno show. Several L.A. Philharmonic concerts are broadcast live from Disney Hall to over four hundred movie theaters across the country, making the celebrity conductor and his orchestra accessible to the multitudes for a fraction of the cost of a Disney Hall ticket. And there is a flurry of publicity over the announcement that Dudamel has extended his Los Angeles contract to 2019—and an even bigger flurry over the arrival, on April 1, 2011, of Martín Dudamel Maturén, the first child of the Maestro and his wife, Eloisa.

During Dudamel's second season with the Los Angeles Philharmonic, the orchestra embarks on a major European tour, performing Beethoven, Bernstein, Mahler, and Adams in many of the great continental capitals. As on their U.S. tour, Dudamel is met with a mixed critical reaction: the maestro's conducting is variously critiqued as electrifying, disappointing, precise, chaotic, a unique joy, and a distinct disappointment. Meanwhile, in a number of reviews for the L.A. Phil's stateside movie-house broadcasts, critics were back to raving about the brilliance and vibrancy of Dudamel's performances.

More interesting than the story of the boom-and-bust nature of critical and media attention to Dudamel, perhaps, is the story of the conductor's reaction to it. When critics and commentators wax rapturous, he remains modest, appreciative of the attention but not terribly interested in its hyperbolic quality. And when negative reviews come in, he is equally unfazed. "Sure," he says to a reporter who asks him about a bad review. "I'm not perfect. I have a lot to learn."

It's rare in our culture that a media celebrity is able to remain genuinely impervious to the debilitating effects of fame. How has Dudamel managed it? One can conjecture that his ongoing ties to family and home in Venezuela may contribute to his psychic balance; he remains very close to his parents, who often travel from Venezuela to see him perform or receive prizes, and to his childhood friends, many of whom he still conducts in the Simón Bolívar Orchestra.

But it's also probable that growing up within El Sistema provides a sturdy protection against the vicissitudes of celebrity. The Sistema's commitment to the values of community and interdepedence, and to individual growth within the context of a harmonious whole—its "infectious creative generosity," in the words of Simon Rattle—have shaped Dudamel's musical life since the very beginning; when he takes his bow from the middle of the orchestra rather than the podium, it is not false modesty, but simply an expression of how he experiences himself in the world. In the Sistema, no one is a celebrity, and everyone is celebrated.

Throughout his hectic and heavily scrutinized beginning seasons with the L.A. Philharmonic, Dudamel has remained overwhelmingly interested in one thing: the process of making orchestral music. "The L.A. Philharmonic and I are still in our meeting phase," he tells me. "One year, two years—it's a very short time. But I can tell you that the response of this orchestra is amazing. I'm really, really, really happy with what we are doing here."

Orchestra members I speak with echo this triple-intensity affection. Says violinist Elizabeth Baker, "He has complete engagement with us from the moment he steps on the podium. He works with such a powerful vocabulary of imagery and feeling—it makes it easy for us to connect with the world of his emotion about the music." His engagement, she adds, is always positive. "He never says 'Don't'—he just leads us toward what he wants. And the direction is all through love."

# Loving Needy Children Well

ACK HOME IN MY EAST COAST PIANO STUDIO, I REAL-
ize that my exploration of El Sistema has reinvigorated
my thinking about my own music-teaching. I had not
anticipated how this exporation would rekindle my awareness of the
deep connections between music-learning and psychic wholeness,
communal vitality, and social well-being. As I work with my piano
students in private lessons, I begin to look for ways—even modest
ones—to bring the spirit of El Sistema into my suburban New Jersey teaching studio. My students are encouraged to play duets more
often—a pale imitation of Doralisa's seven-piano ensemble, to be
sure, but a step in the right direction. I create a series of informal
performing opportunities for small groups of my students, encouraging them in some informal peer teaching. I make extra efforts to
ensure that my minority students feel comfortable and welcome in
this setting where they are, indeed, very much in the minority. And
my students and I are perhaps more alert than we have been before

to the possibility of joy breaking out, at unexpected moments, in the course of making music.

But my feeling of reinvigoration goes deeper than simply the impact of El Sistema thinking on my own work. I find myself with a newfound excitement about what might be possible in this country—in every country, for that matter—through a widespread commitment to the idea that teaching children to play orchestral music together can save lives and heal societies.

"If you put a violin in the hands of a needy child," says José Antonio Abreu, "that child will not pick up a gun." It is this clear and simple truth that lies at the heart of El Sistema. A child who holds an instrument feels entrusted with something of value. A child who is lovingly taught to play an instrument feels competent, worthwhile, and empowered to teach others. And a child who plays an instrument in an orchestra of friends feels a sense of belonging to a community, in which mutual repect and the creation of beauty are inseparable.

That child, says Abreu, will not need to pick up a gun. A million Venezuelan children, over several generations, have proven him right. And if it can happen in Venezuela, it can happen elsewhere. It can, I believe, happen here.

At the end of my interview with José Antonio Abreu, the Maestro spoke of his high hopes for El Sistema USA. "You have such incredible resources in the United States," he told me. "Excellent instruments, excellent buildings. And most important: so many excellent teachers!"

The Maestro is right, and especially about the teachers. The United States has excellent, highly motivated music teachers by the hordes. They are working in public and private schools, in universities and in private studios, in community music schools and in after-school programs. While their effectiveness is often limited by a cultural consensus that puts arts education at the bottom of the educational priority list, many remain stubbornly committed and idealistic. Just as do the teachers in the núcleos of Caracas, our music teachers care greatly about the children they work with, and take intense personal pleasure and pride in their students' accomplishments. They have heart and spirit and intensive training. And they believe in the power of music to change lives.

El Sistema provides formidable affirmation for this belief. And it inspires us to go further, and to marry our conviction that music can be life-transformative with an urgent social imperative: to rescue our neediest children. It is this dimension of the Sistema's vision that feels new to us: an all-encompassing cultural and social commitment to using music on a vast scale to address the self-perpetuating crises of poverty.

In his essay "El Sistema's Open Secrets," Eric Booth writes: "The single most challenging statement about El Sistema's success is that they have learned how to love their neediest children well in the twenty-first century. In the U.S., we must pause and admit that we do not know how to do this." Indeed, we in the United States in the twenty-first century are unaccustomed to imagining the potentially powerful connections between art and social change.

Yet that is how Abreu and Dudamel and their followers have imagined and thought, for thirty-five years. The results of their thinking are clear to anyone who witnesses young people playing music in Venezuela, from the Simón Bolívar Orchestra in the splendor of the Center for Social Action Through Music concert hall to a dusty classroom full of very small string players in a provincial town. The intense level of social and artistic engagement, and the through line of positive energy, never varies.

To be sure, Venezuela still struggles with widespread, intractable poverty, made worse by the intense fluctuations of its oil-dependent economy. El Sistema has never claimed the capacity to end poverty. But it can, and does, claim to have rescued hundreds of thousands of children from the worst depredations that poverty can cause, and given them skills and hope, self-confidence and community, and the experience of beauty. That is a triumph of the human spirit perhaps without equal in our modern world.

And it is a triumph that has lifted the hearts and roused the imaginations of so many musicians, teachers, and social welfare activists in the United States that the number of active El Sistema–inspired programs here has increased almost tenfold in a single year. As of this writing, at least fifty "núcleos" are open and active, and it's probable that the number will be considerably greater by the time this book goes to print. The directors and teachers of these programs are as committed to their work as any Venezuelan núcleo leader, and they clearly identify themselves as a movement.

Inevitably, El Sistema USA will look different from El Sistema in Venezuela. The Venezuelan system began in a centralized way, with government support almost from the beginning. Here in the United States, núcleos are arising spontaneously through autonomous self-invention, and finding a wide variety of ways to grow and sustain themselves. The network of connections among them is strong, and growing stronger, but it may always have an informal quality.

We in the United States will necessarily be more interested than the Venezuelans in creating quantifiable measurements of success, and in gathering data for purposes of evaluation—even though the most potent elements of Sistema pedagogy are precisely the least measurable. It is not easy to create rubrics for love and joy. But measurements and assessment data will be critical for garnering both public and private support in the United States.

There may be repertoire differences, as well, between El Sistema programs in the United States and in Venezuela. Just as the Venezuelan Sistema has balanced its classical orchestral orientation with an exploration of Venezuelan traditional and folk music, Sistema-inspired programs in the United States may explore a mixture of orchestral classics, jazz, musical theater, and other genres indigenous to our culture.

But these are relatively minor differences. And as we have learned from Abreu, infinite flexibility as to means and methods is a key element of El Sistema's success. The central and defining characteristic of all the emerging programs in the United States is the core vision they share with the Venezuelan Sistema—a vision that insists on the primacy of both musical and social goals, and on the mutually reinforcing nature of the two.

The idea that bringing joy, love, and orchestras into children's lives can be a key element of social reform is far removed from the ways we have been used to thinking about both music and social change. But I would argue that it is not a complicated idea, or an implausible one. Every advocate for social change knows that there is a subtly self-perpetuating aspect to poverty, which begins in a child's experience of worthlessness and emptiness. And every musician knows that intense musical learning can fill a child's life and nourish his spirit. José Antonio Abreu has combined these two spheres of understanding to create a vision of combustible force. "Music has to be recognized as an agent of social development, in the highest sense," he has written, "because it transmits the highest values—solidarity, harmony, mutual compassion. And it has the ability to unite an entire community, and to express sublime feelings."

I have seen the truth of Abreu's idea, in very concrete ways. I have watched Esteban in Caracas, DeeShay in Baltimore, and Martin Luther King Aubrey, Jr., in Los Angeles, in the process of discovering that they are valuable, talented, skilled, and loved. I have watched hundreds of young children playing in orchestras together with intense focus and equally intense pleasure, learning as they play that they are essential to their musical communities, and capable of working with others to make something beautiful.

Unquestionably, these children's lives will be transformed by their discoveries, as will the lives of their families. "You cannot imagine," Dudamel has said, "how it changes the life of a kid when he is given a violin or a cello or a flute. You feel you have your world. And it changes your life. This happened to me."

In fact, we can imagine it. Now let us try to imagine an El Sistema USA movement grown so large and strong that a national youth orchestra emerges, and makes its debut at Carnegie Hall or the Kennedy Center or Walt Disney Concert Hall.

Finally, let us try to imagine three or four or five orchestras of children and teenagers in the ghettos and forgotten neighborhoods of every city in the United States, working and playing together every day, teaching and learning from one another, and discovering the "huge spiritual world," as Abreu says, "that music produces in itself, and that ends up overcoming material poverty."

If we can imagine that, persistently and tenaciously and creatively and even joyfully, perhaps it can happen. We owe it to our children to try.

# Acknowledgments

The story of El Sistema is so multifaceted, and unfolds on so grand a scale, that I could never have told it without the help of many people in both Venezuela and the United States. I owe special thanks to the wonderful people of FESNOJIV (now FMSB), the foundation that administers Venezuela's El Sistema. I am particularly grateful for the endlessly generous support and help of Bolivia Bottome, Rodrigo Guerrero, and Norma Núñez Loaiza.

Thanks go as well to the many Sistema leaders and associates who shared their stories with me. The rich recollections of David Ascanio, Luis Rossi, María Guinand, Frank Di Polo, Susan Siman, Alejandro Carreño and Verónica Balda de Carreño, Roberto Zambrano, Lydie Pérez, David Walters, and Paul Goldberg have given shape and personal meaning to the story of El Sistema's birth and growth.

Heartfelt thanks to Mark Churchill for support of many kinds: connections made, meetings enabled, and stories told. Thanks also to Stephanie Scherpf, for help with my Venezuelan travels and my access to the inaugural class of Abreu Fellows; and to the Abreu Fellows themselves, for allowing me to share their deepening understandings of El Sistema in Venezuela and in the United States.

I owe much gratitude to the directors of El Sistema–based programs in the United States. Leni Boorstin, Gretchen Nielsen, and Dan Berkowitz of the L.A. Philharmonic's YOLA; Anne Fitzgibbon of New York's Harmony Program; Dan Trahey of the Baltimore Symphony's OrchKids; Steven Payne of San Antonio's YOSA Music Learning Center; and many of the teachers and administrators involved in these programs—all were tremendously generous with their time and energy, welcoming me into their programs and inspiring me with their dedication. Dani Bedoni's energetic and wholehearted support is much appreciated as well.

My thanks to Deborah Borda, president of the Los Angeles Philharmonic, and to Marin Alsop, music director of the Baltimore Symphony, for sharing with me their stories of being moved to action by the example of El Sistema. Jesse Rosen, Polly Kahn, and Jessica Balboni of the League of American Orchestras also offered valuable perspectives on the meaning of El Sistema for the orchestral world in the United States.

My editor, Maribeth Payne, provided incisive and constructive feedback during the writing process. Thanks also to her assistant, Ariella Foss, for contributing to the process in many ways large and small. And special thanks to my agent, Rick Balkin, whose relentless perfectionist impulse I value ever more highly.

The transcribing skills of Frankie Thomas, Sheila Munson, and Robert Zacharias were an essential contribution to my work. In addition, Robert deserves abundant thanks for helping me navigate the Spanish-speaking world with both translational fluency and unflagging high spirits. And Eva Marin tutored me in Spanish with admirably stubborn optimism.

Thanks, always, to my consistently supportive and inspiring sons: to Evan Johnston, whose continual reimagining of new ways to experience and understand music pushes me to listen harder and think more flexibly; and to Adam Johnston, whose work in creating an El Sistema–based program has shown me firsthand the courage and creativity required to put the ideals of this book into action.

Finally, there are several people whose central contributions to this book cannot be overestimated. Deep thanks go to my longtime friend Margaret Mercer, who kindled my first sparks of interest in El Sistema. To Alexander Bernstein and the Bernstein Foundation, many thanks for vital support in helping to launch the project.

To Jamie Bernstein, who has brought me into the world of El Sistema and shared her experiences with a typically generous and infectious spirit, I am forever grateful. This book would not have been possible without her.

And to Eric Booth, whose work in arts education so powerfully resonates with the ethos of El Sistema, I owe an inexpressible debt of gratitude. For countless introductions made, connections established, and doors opened into the evolving world of El Sistema in the United States . . . for a wealth of knowledge and insights so generously shared . . . for a steady flow of inspirational energy . . . and most of all, for your inexhaustible enthusiasm and support throughout the writing process: thank you, Eric.

The distinctive voices of Gustavo Dudamel and José Antonio Abreu are essential to the vision of this book. For their willingness to share their thoughts and stories with me, I am exceptionally grateful. Their words and their wisdom have guided me continually toward the vital truth that engagement with beauty through community can transform the lives of children everywhere.

# Index